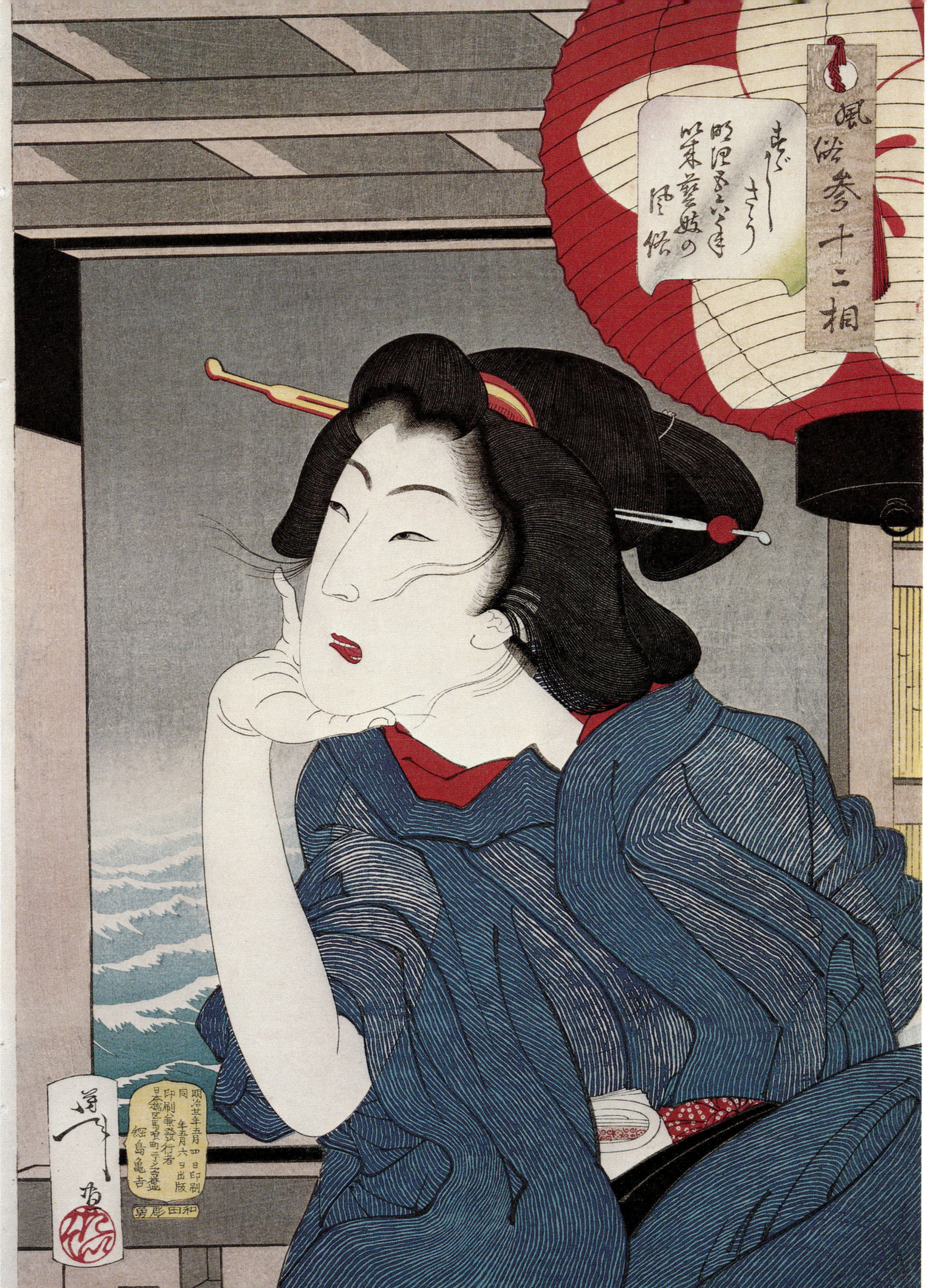
風俗参拾二相
むしあつさう
明治年間女郎の
笑素盡娯の風俗

Cover:
2. Memories of Kikugorō (detail)

Overleaf:
40. Cool: The Fashion of a Geisha in the Early 1870s

THE BIZARRE IMAGERY OF
YOSHITOSHI

THE
HERBERT R. COLE
COLLECTION

ROGER KEYES
GEORGE KUWAYAMA

Published by the
Los Angeles County Museum of Art
5905 Wilshire Boulevard
Los Angeles, California 90036

Library of Congress
Cataloging in Publication Data

Keyes, Roger S.
   The bizarre imagery of Yoshitoshi.

   Catalog of an exhibition held at the Los
Angeles County Museum of Art, July 10–Sept.
7, 1980, and at four other museums during
1980 and 1981.
   Bibliography: p.
   1. Tsukioka, Yoshitoshi, 1839–1892—
Exhibitions. 2. Cole, Herbert R.—Art
collections—Exhibitions.   I. Kuwayama,
George, joint author.   II. Los Angeles Co.,
Calif. Museum of Art, Los Angeles.   III. Title.
NE1325.T76A4   1980   769.92'4   80-15938
ISBN 0-87587-096-1

Edited by Jeanne D'Andrea
and Alison Duncan Hirsch
Designed in Los Angeles by Anna Tartaglini

Text set in Helvetica typefaces by
R S Typographics, Los Angeles
Printed on Lithofect Suede paper by
Alan Litho, Inc., Los Angeles

First Printing 1980, 2000 copies
Second Printing 1980, 2000 copies
Third Printing 1982, 3000 copies

Circulated by
E.D.O. Comprehensive Exhibition Services
Los Angeles, California

Los Angeles County Museum of Art
Los Angeles, California
July 10–September 7, 1980

Glenbow Museum
Calgary, Alberta, Canada
October 25–December 28, 1980

Saskatoon Gallery and Conservancy Corporation
Saskatoon, Saskatchewan, Canada
February 5–March 20, 1981

San Jose Museum of Art
San Jose, California
May 18–July 19, 1981

University Art Gallery
The University of Texas at Arlington
October 7–November 8, 1981

The Fine Arts Museums of
San Francisco, California Palace
of the Legion of Honor
February 27–May 2, 1982
(shown with selections from the
Achenbach Foundation for Graphic Arts)

CONTENTS

ACKNOWLEDGMENTS

Few collectors have acquired the works of an artist as successfully as has Herbert Cole. His appreciation of Tsukioka Yoshitoshi's art was instantaneous and began when he read a periodical article on Meiji prints. With high interest he embarked on the hunt, relishing each adventure. He contacted print dealers and collectors around the world and within a few years amassed a collection of Yoshitoshi prints remarkable for its quality and comprehensive scope. This exhibition and its catalog are the result.

Art exhibitions are complex undertakings which require the cooperation of many people. The publication of this catalog would not have been possible without the encouragement and tangible support given by Mr. Cole. The photographs that appear in the catalog were produced by John Gebhart, Adam Avila, and Kent Kiyomura; its handsome design is due to the artistic talents of Anna Tartaglini; and its readability was enhanced by the judicious editing of Jeanne D'Andrea and Alison Hirsch. All phases of the exhibition received the unstinting assistance of Leslee Leong and Jane Burrell of the Far Eastern Art Department.

While the actual installation of the exhibition will occur after the publication of this catalog, I would like to thank the Conservation Department and the Operations Division, headed by James Peoples, for their assistance in conserving, preparing, constructing, installing, and lighting the display.

(G.K.)

The Japanese adopted the Western calendar on January 1, 1873. Before that they used a lunar calendar which began about a month or a month and a half later than the corresponding Western year and required the frequent addition of intercalary months. To eliminate confusion, dates prior to 1873 are read in Japanese style: 9/1867 means the ninth month of the year that began on February 5, 1867, in the Western calendar. Early dates may be converted to the Western calendar by consulting Paul Tsuchihashi, *Japanese Chronological Tables,* or other reference works. Dates from 1873 on are given in Western style.

The Japanese traditionally counted age by the number of calendar years in which a person lived, rather than the number of years he or she had completed. A Western child is one year old on his or her first birthday, but a Japanese child, until very recently, was one year—that is to say, in his or her first year—the day he or she was born, and two on January 1 of the following year. A child born at Christmas, in other words, would be two a week later on New Year's Day (and would be two for the rest of that calendar year). Yoshitoshi was born in 3/1839. His first print was published in 6/1853, when he was fourteen by Western count but fifteen by the Japanese method. The general rule is to subtract one from the age of pre-modern personages in Japanese publications to arrive at their Western age.

Japanese place their family names before their personal or professional names; hence we have Tsukioka Yonejirō and Tsukioka Yoshitoshi. Artists regularly used secondary names that preceded the names by which they were known professionally, for example, Ikkaisai Yoshitoshi, Taiso Yoshitoshi. Any name or phrase could be used as a seal, which usually followed the artist's signature. In the catalog entries, the names of publishers and engravers as well as of the artist are transcribed exactly as they appear on the prints.

Japanese woodblock prints were printed on papers of many different standard sizes. At the end of the nineteenth century, the most common was a sheet slightly larger than 15 x 10 inches (38.1 x 25.4 cm.) called *ōban,* or "large format." Most Yoshitoshi prints, and all of them in this exhibition, were printed on sheets in this format, although many were designed as larger compositions of two, three, or more sheets. In most of Yoshitoshi's polyptychs the individual panels are verticals placed side by side to form a horizontal composition, although he designed one triptych and several diptychs to be combined in a vertical arrangement. All the prints in the exhibition are *nishiki-e,* or colored woodblock prints.

Yoshitoshi's woodblock prints usually have a printed title and often bear the additional title of a set. The Japanese titles have been romanized and then translated. The transcriptions follow modern pronunciation, using a modified Hepburn system of romanization. Long vowels are indicated by diacritical marks, except in the case of names and modern cities like Tokyo where this would be an affectation. Unfamiliar Japanese words are italicized. In cases where there is no printed title on the prints, we have given a descriptive title in English.

The catalog entry on the painting (cat. no. 1) was written by George Kuwayama; all the remaining entries were written by Roger Keyes.
(R.K.)

YOSHITOSHI AND HIS ART

George Kuwayama

Introduction

During the mid-nineteenth century Japan underwent radical social and political change, accompanied by incessant chaos and war, as it was transformed from a medieval to a modern society. It was a brutalizing period with shifting values: the established order was in decline, and unpredictable new forces were emerging. The past was being irreparably destroyed, and, while for some artists it was an era of bitter disappointment and frustration, for others it was a time of liberation and hope.

For Ukiyo-e artists like Utagawa Kuniyoshi (1798–1861) and his young apprentice Tsukioka Yoshitoshi (1839–1892), it was a tumultuous period. The classic *nishiki-e* (multicolored prints) of languid courtesans and grimacing actors no longer suited the changing tastes of the times, and the soft natural colors of Ukiyo-e were supplanted by gaudy dyes imported from the West.

Yoshitoshi was one of the print masters who survived the turmoil and went on to create masterpieces. Although much admired during his mature years as the leading print artist of his day, subsequent generations have not been as kind: after his death his works were largely forgotten. A reevaluation began in the late 1960s, and today he is much admired along with Kiyochika and Kunichika as one of the three leading Ukiyo-e masters of the Meiji period.[1]

A vigorous draftsman and an accomplished print master, Yoshitoshi used his enormous talents to revive old modes and adapt new concepts of space, texture, light, and color to the print medium. Deeply introspective and for a period mentally ill, he often seems to reveal his inner torment in his work. His art delved into realms that appeal to modern audiences: themes dealing with the occult, with demonic violence, sexual sadism, and hallucinatory imagery. Although some of his contemporaries occasionally touched on these subjects, none approached them with the incredible intensity of Yoshitoshi.

Early Works

Extraordinarily capable and prolific in output, Yoshitoshi continued the popular Ukiyo-e tradition, giving it new vitality. He produced more than five hundred titles; if one counts each print in every series, illustrated book, and newspaper supplement, the total is in the thousands.[2] The enormous range and variety of his work defies a simple linear analysis of his stylistic development, for any given period reflects continuities as well as startling innovations in works covering a bewildering array of themes. Nevertheless, one can compare his early formative years with those of his stylistic maturity which began after the mid-1860s, noting progress toward greater technical mastery and the development of a more personal content.

About 1850 Yoshitoshi was apprenticed to Kuniyoshi, one of the leading Ukiyo-e artists of the time, under whose tutelage he learned and grew. In 1853 at age fourteen he signed his first work—a *nishiki-e* entitled *In 1185 the Heike Clan Sank into the Sea and Perished (Bunji gannen heike no ichimon bokaichu ichiru)*—with his artistic name, Ikkaisai Yoshitoshi (fig. 1). This work, commissioned by his foster father to commemorate Yoshitoshi's coming of age,[3] depicts a popular subject made famous by Kuniyoshi and his followers. Although he had begun to receive guidance from his teacher, Yoshitoshi displayed his own promise in this early work, using a triangular composition of three warriors against a background of concentric or radiating lines interspersed with figures and crabs. Another contemporary work bearing the name Yoshioka Yoshitoshi is an illustrated textbook *(sashi-ehon)* for children, *Illustrated Primer for Language Students (Ehon jitsugoyō dōshikyō yōshi)*.[4] Its execution reveals considerable technical facility by a youthful artist in a style revealing Kanō influence. Subsequently there is a hiatus of five years among his known works, until 1858, reflecting a period of training in Kuniyoshi's studio.

At twenty Yoshitoshi became an independent artist and his output of prints grew. There are a number of works dated 1858 and 1859, mainly comic prints *(kyōga)* or children's prints *(omocha-e),* which adapted techniques he undoubtedly learned from Kuniyoshi, who liked to do caricatures *(fūshi-ga).* Although Yoshitoshi executed these subjects primarily before the Meiji Restoration in 1868, he returned to them at the end of the 1870s and during the 1880s.

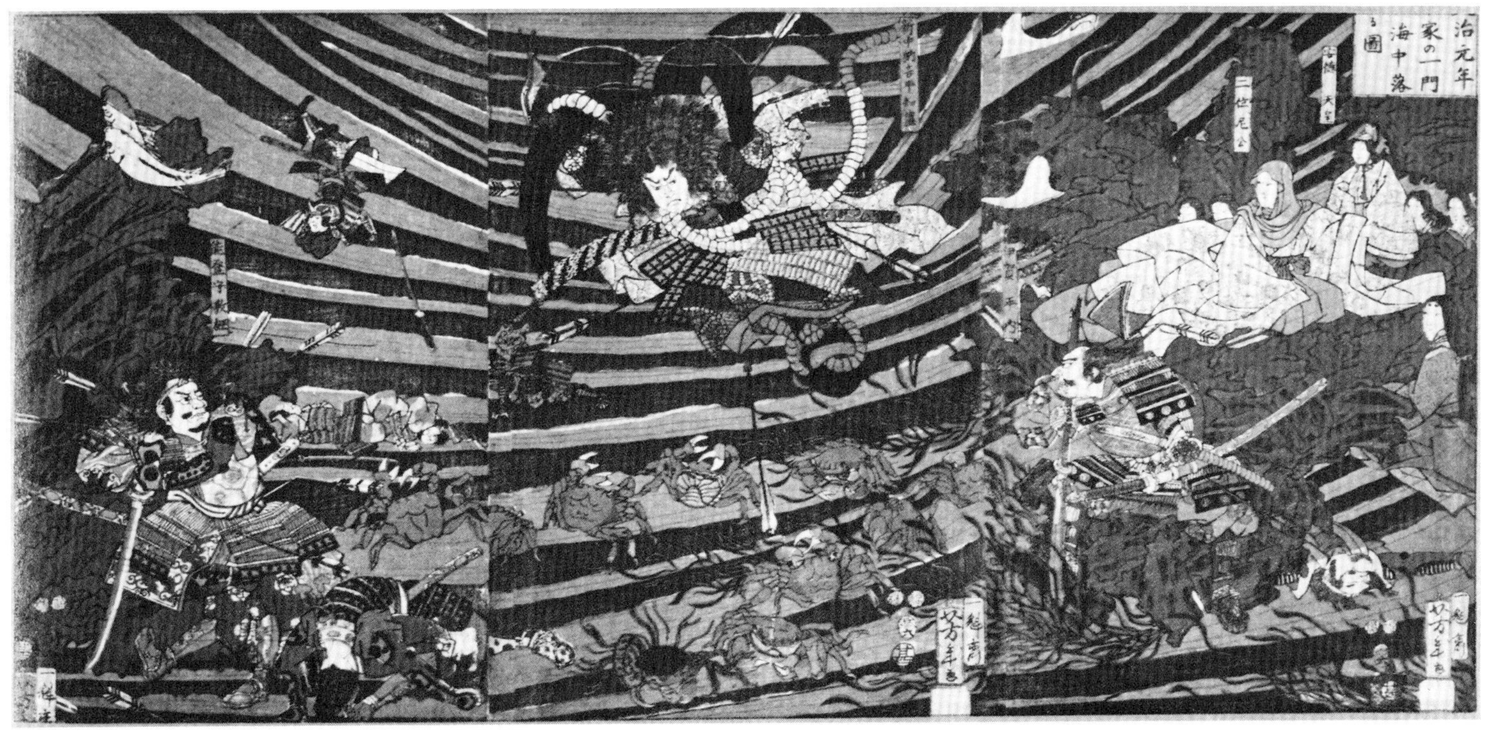

Fig. 1

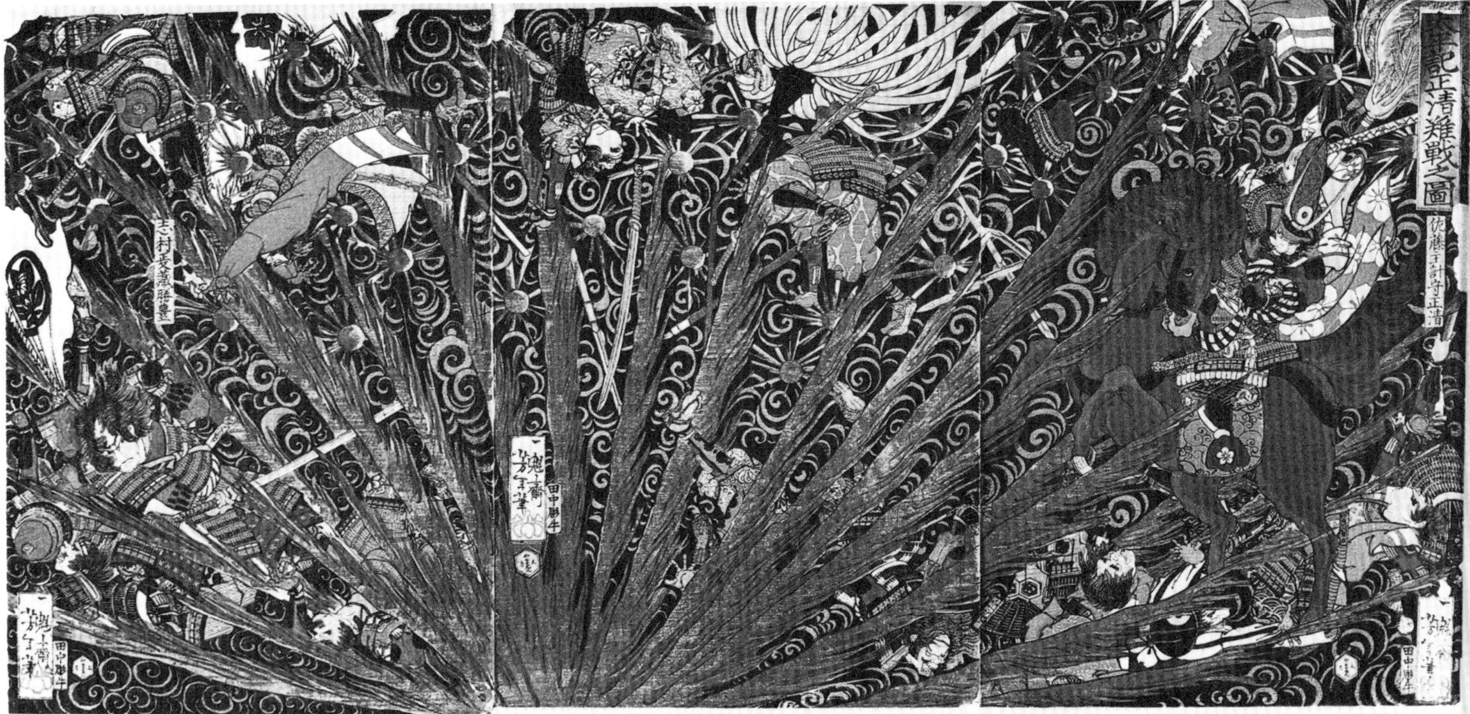

Fig. 2

Actor Prints

Kabuki drama, Ukiyo-e prints, and *kusa-zōshi* (picture books for commoners) were the popular diversions of Edo towns-people with their human, earthy culture. Drawing heavily from the theater as a thematic source for his art, Yoshitoshi produced actor prints which were widely sought. His techniques and expressive mode were strongly influenced by tradi-tional theatrical prints, but he reinterpreted this tradition creatively, broadening its scope with novel uses of space, texture, and color. Although Yoshitoshi seems to have preferred portraying warriors to creating actor prints, he nonethe-less produced a good number of actor prints beginning in 1859 and during the early 1860s.

Historical and Warrior Prints

From his initial repertory, Yoshitoshi branched out to treat a wide variety of subjects including wars, legends, social customs, geisha, and historical person-ages. These works reflect a broad, gen-eral familiarity with Japanese literature and history.

In 1863 and 1864 he illustrated historical subjects *(haishi-e),* and in this process he began to establish his own style. With these and the warrior subjects, his rep-utation as a Ukiyo-e artist grew. He was critically acclaimed for some of his most successful *haishi-e, One Hundred Ghost Tales from China and Japan* (cat. nos. 4–6) and *Biographies of Modern Heroes (Kinsei kyogiden)* of 1865.[5] The journal *Edo saiseiki* of that year ranked him tenth among the leading Ukiyo-e artists of the day.[6]

It was fortunate for Yoshitoshi that, during the tumultuous Bakumatsu years (1853–68), his special preference for illustrating warriors was fostered by Kuniyoshi, who also excelled in this subject. Prints of warriors and famous historic battles be-came increasingly popular as a reflection of unsettled contemporary conditions. Beginning in 1862 Yoshitoshi produced warrior prints *(musha-e)* in considerable numbers. He illustrated incidents from Hideyoshi's expedition to Korea, the Gempei Wars, Nobunaga's campaigns, and the battles between Takeda Shingen and Uesugi Kenshin.

Kuniyoshi's tutelage is apparent in Yoshi-toshi's early warrior prints as evidenced in the compositional treatment of *The Descent from Hiyodorigoe in the Battle of Ichi-no-tani (Ichi-no-tani hiyodorigoe saka otoshi no zu)* of 1864.[7] Also apparent in the costumes and facial expressions is the influence of Kabuki actor prints. Yoshitoshi's emerging individuality can be seen in his skillful handling of a complex series of actions on a battlefield in *The Night Attack at Horikawa from Gempei Seisuiki (Gempei seisuiki horikawa youchi no tatakai),*[8] a precursor of the startlingly bloody scenes he was to do later. In 1866 with the superlative *Masakiyo's Difficult Battle in the Taiheiki (Taiheiki masakiyo nansen no zu)* he displayed his emerging artistic maturity and individual creativity (fig. 2). There are figures in startling perspective, dramatically foreshortened bodies flying through space, and a modern approach to composition in the abstract relationship of pictorial elements. In the late 1860s the government ban on illustrating contemporary events was re-moved, and Yoshitoshi depicted murders as well as the savage acts of war with increasing realism. These are no longer traditional samurai scenes with warriors engaged in romantic battles of ancient legend, but rather samurai fighting in actual combat.

Blood and Violence

The most renowned of Yoshitoshi's prints are those that illustrate savage cruelty with a profusion of blood and gore. This is best exemplified by *Twenty-eight Famous Murders with Poems (Eimei nijūhasshūku)* (fig. 3) and *One Hundred Warriors in Bat-tle Selected by Yoshitoshi* (fig. 4; cat. no. 8), published in 1866–67 and 1869 respec-tively. *Twenty-eight Murders* was a collabo-rative work with Yoshiiku, a fellow apprentice from Kuniyoshi's studio, with each artist producing fourteen prints. These are not the ordinary warrior prints that Yoshitoshi produced under Kuniyoshi's influence earlier in this decade, but savage and chilling images. Perhaps their closest Western analogy is Goya's series on the *Disasters of War* which depicts the ravages of the Napoleonic invasion.[9] Ostensibly each episode illustrated in *Twenty-eight Murders* was taken from the theater, and the prose accompanying each print was written by two of the lead-ing playwrights of the day, Segawa Jokō III and Kawatake Mokuami.[10]

One Hundred Warriors in Battle takes these bloody scenes a step further. Having witnessed the mutilated bodies and the wounded, dying samurai at the Battle of Ueno in 1868, Yoshitoshi intensified the sense of realism in this series. Acute observation was a trait Kuniyoshi tried to instill in his apprentices, who sketched from live birds, cats, turtles, and monkeys. Yoshitoshi's figures reflect a familiarity with nature and a knowledge of human forms in motion.[11] Access to Kuniyoshi's large collection of Dutch graphics with their illusionistic illustrations further broadened Yoshitoshi's acquaintance with representational art. A heightened realism also extended to some of his techniques: he mixed glue and alum into a special pigment with an eerie luster to represent blood.[12]

The fascination with bloody scenes continues a practice already established by Hokusai[13] and Kuniyoshi.[14] Yoshitoshi's works, however, achieve an unmitigated violence never seen before. During the closing years of the Edo period, the Tokugawa shogunate was no longer able to maintain civil order, and physical insecurity and economic depression produced feelings of paranoia and desperation in the populace. Tragic and gruesome acts were now daily occurrences and were frequently depicted in Kabuki plays with scenes of bloody killings.[15] The decadence and chaos during the years before the Meiji Restoration reduced many to a primeval struggle for survival. *Twenty-eight Murders* and *One Hundred Warriors in Battle* reproduced the violence of the age as revealed through an artistic personality that enjoyed sadistic acts of brutality, for Yoshitoshi is known to have derived pleasure from acts of cruelty toward women. These prints are expressions of Meiji "romanticism," concentrating on the grotesque, which combines the turbulence of the age and its suppressed feelings and tensions with the individual personality of Yoshitoshi. After the Meiji Restoration in 1868 and especially during the early 1870s, the popularity of warrior prints declined. In 1877 the Satsuma Rebellion and the Seinan Wars rekindled the demand for battle scenes. The warrior and battle prints produced by Yoshitoshi after the restoration of the emperor are rendered with a sense of reality that could only come with actual observation and deeply felt experience.[16]

Newspaper Illustrations

After a mental breakdown in 1872–73 Yoshitoshi gradually regained his health, and he celebrated his recovery by adopting the new name Taiso (Great Resurrection). In 1874 he was retained by the *Meiyo shimbun (Illustrious Newspaper)* and in the following year by the *Yūbin hōchi shimbun (The Postal News)* to do *nishiki-e* (see cat. nos. 10, 11). These *nishiki-e,* distributed by newspapers, became an important source of commissions and provided Yoshitoshi with a secure income. After the Meiji Restoration, newspapers were published for the first time in large numbers and Ukiyo-e supplements were distributed to subscribers. Yoshitoshi is generally credited as being the first Japanese to do topical newspaper illustrations.[17] With these successes, he again became one of the most popular graphic artists in the country.

Style

A distinct stylistic change may be observed in a comparison of Yoshitoshi's works signed "Taiso" of the 1870s and those before the Meiji Restoration. His earlier work was strongly influenced by Ukiyo-e masters like Hokusai, Eisen, and of course Kuniyoshi. Facial features and figures conform to generalized classic types with curved calligraphic lines. In contrast, the works executed after the mid-1860s, and especially those signed "Taiso," have more individualized features executed with lines that are slender, angular, and free and that zigzag at a quicker tempo. The rendering of subject elements now reflects studied observation and an artistry enriched by experience. Yoshitoshi was not immune to the influences of Westernization, and its stimuli led him to experiment with novel uses of spatial recession, human forms seen in unusual projection, dissonant color combinations, and rich textural patterns and surfaces. Although he occasionally used tonal shading on the folds of Western clothing by overprinting shadows, he declined to explore the illusionistic use of light and atmosphere or of optical realism. Despite these experiments, Yoshitoshi was essentially a Ukiyo-e traditionalist in his choice of native themes and his preference for classic linear techniques and flat planes of color.

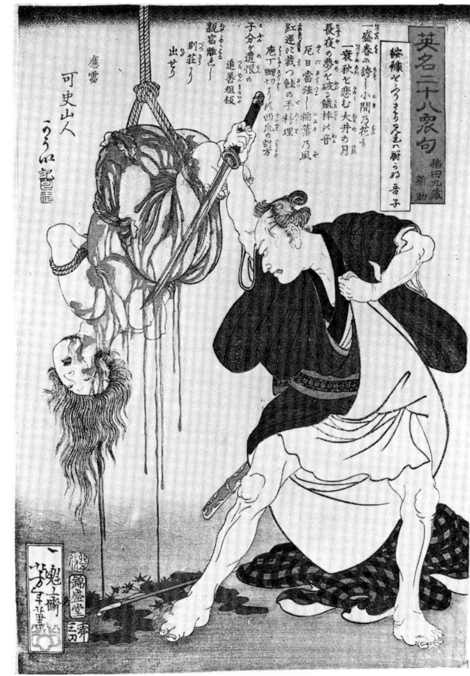

Fig. 3

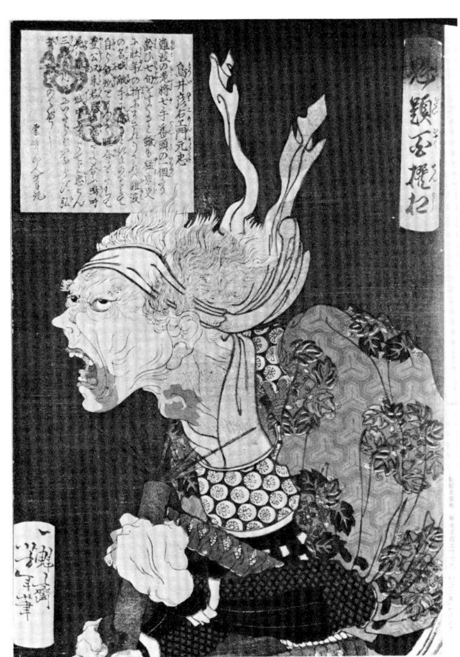

Fig. 4

Artistic Maturity

The years after 1877 saw growing self-confidence and increasing public esteem. By the early 1880s Yoshitoshi was the most popular and best-known artist of his time, secure in his position and successful in the sale of his works. In 1882 he was hired by the *Eiri jiyū shimbun (Illustrated Free Newspaper)* to illustrate its special supplements at an exceptional salary. At about this time Yoshitoshi embarked on a number of series that would be counted among his most significant works. These are the products of his artistic maturity and include *A New Selection of Eastern Color Prints* of 1885 (cat. nos. 30–33), *One Hundred Aspects of the Moon* (cat. nos. 48–67) of 1885–91, *Lives of Modern People* (cat. no. 39) of 1886, and *New Forms of Thirty-six Ghosts* (cat. nos. 42–47) of 1887. Their artistic success elevated Yoshitoshi to the position of the foremost Ukiyo-e master of his time.

In his late years Yoshitoshi executed a number of commissions in various media. Most of his paintings date from the 1880s, and he experimented with the soft tonal brushwork of the Shijō School whose influence is apparent in some of the prints of *One Hundred Aspects of the Moon* and *A New Selection of Eastern Color Prints,* and in the *Demons of Illness and Poverty Stalking the Lucky Gods* (cat. no. 25). He also started a new trend in book illustration, providing pictures for translated foreign novels and popular literature, and he designed covers for printed books.

Painting

The extant paintings by Yoshitoshi are relatively few; they number at most thirty. The oldest painted work is *The Great Tapestry (Daimammaku-e),*[18] produced for a Shinto Festival in Kōfu in 1865. It is painted in Kanō School style, confirming that the young Yoshitoshi had learned this manner.[19] It is probable that the Cole painting *January: Celebrating the New Year* (cat. no. 1) was executed shortly after 1865 in Ukiyo-e style. During his travels in 1871 Yoshitoshi is known to have painted a large number of works in Kōfu, but only one of these remains today.[20] It is also recorded that he painted a number of memorial *ema,* or votive paintings on wood, to be hung in temples there.[21]

In 1977 the organizer of a comprehensive Yoshitoshi exhibition at the Seibu Museum could find only sixteen paintings.[22] Most of these were from his late years, and stylistic analogies can be found for many of them among his extant block prints. Some of his works were produced in the Shijō School manner, and he even painted a Nanga screen, much admired in its day but now lost. In his last few years he produced several unique paintings remarkable for their ghostly qualities reminiscent of Noh drama; these paintings are typified by *An Apparition (Yūrei no zu).*[23]

Ghosts

Ghosts are a common subject in Yoshitoshi's prints, and his lapses into emotional instability gave tangible reality to his apparitions. Although Yoshitoshi was usually lucid and brilliant, one sometimes senses a blurring of the distinctions between illusion and reality in his work.

In pre-modern Japan, spirits, ogres, ghosts, and goblins were part of traditional folklore and integral to the superstitious beliefs of everyday life. Through the centuries, ghost paintings in a variety of styles continued as a major artistic tradition until the end of the Tokugawa period. Prior to the empiricism fostered by industrialization, supernatural beings described in folklore and common religious beliefs attained a palpable reality. For many nineteenth-century Japanese, the witches of Adachigahara and the ogres of Mount Ōe were real, and the ghosts of Heike warriors still haunted the watery depths of Dan-no-Ura. It is reported that Yoshitoshi himself during a depressed state saw the ghost of his former mistress Okoto.[24] Apparitions in Yoshitoshi's art are perceived as actual entities and are rendered convincingly.

Ghosts reappear thematically throughout Yoshitoshi's artistic career, from *In 1185 the Heike Clan Sank into the Sea and Perished* (1853) and *One Hundred Ghost Tales from China and Japan* (1865) to his last works, *One Hundred Aspects of the Moon* (1885–91). His early ghosts and monsters continue Ukiyo-e traditions inspired by the works of Hokusai[25] and Kuniyoshi,[26] and Yoshitoshi retained some of their macabre humor and a certain theatricality. In his later years, when drawn toward the demonic and the occult, he created ghosts in a different vein.

In *New Forms of Thirty-six Ghosts* (1889), demonic themes are expressed in weird, powerful, and skillfully executed images climaxing this tradition; he not only illustrates what one cannot ordinarily see, but he also gives awesome reality to incomprehensible things.

Bijin-e

In the years following the Restoration, Yoshitoshi produced prints of a traditional Ukiyo-e theme, famous beautiful women *(bijin),* exemplified by *Fancy Dishes at Tokyo Restaurants (Tōkyō ryōri sukuburu beppin)* of 1871.[27] In this work he used live models for the first time and showed women in their day-to-day activities; he was very fond of Suzukiya Okiku, who worked at the Shōeitei Restaurant and is portrayed in this series.[28] This element of realism is best exemplified by the use of his mistress Maboroshidayū as a model for a number of his later works. Prints of women were frequent subjects during the 1870s and 1880s, contrasting sharply with his earlier preoccupation with warrior prints. His prints of women differ from the usual Ukiyo-e *bijin-e* in their realism and contemporaneity. Women of the past or present are depicted as figures from everyday life. The year 1877 marks an important development in Yoshitoshi's *bijin-e.* In *A Collection of Desires (Mitate tai zukushi)* there is an expression of mood and feeling in an illustration of women as real people (fig. 5).[29] These were not mere portraits, but portrayals reflective of inner emotions.

In 1888 with *Thirty-two Aspects of Women* (cat. nos. 40, 41), Yoshitoshi turned the time honored Ukiyo-e theme of beautiful women in a new direction: unlike classic Ukiyo-e prints, depicting prominent ladies of the gay quarter often depicted intimately with their male lovers, this series objectively portrayed women of different backgrounds and social status as people. Yoshitoshi included portraits of actual women who lived from 1800 to the 1880s. He showed them as coquettes or as cruel and cold; they were from all walks of life, casually and candidly viewed carrying out their daily activities. The distinguishing feature of each subject was chosen to create individualized portraits, in contrast to the generalized and idealized Ukiyo-e beauties.

This innovation became an important development in the modern history of Japanese prints, creating a style that continued to flourish during the twentieth century. One of Yoshitoshi's best apprentices was Mizuno Toshikata, noted for his *bijin-e*; his disciple Kaburagi Kiyokata, also famous for his illustrations of women, taught Itō Shinsui, a celebrated twentieth-century master renowned for his female subjects.[30] The Utagawa School, from which Yoshitoshi descended, was the leading group of Ukiyo-e print artists in the nineteenth century. It was fated to decline with the Meiji period, and the collateral Toyokuni School was soon afterward eclipsed with the advent of photography. Only the Utagawa Kuniyoshi line, which began with warrior and historical prints, survived in the *bijin-e* of Yoshitoshi.

Later Historical Prints

Profiting from his earlier experience with prints of warriors and historical legends, Yoshitoshi again illustrated these subjects. In the late 1870s he first treated historic events of the Tokugawa reign and the Bakumatsu years (1853–68). He turned then to themes from historical romances such as *A Mirror of Famous Generals of Japan* of 1878–82 (cat. nos. 13, 14), *Short Illustrated History of Japan (Dai nippon shi ryaku zue)* of 1879–30,[31] *Yoshitoshi's Warriors Trembling with Courage* of 1883–86 (cat. nos. 20, 21), and *Lives of Modern People* of 1885 (cat. no. 39): these are among his most celebrated works. Historical literature of all sorts provided thematic sources for Yoshitoshi's historical prints, which included the classic theater of Kabuki, Noh, and *kyōgen,* or short satirical interludes performed between Noh plays; the popular literature of traditional folk tales, *kusazōshi* and *kōdan* (historical tales); as well as translations of Chinese literature widely disseminated during the Bakumatsu period. Historical romances were a common genre in Japanese literature and art, and by the end of the Edo period they were printed in large editions. Publishers commissioned Ukiyo-e artists to provide suitable illustrations for them as well as *nishiki-e* prints of historical heroes or famous events. During his last years Yoshitoshi was strongly influenced by contemporary popular literature which inspired many of the prints in *A New Selection of Eastern Color Prints* (cat. nos. 30–33).

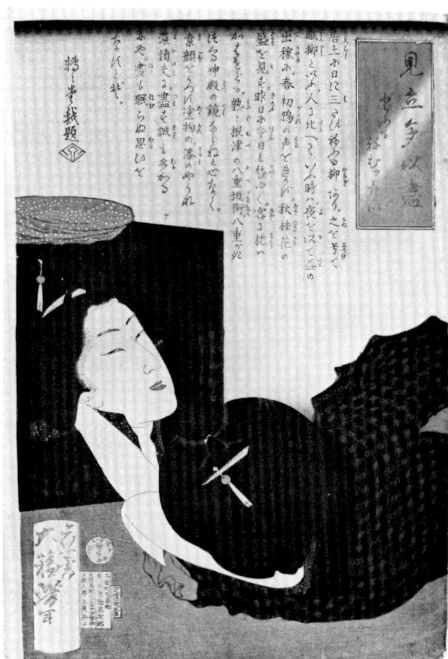

Fig. 5

Later Actor Prints

After a hiatus in the production of actor prints during the early Meiji years, Yoshitoshi returned to them in 1876. His renewed fame and fortune allowed him to indulge his love of Noh and Kabuki as well as of dance and music, and he developed close friendships with leading actors and playwrights. Not only did he execute prints of actors, but he also created billboards for plays, lantern illustrations for Kabuki, and painted stage sets. He produced several marvelous triptych portraits of actors, including Ichikawa Danjūrō IX in the part of Benkei of 1887 (cat. no. 38) and Onoe Kikugoro V, Danjūrō IX, and Ichikawa Sadanji in *Snow, Moon, Flower (Yakusha setsu gekka no uchi),* printed in 1890.[32] These were all monumental bust portaits placed in a triptych format and set dramatically against an unobtrusive background. His compositions were inspired by what he saw on the Kabuki or Noh stage; he derived subjects from the plots of plays and found visual suggestions for compositional schemes. Conversely, actors such as Ichikawa Danjūrō were influenced by the visual images they saw in Yoshitoshi's prints.

Noh Aesthetics

Noh and Kabuki were to remain a continuing thematic source for Yoshitoshi: this is particularly evident in *Umewaka and the Child Seller beside the Sumida River* (cat. no. 23), *One Hundred Aspects of the Moon* (cat. nos. 48–67), and *New Forms of Thirty-Six Ghosts* (cat. nos. 42–47). In 1885 he began to design his spectacular series of vertical diptychs, among which are *Genji in the Countryside (Inaka Genji)*[33] and *The Lonely House on Adachi Moor in Northern Japan* (cat. no. 29). Many of the subjects in this series were drawn from Kabuki and Noh. Yoshitoshi took lessons in reciting the *utai* (chanted interlocution) of Noh and often chose subjects from *utai* texts. He is perhaps the first Ukiyo-e artist to produce pictures inspired by Noh plays for popular consumption.

Yoshitoshi's art came to fruition under the influence of Noh aesthetics in which the principle of *yūgen* affected his work, infusing it with subtlety and restraint, a feeling for the impermanence of life, and an awareness of the innate pathos in all things. *One Hundred Aspects of the Moon* typifies the poetic sensibility that pervades his later works that are free of the intense violence, blood, and unrefined decorativeness found in some of his earlier prints. Color selections are harmonious, emotionally evocative, or expressive of mood. This series is wide-ranging in its variety of subjects, styles, and modes of expression. But throughout the series there is a sense of mystery, passive in its tranquility and detachment.

Techniques

Yoshitoshi's catholic interests, combined with an unstable emotional condition, resulted in disparate works ranging from happy humor to savage cruelty or from poetic lyricism to the macabre. His compositional devices are many and varied for he was an eclectic as well as an experimenter. By the later 1860s and 1870s Yoshitoshi had already tried a variety of techniques and styles; his subsequent developments became more personal, reflecting his artistic maturity. Technical means became adapted to a changed content, one that was more introspective, poetic, or reflective of his own personal experiences and observations.

Dramatic suggestion was often used to great effect, and *The Party at the Etsuda Palace (Estuda goten shuen no zu)* from the series *A New Selection of Eastern Color Prints* is a particularly successful example.[34] It is a parody of Princess Sen's Yoshida Palace in which the eyes of the princess's ladies-in-waiting are turned upon the folding screen at the left, suggesting what is happening behind it. This use of suggestion, encouraging the viewer to participate in the event depicted, is effectively used in his violent prints. The scene illustrated is the moment before bloodshed, increasing the sense of horror. Although *shunga,* or pornographic prints, were popular during the closing years of the Edo period, Yoshitoshi does not seem to have designed any himself. The erotic themes in his prints are not depicted directly but are witnessed by a voyeur, as in *Peeping at Kaoyo through the Hedge in Moonlight (Kaoyo kakimami no tsuki)* of *One Hundred Aspects of the Moon,*[35] or in *The Story of Priest Nitto of Emmei-in Temple (Emmei-in nitto no hanashi),* of *A New Selection of Eastern Color Prints.*[36]

Yoshitoshi constantly made study sketches to plan his compositions and improve his skill. He also studied the published sketchbooks of the great works of the past. The main schema for the triptych of Benkei and Ushiwaka on Gojō Bridge (cat. no. 15), published in 1881, is taken from a sketchbook. His keen interest in sketching resulted in an increasing mastery of technique. The cursive, sweeping outline of varying width, characteristic of Ukiyo-e, with which Yoshitoshi first drew his figures, was replaced by a more controlled line that was sensitive to form. Inner contour lines are looser, freer, and more spontaneous, drawn often with a nervous tempo reflecting the action of their subjects. Colors are selected to express the emotional ambience of a scene with the subtle use of secondary hues. No longer are the harsh aniline dyes applied with the abandon evident in earlier prints.

Meticulously planned, two-dimensional compositions set dynamically in asymmetrical balance are a traditional feature of Japanese art perfected by the masters of the Rimpa School. Yoshitoshi adapts these principles in a new way by consciously considering textures. His compositions are often densely filled with colorfully patterned surfaces in an interplay of shapes and forms exemplified by *A Woman Saving the Nation: A Chronicle of Great Peace* (cat. no. 34).

Conclusion

The rediscovery of Yoshitoshi and the enthusiasm for his work within the last decade is an unusual occurrence. The popular appreciation of the bizarre and the occult, of blood and violence, is an international phenomenon of the 1970s fostered by film and television. For the Japanese there is a sense of nostalgia in seeing Yoshitoshi's prints. In an industrial age, traditions and legendary heroes are being forgotten, but the encyclopedic range of Yoshitoshi's subjects provides a kaleidoscope of Japan's past. As the last major master of Ukiyo-e, he utilized the vast thematic resources of the theater, popular lore, and historical legend. He personifies the transition and the upheaval that Japan experienced during the second half of the nineteenth century in its change from a traditional Far Eastern culture to an industrial society. Born to a lower-ranking samurai family in the heart of Edo, Yoshitoshi could understand the traditions and the life of the samurai as well as that of the *chōnin* (townsman), and he could interpret the character of both with insight and sympathy. It was the members of the lower samurai class who suffered most from the changes wrought by the Meiji Restoration, the wrenching of values, and the destruction of their life style. Yoshitoshi's art is nostalgic yet universal, drawing its inspiration from Japan's rich cultural past.

Fig. 1 In 1185 the Heike Clan Sank into the Sea and Perished
(Bunji gannen heike no ichimon bokaichu ichiru), 1853

Reproduced from Seibu Museum of Art, *Saigo no ukiyo-e shi saishō no gekigaka tsukioka yoshitoshi no zemboten* [A representative exhibition of the works of Tsukioka Yoshitoshi, the last master of Ukiyo-e and the first theatrical artist], exh. cat., Tokyo, 1977, unpaginated.

Fig. 2 Masakiyo's Difficult Battle in the Taiheiki
(Taiheiki masakiyo nansen no zu), 1866

Reproduced from Shinichi Segi, *Tsukioka yoshitoshi gashū* [A Collection of pictures by Tsukioka Yoshitoshi], Kodansha, Tokyo, 1978, pl. 7.

Fig. 3 Inada Kyuzo Shinzuke
1866
Series: *Twenty-eight Famous Murders with Poems (Eimei nijūhasshūko)*

Reproduced from Segi, *Yoshitoshi gashū,* pl. 41.

Fig. 4 Torii Hikozaemon Mototada
1869
Series: *One Hundred Warriors in Battle Selected by Yoshitoshi (Kaidai hyaku senso)*

Reproduced from Seibu Museum of Art, *Yoshitoshi no zemboten.*

Fig. 5 I Want Very Much to Sleep
(Domo nemutai), 1877
Series: *A Collection of Desires (Mitate tai zukushi)*

Reproduced from Segi, *Yoshitoshi gashū,* pl. 95.

THE LIFE OF TSUKIOKA
YOSHITOSHI, 1839–1892

Roger Keyes

Family Background

Almost nothing is known about Yoshitoshi before he designed his first woodblock print at the age of fourteen, but we do know something of his family—or families, as he was adopted in childhood by his uncle. Yoshitoshi was born in the city of Edo, modern Tokyo, on the seventeenth day of the third month of the year of the dog, the tenth year of the Tempo period, which corresponds to April 30, 1839, in the Western calendar. He was given the personal name Yonejirō. His father was a merchant named Owariya Kinzaburō (1815–1863) who was wealthy enough to buy a position for himself in the family of the samurai Yoshioka Hyōbu (1796–1855), a relatively common form of social mobility in Japan during the Tokugawa period. After Kinzaburō changed his family affiliation, his children were also entitled to use the new family name, and Yoshitoshi's first illustrated book published around 1853 is signed "Yoshioka Yoshitoshi."

The name "Yoshitoshi" was given to the artist by his mentor, Kuniyoshi. It was customary for Ukiyo-e artists to give their pupils working names to sign their pictures, and Kuniyoshi gave his students names which began with Yoshi, the last two syllables of his own name. The pupils then chose—or were given—secondary, or "studio," names modeled on the secondary names used by their teacher, Ichiyūsai or Chōōrō. Yoshitoshi used the secondary name Ikkaisai (or Ikkai) in his signature from 1853 through late 1873 when, to mark his recovery from illness, he adopted the name Taiso, The Resurrected. He also used the secondary name Gyokuōrō (or Gyokuō) for a brief period around 1860.

Yoshitoshi lost his mother at an early age, perhaps by divorce rather than death, since her name does not appear on the tombstone of the Yoshioka clan. Kodō Yamanaka, one of Yoshitoshi's pupils who compiled a biography of the artist in 1930,[1] wrote that afterward, when Yoshitoshi's father brought his mistress home to live with them, the boy could not endure her and fled to the home of his uncle, Kyōya Orizaburō, a successful druggist.

The third family to which Yoshitoshi felt related was the Tsukioka clan, descended from Tsukioka Settei (1710–1786), the Osaka painter. Settei's eldest son, Sessai, was born in the eighteenth century in Osaka and worked there much of his life; eventually he moved to Edo where he died in the second month of 1839, the year of Yoshitoshi's birth. In the death register of Ryūsenji, the Shingon sect temple where Sessai was buried, he is described as the younger brother of Kyōya Jūgorō, the father of the druggist Orizaburō, who had died in 1815. This relation was biologically impossible since Jūgorō's father was an Edo fishmonger, not an Osaka painter, but given the flexibility of kinship arrangements in Japan in the Tokugawa period, the families probably had some formal relationship. Kodō suggests that Yoshitoshi became the heir of Settei's branch of the Tsukioka clan.[2] In any case, soon after Yoshitoshi's father died in 1863, the artist began signing some prints as "Tsukioka Yoshitoshi," and in the mid-1870s, when the Japanese government required woodblock print designers to supply their official name and address on their prints, the artist always gave his name as "Yonejirō Tsukioka." Yoshitoshi's only sibling was a sister, or half-sister, who is mentioned on one of the Yoshioka gravestones and about whom nothing more is known. He may have known his foster father's daughter, although she died in 1851 when he was twelve. He never knew Orizaburō's son, who had died in 1842 when Yoshitoshi was three.

Relationships with Women

Nothing definite is known about Yoshitoshi's early adult relationships with women. Segi reports on uncertain authority that Yoshitoshi may have married the daughter of a *kiyomoto* (ballad) singer in the early years of the Meiji period—that is, in the late 1860s or early 1870s—and that he had a daughter who died at the age of two in 1864.[3] Before the Meiji period, Japanese counted a person's age as one year the day he or she was born, and two years old on the next New Year's Day. If indeed Yoshitoshi had a child, she would have been born in 1863.

The warmest and most devoted woman in Yoshitoshi's life was Okoto, who lived with him for some time in great poverty, cared for him during his illness in 1872 and 1873, sacrificed her own few possessions to help make ends meet, and prayed to St. Nichiren for Yoshitoshi's success and recovery. Okoto endured much misery in the belief that things would improve when the artist recovered from his illness, but she was disappointed and soon afterward returned to her parents' village in the countryside.

During the Tokugawa period, most prostitution was conducted from established brothels. Women were engaged by contract and served a stipulated time for a previously agreed amount of money. Poor parents often sold attractive children into such establishments, and women could sell themselves for set periods of time to raise money. After returning to her parents' village, Okoto is said to have sold herself to an establishment called the Daikokuya, perhaps to raise more funds and help Yoshitoshi. In 1877 Yoshitoshi earned enough to send 20 or 30 yen to her. By 1880 she must have died, since about that time Yoshitoshi reported that he saw her ghost in the alcove of the guest room next to his studio in his new quarters in Nezu. Her apparition is said to have prompted him to design a series of ghost prints. The drawings for these prints were completed, but the set was not published.

Like many men in the Tokugawa period, Yoshitoshi consorted with prostitutes, and it was during a visit with friends to a brothel in Shinagawa in 1871 or 1872 that Yoshitoshi reportedly saw another unfortunate woman's ghost. A waitress at the Shōeitei Restaurant named Okiku was said to have been his occasional mistress for a number of years, and he included her portrait in a set of prints of Tokyo restaurants published in 1871. Her younger colleague Otake also may have had relations with Yoshitoshi from time to time, and the two were friends in the late 1880s, even after Yoshitoshi's marriage.

In the fall of 1877 Yoshitoshi built a small, comfortable house for himself in Maruyamachi, the district in which he had lived with his uncle as a child, and set up housekeeping there with Oraku, a geisha from that neighborhood. Their relationship was quite public, and Yoshitoshi invited his students to a housewarming party, but the romance was shortlived. Within a year Oraku left and sold herself to a brothel in Tochigi prefecture, after disposing of her clothes and other possessions, presumably to help support the artist. Yoshitoshi's neighbors were openly critical, saying that he was to blame for Oraku's departure and "stripped his women bare and tossed them out."[4] Yoshitoshi does

seem to have had further financial difficulty at this time and was helped by the proprieter of Kameya, a geisha establishment, a woman six years his senior. He must have had strongly ambivalent feelings toward Oraku and perhaps toward most women at this time. During their liaison he designed his first woodblock prints of women: they are harsh, openly vulgar, and covertly erotic. In early 1880, after his separation from Oraku, he moved from Maruyamachi to Nezu and abruptly ceased to produce this type of print.

In Nezu, Yoshitoshi formed a liaison with a beautiful young courtesan named Maboroshidayū, The Phantom. Many fanciful stories have been told about their relationship. One night, it was said, The Phantom gave Yoshitoshi permission to perform "some unspecified act" on her body, and the morning after they parted she surprised him with a demand for a hundred yen, a large sum of money. Despite the lurid suggestions of depravity, the woodblock portrait Yoshitoshi designed of The Phantom in 1884 is gentle, lyrical, and tender. It is one of his few pictures of women during this period and bespeaks a far different quality of affection than he felt for the geisha Oraku.

It was also in Nezu that Yoshitoshi met Taiko Sakamaki, a young woman who had two small children (it is unclear whether or not she was still married when they met). Taiko was beautiful, practical, and forebearing, and she married the artist in October 1884, at the height of his public success. Yoshitoshi adopted her children. The daughter, Kinko, became a musician. The son studied with Ogata Gekkō and designed and painted pictures of the Noh theater under the name Kōgyo. Taiko was ill much of the time, and Yoshitoshi continued to see other women. Once his wife asked him sadly why he drew so many pictures of geisha laughing in their sleeves. Well after all, her husband answered, drawing is my business.[5]

Men in Yoshitoshi's Life

The most important men in Yoshitoshi's childhood were his father, Yoshioka Hyōbu, his uncle Kyōya Orizaburō, and his kindly teacher, Utagawa Kuniyoshi. Nothing is known about his relationship with his father, but his uncle was fond of the youth. Orizaburō had lost his own two children and often told Yoshitoshi that the business and household would be his

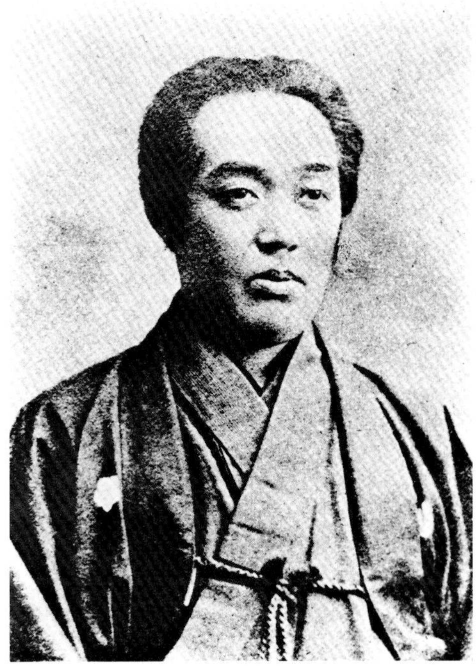

Tsukioka Yoshitoshi (1839–1892)

Reproduced from Seibu Museum of Art, *Yoshitoshi no zemboten.*

one day, although there is no record of a substantial inheritance. It is not known precisely when Yoshitoshi entered Kuni-yoshi's studio, nor precisely how long he stayed there, but he designed his first woodblock print at the age of fourteen in the middle of 1853. When Kuniyoshi died in 1861, Yoshitoshi had been designing prints continuously for more than two years, so it is possible that he became independent in the late 1850s. Kuniyoshi was said to have had a special fondness for his youngest pupil. He once compared him with Yoshiiku, a pupil six years older and Yoshitoshi's rival through much of their adult lives: "Yoshitoshi is awkward, but enthusiastic; Yoshiiku has technique, but not half the enthusiasm."[6] Yoshiiku had a vain, violent, bullying disposition and at Kuniyoshi's funeral is said to have gone out of his way to kick Yoshitoshi, accusing him of blocking his way in a crowd. It is reasonable to imagine that Yoshiiku was jealous of the younger artist and used his seniority to belittle and obstruct him while they were students together. Memories of this and similar incidents may have led Yoshitoshi to tell friends many years later, when his own success had completely eclipsed his rival's, that "at last the stain of shame has been wiped out."[7] Yoshiiku's mistreatment of Yoshitoshi during his late adolescence may even be one of the sources of the murderous rage that flashes out in the violent, bloody prints Yoshitoshi designed in the mid-1860s.

Yoshitoshi had many relations with women, but his most satisfying friendships were with men. From the beginning of his independent career he attracted students, some of them even younger than he had been when he had entered Kuniyoshi's studio. Toshikata, his favorite and most talented pupil, entered his studio in 1879 at the age of fourteen. Toshiyuki, who ran errands for Yoshitoshi as a nine-year-old, grew up to be a colleague and a lifelong friend. His pupils were as devoted and loyal to Yoshitoshi as ancient warriors to their feudal lords. During his illness and poverty in the early 1870s, his young students brought what little money they could to their teacher and pilfered rice and pickled vegetables from their own family households to feed him. Throughout his life they accepted his sudden changes of temper and mood with patience and resignation. In the 1880s, Yoshitoshi had more than two hundred pupils, although no more than six or seven lived with him at a time. Most of these were men or boys, although occasionally the daughter of a wealthy household would come for lessons. Yoshitoshi greatly admired the beauty of the boys and the strength and vigor of the young men who surrounded him, and their admiration and physical presence were certainly an inspiration for his work. One anecdote suggests that his pupils knew that the artist was attracted to some of them, although there is no indication that he engaged in open sexual activity with any of his male friends.

Yoshitoshi abhorred rivalry and was more comfortable surrounded by devoted students than in seeking out his peers among artists or others of his own generation. The painter Eitaku, four years older than Yoshitoshi, came to study print design with him, and the two became intimate friends. Their friendship apparently ended during a sketching trip when Yoshitoshi took affront at Eitaku's obviously superior draftsmanship and returned to Tokyo without him.

Although Yoshitoshi did not seek out celebrities, he did have a long acquain-tance with Onoe Kikugorō V and Ichikawa Danjūrō IX, the two leading Kabuki actors of the Meiji period. Both actors staged tableaux based on Yoshitoshi's prints, and both engaged the artist on occasion to paint their costumes (see cat. no. 24). Kikugorō invited Yoshitoshi to see him perform, and Danjūrō helped the artist construct a float for a festival procession. Most of Yoshitoshi's companions were his own age or younger, but at the end of his life he cultivated friendships with the pub-lisher Akiyama Buemon and the callig-rapher and poet Keíka, both older men.

Residences

Yoshitoshi had several residences during his lifetime, all in various districts of Edo. He was probably born at his father's home in Minami Ōsakachō. His uncle's house where he spent part of his child-hood was in Maruyamachi. Kuniyoshi's studio was in Genyadana. As a young man Yoshitoshi lived in Okemachi, and other sources say that he lived at 2 Oke-machi near Kyōbashi in 1864, in Naka-bashi in 1865, and at 1 Hiyoshimachi in 1869, all districts near the center of Edo.[8] When artists were required at the end of 1875 to give their addresses on their woodblock prints, Yoshitoshi was living in rented quarters at 14 Minami Kinrokuchō, where he had lived during his illness in 1872 and 1873. According to inscriptions on the prints, he remained at this address through September 1877 (although Kodō says he lived at Kanaharu Yokochō in 1875)[9] and then moved to 5 Maruyamachi, where he lived until January or February 1880. From the end of February 1880 to the middle of April 1885, he lived at 35 Miyanagachō in Nezu, a district somewhat to the north. He then moved to larger quarters to accommodate his students, and from May 1885 his address was 2 Sugachō, Asakusa. A geomancer advised him that the house at Sugachō was improperly located, so in 1888 he built a new house at 2-1 Hamachō, Nihonbashi. But this one proved even more unfortunate. It was burglarized soon after he moved in, and he lost his household effects, pictures, and a sum of money. Kodō says that Yoshitoshi moved back to Minami Kinrokuchō briefly before he moved to Nezu,[10] but this is not officially mentioned on the prints. He also says that Yoshitoshi lived at Ontakekura in Honjo before he moved to the Hamachō residence. If this is true, his stay there was very brief. After his release from Sugamo Hospital in the spring of 1892, Yoshitoshi moved to temporary quarters at 3 Fujishiromachi in Honjo, and it was there that he died, although his official residence at the time of his death was still at Hamachō.

Illnesses

Yoshitoshi was seriously ill in the mid-1860s and again in the early 1870s, and he was said to be mentally ill at the end of his life. In the mid-1860s, after he returned to Edo from a trip to Kōfu, he developed an eye disease. Rather than risk dying in the city, he preferred to return to a temple in Kōfu to convalesce. In the early 1870s when he was living in extreme poverty, he suffered from an intermittent illness that may have risen from the combined effects of malnutrition and stress. During this time he was incapacitated for long periods, although he behaved quite normally in between. Since he left his house at Sugachō in 1888 on the advice of a geomancer, Yoshitoshi may have felt that he was suffering from some form of possession or evil outside influence, but nothing more specific is known about the artist's state of mind or mental condition at the end of his life. The onset of his final crisis has been variously attributed to overdrinking, malnutrition (his eyes seem

to have suffered, and he may have contracted beri-beri), to strain caused by the shock of the burglary in 1888 and the loss of his money and possessions, to overwork, and to the stress of serving as guarantor for a loan.[11] He was hospitalized after visiting friends and inviting them to a non-existent gathering of artists. His death was attributed to cerebral hyperemia, or brain congestion *(nōjūketsu),* but one recent writer suggests that he had begun to recover from his nervous condition in 1891 but contracted some other iatrogenic illness during the course of his hospitalization.[12] He was declared incurable and released from the hospital in the spring of 1892; he died shortly thereafter on July 9. His funeral was attended by many well-wishers, including his childhood rival Yoshiiku, and a monument was erected to his memory at Hyakkaen in Mukōjima on the east bank of the Sumida River in 1898.

Appearance and Personality

Yoshitoshi was neither an attractive nor an outgoing child. When he appeared for the first time at Kuniyoshi's studio, one of his fellow pupils, Yoshimune, thought he looked like a drab little shopkeeper's assistant. As he grew older he became more handsome. An old paper merchant remembered him frequenting his store as a young man, "the very image of Yosaburō,"[13] a figure in one of Yoshitoshi's prints (see cat. no. 30). A photograph taken of Yoshitoshi toward the end of his life shows a direct gaze, a full sensuous mouth, and a grave detachment—qualities that also appear in the memorial portrait by Toshikage published soon after the artist's death. (An early newspaper portrait of Yoshitoshi and a posthumous sketch by the artist Kaburagi Kiyokata both seem to be based on the photograph).

As a teacher Yoshitoshi was loyal, devoted, conscientious, and generous, although he was also a demanding perfectionist. He was intense and energetic and underwent extreme, severe changes of mood. His adopted daughter, who knew him only at the end of his life, remembered that he was at times "high as the skies" and at other times deeply depressed.[14] He found release from his moods in work and companionship. At work he was preoccupied, irritable and tense, but with companions he was affectionate and relaxed. He was most comfortable in the company of men and boys, but for most of his adult life he formed brief liaisons with women which were ambivalent and intense. His principal relaxations were drinking, conversation, travel, and sex. He was an excellent player of *shōgi,* or Japanese chess, and toward the end of his life he learned to chant Noh plays and *kiyomoto* recitations. He was intensely interested in history, although there is no indication outside his work that he was widely read. He was attractive but self-conscious, vulnerable but ambitious, determined and proud. He was also vindictive, volatile, selfish, lonely, and obsessed. He was the most brilliant print designer and one of the greatest artists of the Meiji period.

Yoshitoshi's Career

Yoshitoshi designed about two thousand color print compositions and hundreds of illustrations for books and newspapers in the second half of the nineteenth century. His first print was a triptych of the underwater death of the Emperor Antoku and the Taira warriors after the battle of Danno-ura, which was approved by the censor for publication in the sixth month of 1853. Many elements in the print were drawn from earlier pictures by his teacher, Kuniyoshi.

Yoshitoshi's next woodblock prints were published in 1858. In the intervening years he probably continued working in some capacity in Kuniyoshi's studio; perhaps he also lived there. In 1858 he designed a few comic prints, and in 1859 he began designing actor prints. In the early 1860s he designed a few prints of foreigners and several battle triptychs of Japanese warriors repelling foreign invaders. In the mid-1860s he designed many disguised triptychs of battles in the civil wars leading to the Imperial Restoration, the bloody prints of murders which have attracted so much recent attention in Japan, and his first set of ghosts and monsters (see cat. nos. 4–6). It was also during this period that he traveled to Kōfu with a pupil and executed paintings there. In 1868 he introduced Western shading and foreshortening into a series of disguised portraits of combatants at the Battle of Ueno, which he and a pupil had witnessed firsthand (see cat. no. 8). The set was a momentary success and continued through the spring of 1869. In the fourth month of that year the artist's work abruptly ceased until the spring of

1871, when he again adopted a "Western" style and designed several pictures of modern Tokyo and battles in the recent wars. After these prints appeared, Yoshitoshi either chose or was forced to stop work again. His prints were not particularly popular, and he may have lacked commissions, but Kodō reports that he refused commissions to illustrate books and devoted himself instead to study of earlier work.[15] In any case he was desperately poor and fell ill. It was during this illness, from the end of 1872 to the beginning of 1873, that he designed *Ikkai zuihitsu (Free Brushwork by Yoshitoshi)* which was the first mature expression of his personal style. At the end of 1873, after another brief period of inactivity, Yoshitoshi adopted the secondary name Taiso and began designing prints actively once again. In 1874 he began designing "newspaper prints" (see cat. nos. 10, 11) and at the end of that year completed his masterpiece, *The Battle of Ueno* (see cat. no. 9). His interest in current events and his facility at designing documentary prints led to many commissions during the Satsuma Rebellion in 1876 and 1877 (see cat. no. 12). Yoshitoshi received three-and-a-half yen for each triptych he designed at the beginning of the rebellion and five yen apiece when his prints proved popular. The published triptychs themselves were sold publicly for six sen, or six-hundredths of a yen, each. After nearly two decades of poverty, his earnings were large enough to enable him to purchase a house. In the late 1870s he designed many coarse prints of women and began *A Mirror of Famous Generals of Japan* (cat. nos. 13, 14), his lyrical evocations of the Japanese past. This set was a turning point. Fifty years later, his biographer recalled both the excitement he felt seeing the history prints for the first time and the praise and slander they provoked when they appeared.[16]

In 1880 Yoshitoshi moved to Nezu and his prints became more visionary and more personal, although soon afterward he began a public career as staff illustrator for the *Illustrated Freedom Newspaper (Eiri jiyū shimbun)* and accepted larger numbers of commissions for illustrated books. The *Illustrated Freedom Newspaper* hired Yoshitoshi in 1882 for forty yen a month. Before long another paper lured him away with an offer of a hundred yen a month, a large sum at the time. Finally Yoshitoshi felt financially secure enough to leave the newspaper business altogether. By 1885 he had completed most of his major triptychs and had begun the vertical diptychs, *A New Selection of Eastern Color Prints* (cat. nos. 30–33), and the *One Hundred Aspects of the Moon* (cat. nos. 48–67), for which he is said to have received ten yen for each design. The *One Hundred Moons* were extremely popular. Yone Noguchi remembered his disappointment upon reaching the publisher's shop to buy a new print at 7:00 a.m. on the day of publication and finding that the entire edition was already sold out. In 1887 Yoshitoshi designed the *Thirty-two Aspects of Women* (cat. nos. 40, 41), and he began the *New Forms of Thirty-six Ghosts* (cat. nos. 42–47) in 1889. The last prints in the *One Hundred Moons* set were published two months before his death, and the last three of the *Thirty-six Ghosts* were published posthumously.

In addition to the color prints and book and newspaper illustrations, many sketches and a few paintings by Yoshitoshi have survived. The earliest drawings may be the block copies for a group of unpublished warrior prints in half-block format which were done around the mid-1860s and are in the Spencer collection in the New York Public Library. The latest drawings may be those in a sketchbook which includes wash and pencil sketches for prints published in December 1885. Matsui Eikichi, a pupil of Yoshitoshi who became a print publisher in the 1880s, opened a gallery and exhibited printings on silk by his teacher. Most of the dozen or so paintings in Yoshitoshi's style that have come to light in recent years seem to have been done around this period. The most convincing are those which are unrelated to the artist's prints. Yoshitoshi also painted a rough historical scene on a trip to Kōfu in the mid-1860s and a number of votive pictures for temples, some of which have disappeared; others survive in varying degrees of preservation.

1. January: Celebrating the New Year
Mid-1860s

Ink and colors on silk
14¾ x 21¾ in. (37.5 x 55.2 cm.)
Signature: Yoshitoshi
Seal: Go Kaisai

The two women in this painting are engaged in
the traditional New Year's game of *hanetsuki*
with battledores and shuttlecocks. All the elements illustrated pertain to the New Year: pines
which symbolize longevity decorate the front of
the house, and an early blossoming plum tree
is a harbinger of spring. Behind the women,
three boys play with a kite. The Cole painting
may be the first of a series of twelve celebrating the months of the year, or it may be part of
a series illustrating the *gosekku,* the five main
festivals held in the months of January, March,
May, July, and September.

Yoshitoshi's signature and seal in the lower
right corner indicate that the painting could
have been a leaf in a large album which
opened from right to left. The calligraphic style
of the signature suggests a work of the middle
or late 1860s, and the seal can be found on
works of the same period. The closest stylistic
parallel among extant Yoshitoshi prints is the
triptych *Boats Returning from the Ryūkyū Is-
lands (Ryūkyū no kihan)* from the series *Eight
Views with Heroic Tales of Warriors (Bidan
musha hakkei)* dated 9/1867. There are similar-
ities in the lines, the figure proportions of
small heads and elongated bodies, the colorful
patterning of drapery, and the facial details.

This rare, early painting is classic Ukiyo-e
executed in the Utagawa tradition of Kunisada
and Kuniyoshi. It is meticulously painted with
strong brush lines and brilliant colors. The patterns on the women's kimono and *obi* (sashes)
are rendered in great detail and with utmost
refinement. Stylistic analogies may be found in
a number of Kuniyoshi's works, including *Eight
Views of Virtuous Women (Kenjo hakkei)* or
Plum Trees at Night (Yoru no ume), which may
have provided models for Yoshitoshi to follow.

January: Celebrating the New Year, painted on
silk, was a major commission for a young artist
which might have gone to his late master,
Kuniyoshi, had he still been alive. Evidently
Yoshitoshi had a special relationship with the
citizens of Kōfu, for he painted a large curtain
(mammaku-e) there in 1865, and shortly thereafter may have been commissioned to do a
series involving seasonal themes. This painting
would have been one of that series.

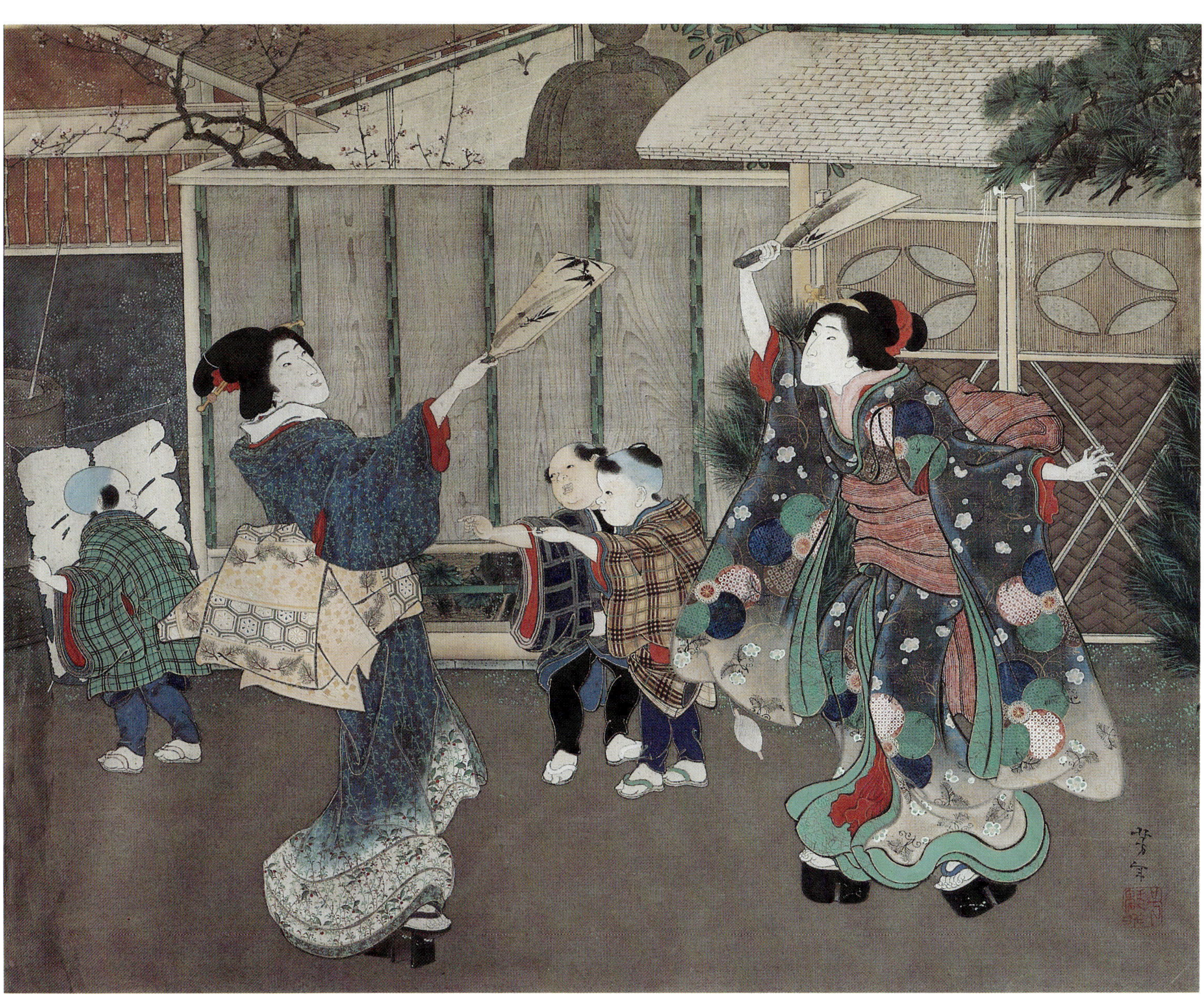

2. Memories of Kikugorō
(Kiku no omokage), 7/1860

Ōban diptych
Signature: Gyokuō Yoshitoshi hitsu
Publisher: Kadokin

The Kabuki actor Onoe Kikugorō IV (1808–1860) died on the twenty-eighth day of the sixth month of 1860; his wife died suddenly the same day. Kikugorō specialized in female roles. In this print he is dressed in a surplice and holds a whisk—a symbol of religious attainment—as he watches a ghostly procession before the tribunal of Ema, the king of hell. The seven figures of women, shown in silhouette, are popular female roles that the actor had performed in recent years: the widow Otaka, Goshiden Okuma, Karigane no Oren, the courtesan Takao, Ofude no Kata, Yokogushi no Otomi, and Kumasaka Ochō. The figures in the tribunal are all recently deceased Kabuki actors. The judge, Nakamura Utaemon IV, died in 1852; the youth at the left, Ichikawa Danjūrō VIII, committed suicide in Osaka in 1854; his father, Ichikawa Danjūrō VII, the nearer figure on the pole, died in 1859. The actor on the right resembles Matsumoto Kōshirō V, who died in 1838, but he may be the subject's father, Onoe Kikugorō III, who died in 1849. Behind the king of hell is the mirror in which each person sees the events of his or her life. On the right are the mountain of needles and the steaming caldron, two of the tortures of hell; in the right distance is the rooftop of Kinryūzan Temple in the Asakusa district of Tokyo, with lotus petals floating about in the sky, a conventional reference to death.

Yoshitoshi's three-quarter-length portrait of the actor is unusual, as are the shadow figures and the judgment bar presided over by other actors. The most striking feature of the picture is the contrast between the brilliantly colored, painstakingly engraved figure of the actor and the dreamlike, monochrome scene of judgment behind.

Yoshitoshi designed four other diptychs in 1860. This one is particularly rare: only one other impression seems to be known.

Detail on cover.

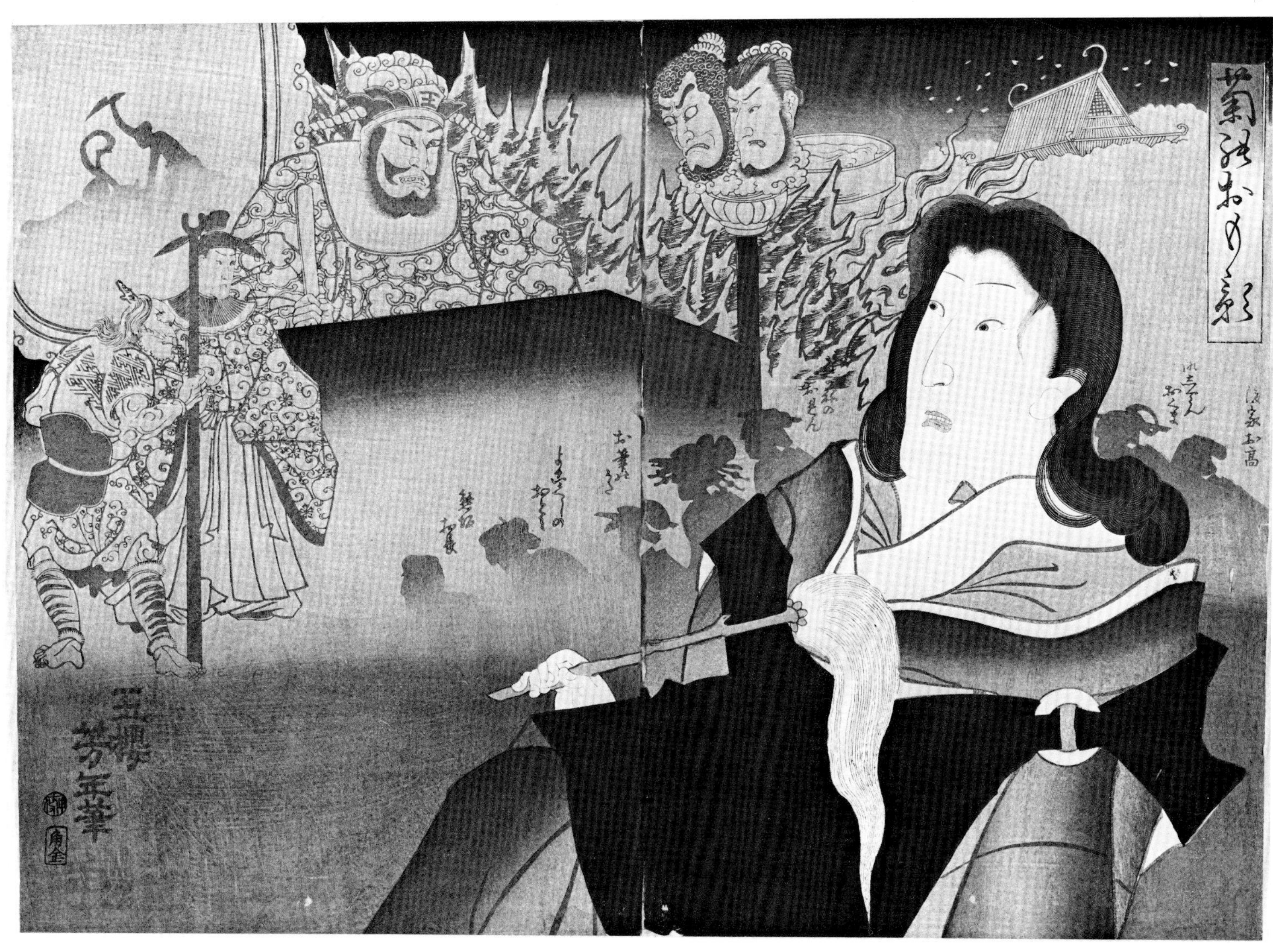

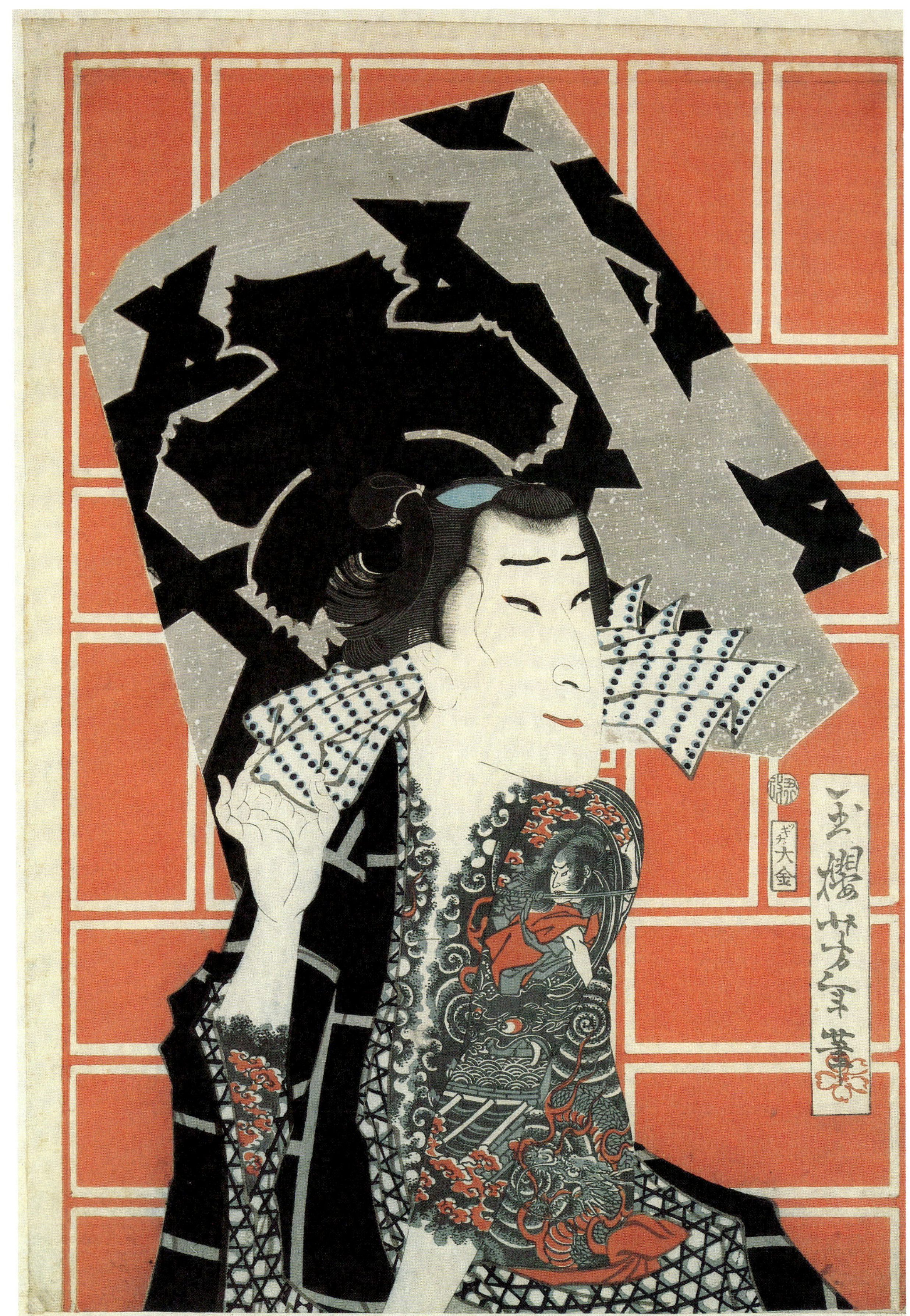

3a.

4. Fuwa Bansaku and the Monster
8/1865

Series: *One Hundred Ghost Tales from China
and Japan (Wakan hyaku monogatari)*
Ōban
Signature: Ikkaisai Yoshitoshi ga
Publisher: Daikin

"Fuwa Bansaku," according to the inscription
by Kanagaki Robun at the top of the print, "was
one of the three bravest samurai of the Mori
clan, a powerful and valiant young man. He
and two other brave men, Takagi and Nagoya,
promised to go together to the ruined temple
to investigate the monster there, and they are
said to have seen it assume its true form."

Bansaku was the beautiful and beloved page
of the shogunal regent Hidetsugu at the end of
the sixteenth century. His exploits, particularly
his rivalry with Nagoya Sanzaburo, one of the
other "brave men," are chronicled in several
popular plays in the Kabuki repertoire. Bansaku's visit to the haunted temple was unfamiliar to Yoshitoshi's audience, and the artist thus
felt free to create a nightmare monster from the
depths of his own imagination. The creature
that glowers at the fearless youth is one of the
first of many horrifying monsters that Yoshitoshi
imagined and depicted in his prints.

The *One Hundred Ghost Tales* traditionally
provided an eerie and entertaining way to raise
a ghost. As the night deepened and one by
one the lights were extinguished, people told
stories of the supernatural. According to tradition, if the group had fallen into a deep state of
fearful expectation by the time the last light
was put out, a ghost would appear. Hokusai
designed a set of five ghost prints with this title
about 1830. This group was Yoshitoshi's first
set of ghost prints. The finest impressions were
printed on heavy paper with special effects like
the polished pattern of black on black on the
monster here.

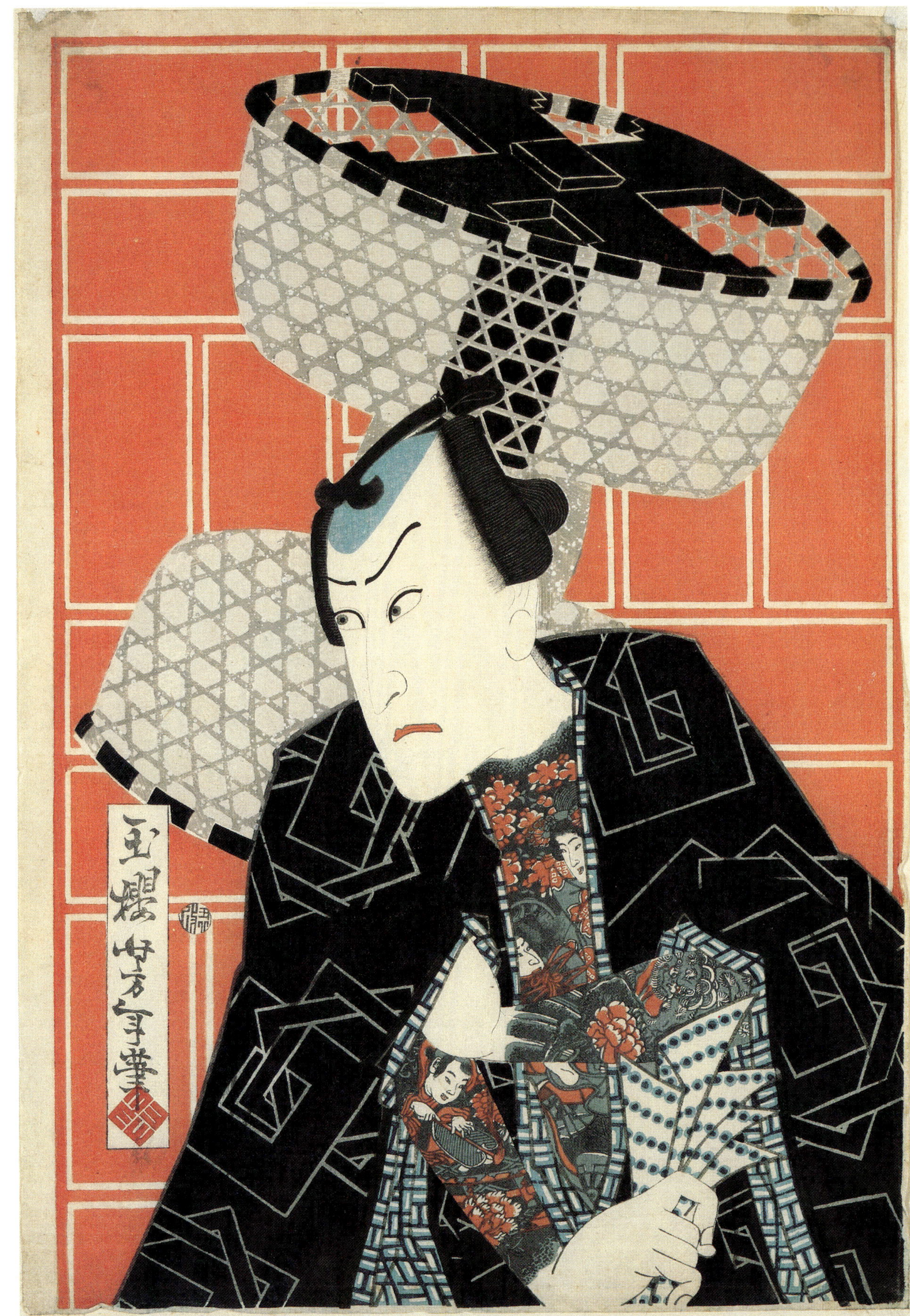

3b.

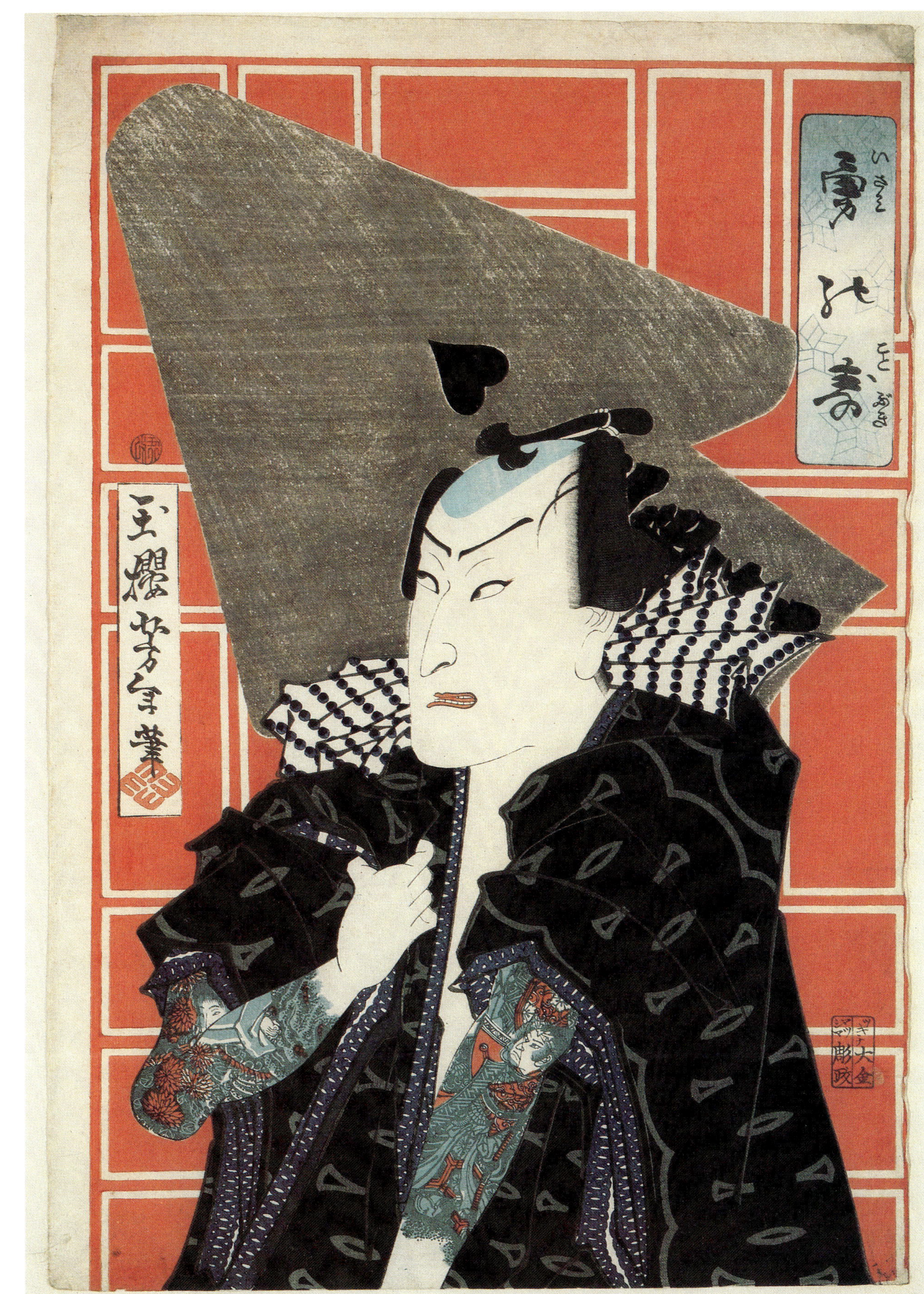

3c.

3. A Celebration of Gallantry
(Isami no kotobuki), 8/1865

Ōban triptych
Signature: Gyokuō Yoshitoshi hitsu
Seals: *Yo* and plum blossom
Publisher: Daikin
Engraver: Matsushima Hori Masa

This triptych shows Sawamura Tosshō (cat. no.
3c), Kawarazaki Gonjūrō (cat. no. 3b) and an
unidentified actor (cat. no. 3a) dressed as
tattooed firemen. Yoshitoshi and his fellow
Edo townsmen in the mid-nineteenth century
shared a particular affection for the rough-and-
ready firemen whose services were required
for so many citywide conflagrations. Firemen
and other members of the lower classes often
wore elaborate tattoos as emblems of vanity
and indifference to pain. Edo townspeople
were as fascinated with these tattoos as
they had been with the extravagant finery of
courtesans in earlier generations. They also
lionized certain handsome young Kabuki actors. In the combination of all these elements
Yoshitoshi found the subject for this print.

Kawarazaki Gonjūrō, later Ichikawa Danjūrō IX
(cat. no. 3b), was the most popular young
actor of male roles during this period. He
and Sawamura Tosshō (cat. no. 3c) were the
subjects of two panels in a similar triptych
Yoshitoshi designed earlier the same year, in
which the tattooed actors were shown beneath
a conventional setting of cherry trees. Here
they stand against deep red backgrounds
holding huge geometric forms, representations
of the *matoi,* or standards, that troops of firemen carried into conflagrations to identify
themselves and to signal movements above
the noise of the flames.

The patterns on the actors' robes are based on
their personal identifying crests; the figures in
their tattoos are taken from history and legend. The boy among the chrysanthemums on
Tosshō's chest (cat. no. 3c) is the eternal youth,
Kikujidō; the standing warrior with the bow may
be Minamoto no Yorimasa. The couple on Gonjūrō's chest (cat. no. 3b) are Yoshitsune's mistress Shizuka and a fox disguised as his loyal
retainer Satō Tadanobu. The Chinese boy
and the lion gamboling among peonies are
allusions to the Noh play *The Stone Bridge
(Shakkyō).* The warrior on the temple rooftop
tattooed on the third actor (cat. no. 3a) may be
Watanabe no Tsuna, who fell onto the roof of
the Kitano Shrine in Kyoto after he cut off the
arm of a demon who had assumed the shape
of a young girl.

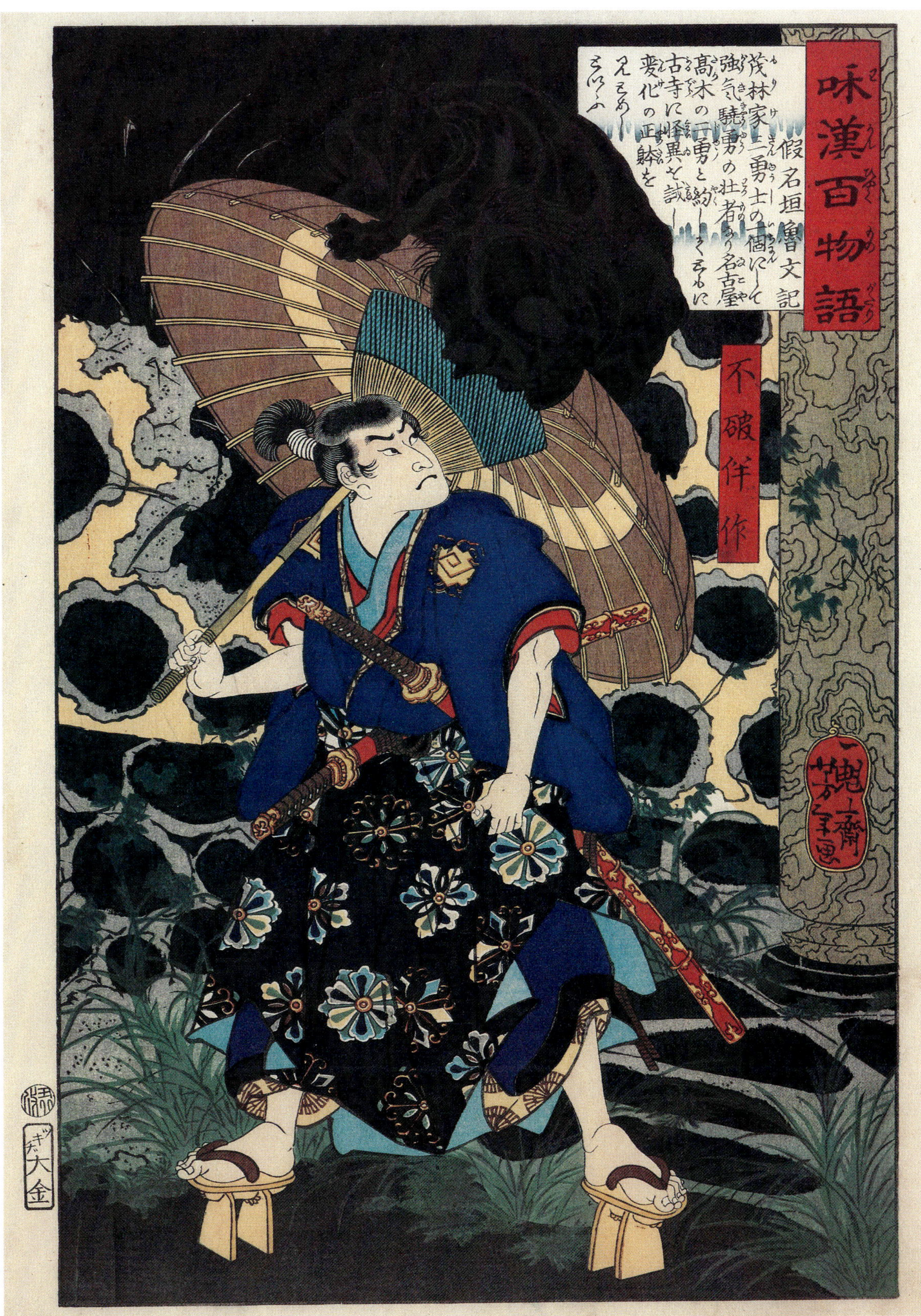
味漢百物語
不破伴作
假名垣魯文記
一魁齋芳年画
ギ
ヅ大金

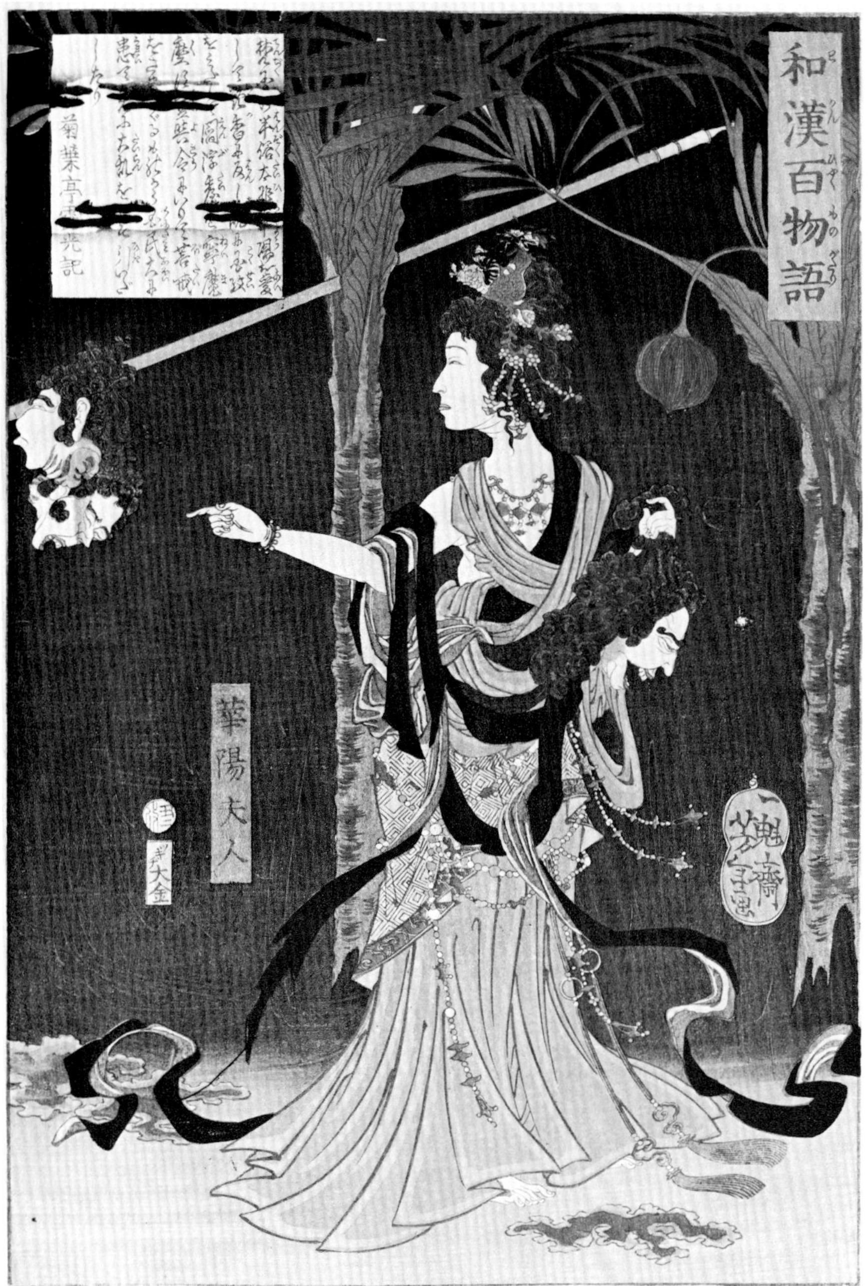

5. Lady Kayō Holding a Severed Head
2/1865

Series: *One Hundred Ghost Tales from China and Japan (Wakan hyaku monogatari)*
Ōban
Signature: Ikkaisai Yoshitoshi ga
Publisher: Daikin

The beautiful but evil woman who ruined a nation by seducing its ruler away from his duties was a familiar subject during certain periods of Chinese and Japanese history. In the popular imagination, the downfall of the T'ang dynasty was caused by the infatuation of the last emperor, Hsuan Tsung, for his consort Yang Kuei-fei, and in Tokugawa Japan courtesans were called *keisei* ("castle destroyers"), an epithet the Sung poet Su T'ung-po had applied to Yang. In the nineteenth century, as Japanese men began to face a crisis of personal power, the image of the powerful and bewitching woman became increasingly common in popular literature and pictorial art.

Lady Kayō was a character in *Ehon yōfuden (The Story of the Magic Fox Woman),* a fifteen-volume novel by Takai Ranzan with illustrations by Teisai Hokuba published between 1804 and 1805 and soon adapted for the Kabuki theater. The book describes the adventures, or misadventures, of a golden fox with nine tails whose various manifestations possessed the consorts of rulers in India, China, and Japan. In each kingdom, the fox caused havoc until it was recognized and exorcised or otherwise dispatched. In the novel, Lady Kayō was the consort of Prince Hanzoku, a ruler in southern India. She took ill, and a physician, suspecting her true nature, gave her a special herb, whereupon the fox assumed its true shape and flew into the air.

Yoshitoshi's Lady Kayō is far more menacing than the character in the novel, who murdered neither the prince nor his councillors. In the print, she is dressed in a vaguely European costume, and the three severed heads with their long curly hair appear to be Caucasian. By 1865 Yoshitoshi had already designed several overtly anti-foreign battle triptychs that obviously appealed to proponents of the imperial restoration, whose slogan was "Respect the emperor, expel the barbarian" *(Sonnō jōi).* The text on the print is by Kikuyōtei Rokō.

6. Kiyohime Turning into a Serpent
9/1865

Series: *One Hundred Ghost Tales from China
and Japan (Wakan hyaku monogatari)*
Ōban
Signature: Ikkaisai Yoshitoshi ga
Publisher: Daikin

Every year a monk named Anchin from Dōjōji
Temple visited the village of Masago on his
annual pilgrimage to Kumano. At the inn where
he stayed, the innkeeper's daughter, Kiyohime,
fell in love with him. As a monk, Anchin could
not marry, but Kiyohime would not accept this.
He retreated to his temple on the banks of the
Hidaka River, and she followed in pursuit. When
she reached the river it was flooded, and the
ferryboat was on the other side. Nevertheless,
she flung herself into the water; her passion
and jealousy were so great that she began
to change into a serpent and arrived safely on
the other side. In the end, Anchin hid himself
inside the great temple bell, but Kiyohime,
completely transformed into a serpent and
furious over his rejection of her love, surrounded the bell with her coils. She melted the
bell with the heat of her anger and the priest
died.

This tenth-century story reportedly was recorded by the Emperor Go-Komatsu (1377–
1433) and was the basis for the Noh play
Dōjōji.[1]

Yoshitoshi shows the girl emerging from the
river in the dead of the night, holding strands
of her hair in a gesture of determination. The
patterns of her sash and robe are meant to
suggest a serpent's scales. The falling cherry
blossoms indicate the season of spring, as well
as the fragility of human life. The finest impressions of the print have a polished pattern for
the water dripping from Kiyohime's hair. The
text on the print is by Sumida Ryōko.

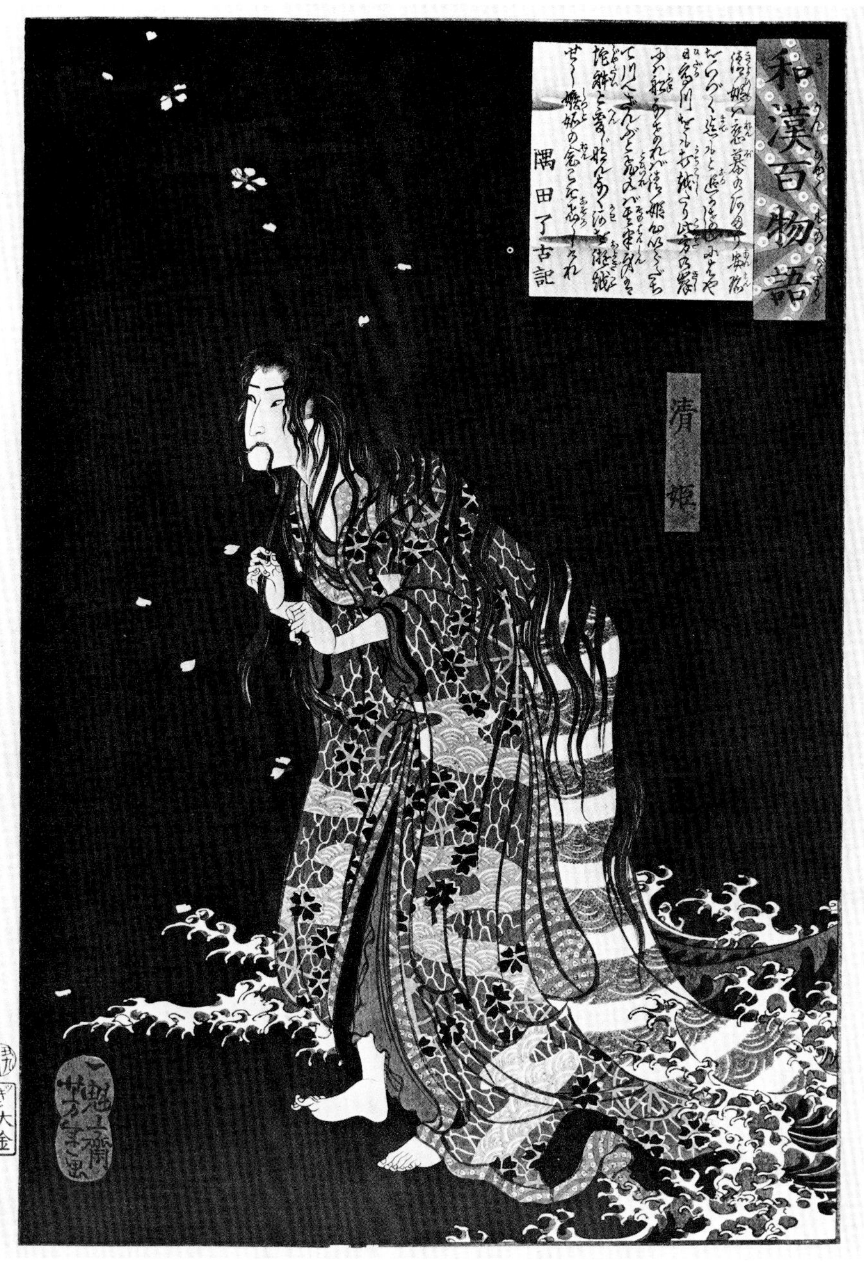

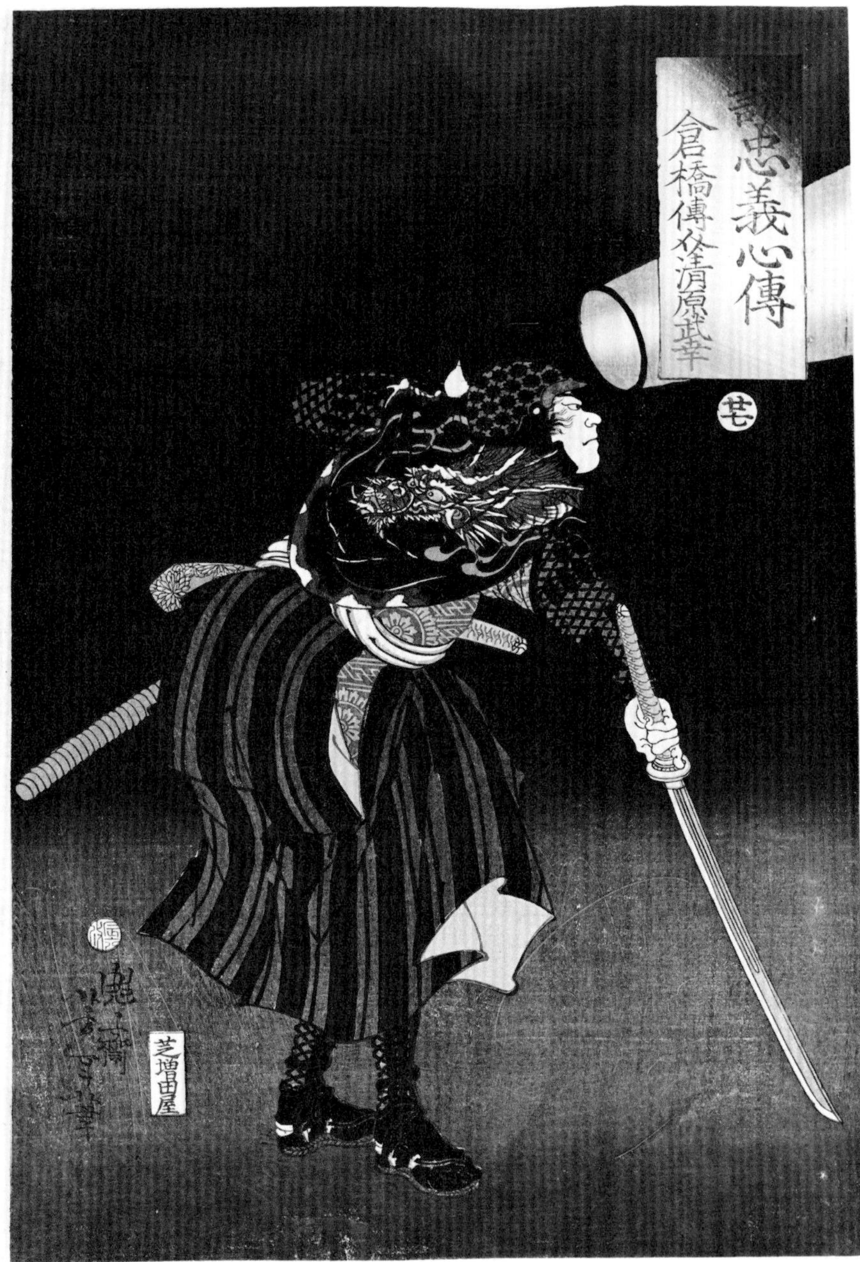

7. Kurahashi Densuke Kiyohara no Takeyuki Holding a Lantern
6/1868

Series: *Portraits of True Loyalty and Righteous Hearts (Seichū gishinden),* no. 27
Ōban
Signature: Kaisai Yoshitoshi hitsu
Publisher: Masudaya

Japan had been at peace for more than two centuries when civil war broke out in the mid-1860s between supporters of the military government of Edo and adherents of the emperor in Kyoto. The tumultuous events of this period seized the popular imagination, and Ukiyo-e artists were asked to design numerous prints of military subjects. At the beginning of its administration in the early seventeenth century, however, the Tokugawa government had forbidden artists and writers to draw, or discuss, contemporary events. These restrictions, theoretically, were still in force in the 1860s, and no artist dared explicitly to portray any momentous current event. Printmakers therefore turned to historical themes that held allegorical significance for the contemporary military scene.

This portrait was one of a series of the forty-seven *rōnin,* or masterless samurai, who avenged their master's death in an attack on his enemy's mansion. Afterward, they all committed ritual suicide. This incident took place in Edo at the beginning of the eighteenth century and was perpetuated, first in the *jorūri* puppet theater and soon thereafter in the enormously popular Kabuki play *A Treasury of Loyalty (Chūshingura).* The forty-seven *rōnin* became romantic symbols of loyal warriors who sought justice outside the established legal system and willingly accepted their own deaths as a consequence. They became popular models for soldiers on both sides of the civil war, especially for the imperial insurgents.

All the prints in Yoshitoshi's series have black backgrounds, indicating the nighttime attack of the forty-seven *rōnin.* The samurai carries a hooded lantern that sends out a strong, directed beam of light but can be covered up for travel in total darkness. He is dressed in the traditional black zigzag-patterned robes of the forty-seven *rōnin.*

8. Shigeno Yozaemon and a Bursting Shell
1/1869

Series: *One Hundred Warriors in Battle
Selected by Yoshitoshi (Kaidai hyaku sensō)*
Ōban
Signature: Ikkaisai Yoshitoshi hitsu
Publisher: Ōhashi

In the fifth month of 1868, just before the
victorious entry of the emperor into Edo, a
troop of soldiers loyal to the shogun made a
final stand at Tōei Temple on a hill in the Ueno
district, near the present site of the Tokyo
National Museum. Yoshitoshi and his pupil
Toshikage went to Ueno to observe the bloody
fighting firsthand. Two months later he published the first prints in a strange set of soldier
portraits which combine Western techniques of
drawing, shading, and foreshortening (seen
here) with an overwhelming abundance of
blood and gore (seen in other prints).

Artists could circumvent the government ban
on portraying contemporary events by pretend-
ing that the events took place in the distant
past. The soldiers in this set, for example, are
given the names of warriors who figured in civil
wars of the fourteenth and sixteenth centuries,
before the Tokugawa clan came to power. This
is a complete fiction, however, since the soldiers are depicted in modern costume, and the
Western effects deliberately give the pictures
a modern touch. The set was successful at first
but became repetitious, and it was discon-
tinued in the third month of 1869 after fifty-eight
of the projected one hundred prints were
published.

The text here, by Umpō Sanjin, gives a brief
biography of the supposedly medieval subject,
ending with a note that Shigeno was wounded
in the hand by a large Western-style gun.

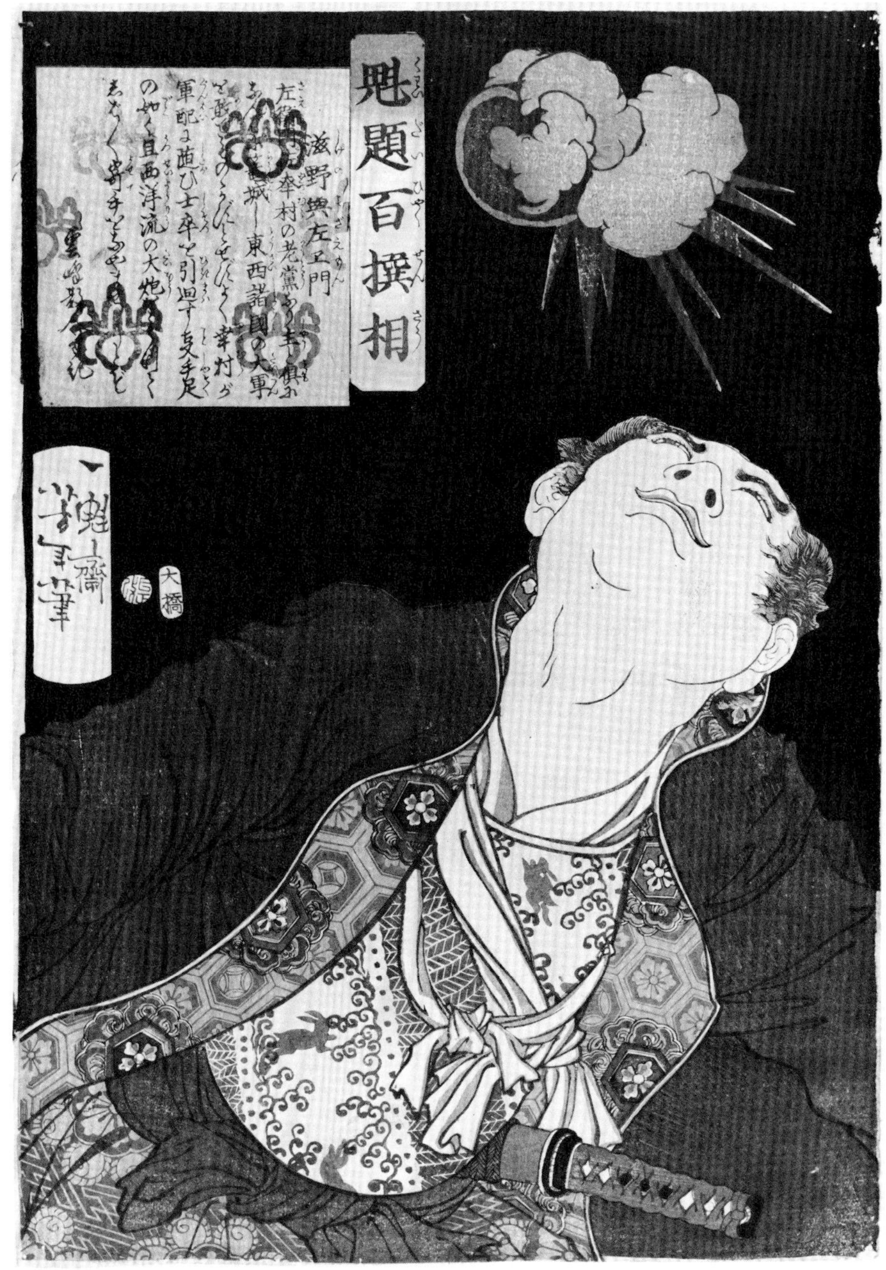

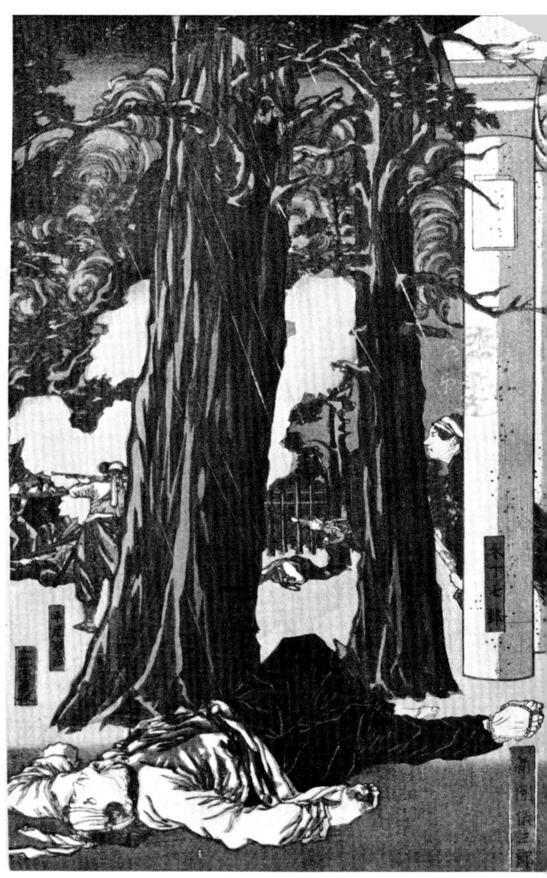

9. The Battle of Sannō Shrine

(Tōdai sannōzan sensō no zu), c. late 1874

Ōban triptych
Signature: Ōju Taiso Yoshitoshi
Publisher: Rokkaen
Engraver: Horikō Tomekichi

Yoshitoshi celebrated his recovery from illness at the end of 1873 by adopting the secondary name Taiso, which means "resurrected," or "returned to health after a serious illness," but he did not strike a successful balance in his work until the end of 1874, when he designed a group of battle triptychs based on his firsthand memories of the actual fighting at the Battle of Ueno in 1868. This print is unquestionably the finest of the group. The horror of the scene is made just bearable by the indifference of the landscape; the violence is balanced by the geometric composition, and the blatant red is subdued by the delicate colors of the strange trees and the background. In this print Yoshitoshi seems to have come to terms with his obsession for blood and violence, and his imagination has become freed for other tasks. The figures in the print are historical personages, all soldiers loyal to the shogun Tokugawa Iemochi. From left to right their names are given as Amano Hachirō, Sakai Saisuke, Kondō Takeo, Ishikawa Zenichirō, and the fallen Niibiraki (Shinkai) Gisaburō. Kinoshita Shichirō is shown running through the stone gate, and Hirao Iwanosuke is firing a rifle in the background.

The print is particularly interesting because it became the property of Mizuno Toshikata, Yoshitoshi's favorite and most talented pupil, and bears Toshikata's seal dated 1879, only five years after the print was designed. Toshikata was born in 1865 and became Yoshitoshi's pupil at the age of fourteen in 1879. Yoshitoshi must have given the boy this print soon afterward, and Toshikata stamped each sheet with his new seal with a child's carelessness and disregard.

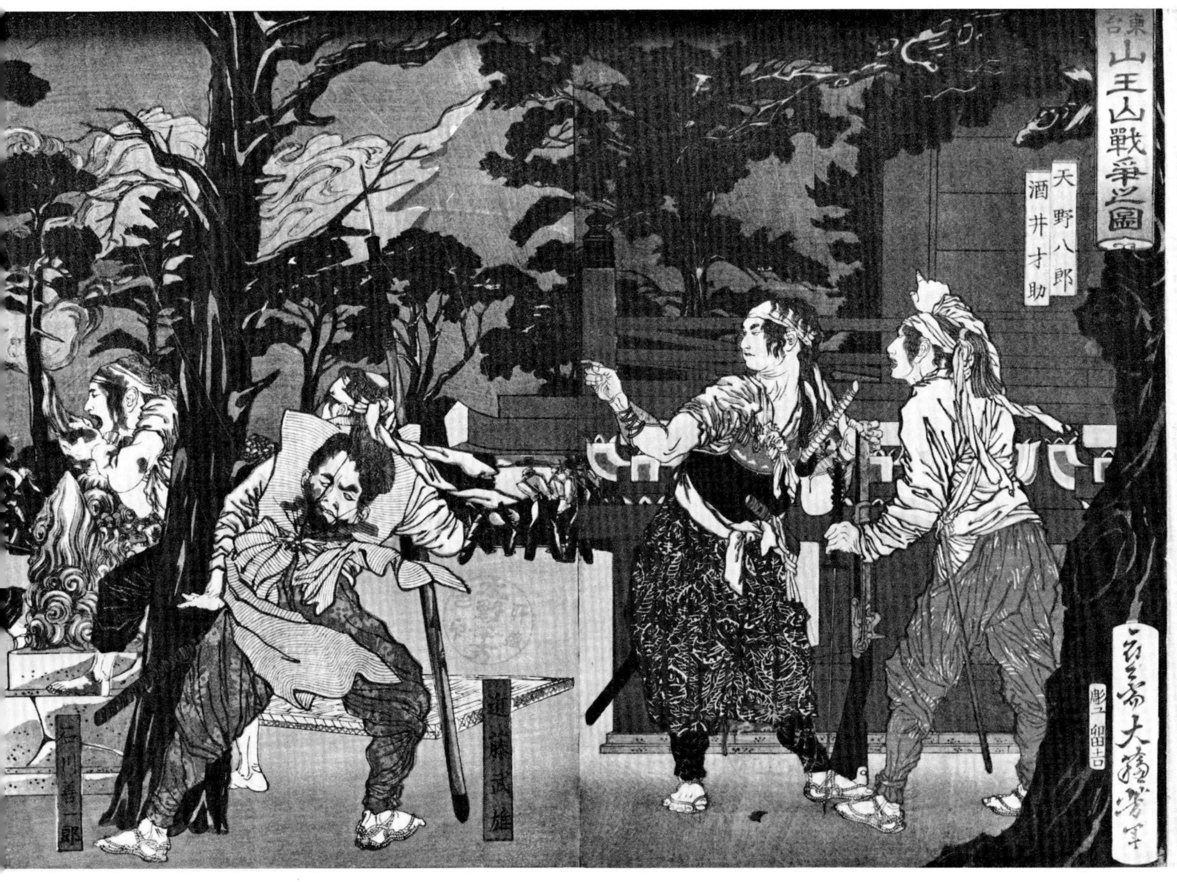

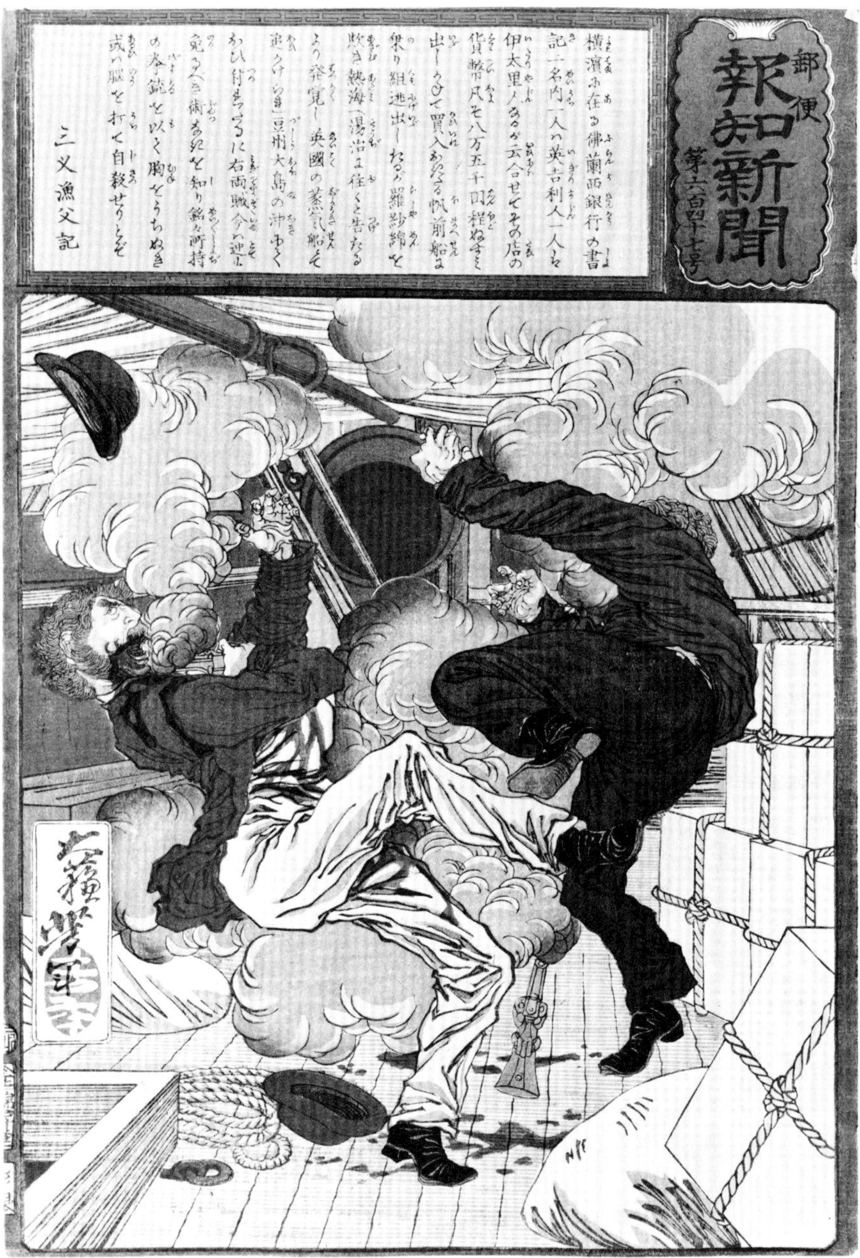

10. The Suicide of Two Foreign Clerks

c. August 1875

Series: *The Postal News (Yūbin hōchi shimbun),* no. 647
Ōban
Signature: Taiso Yoshitoshi
Seal: Yoshitoshi
Publisher: Kinshōdō
Engraver: Horikō Gin

Yoshitoshi established himself as a popular artist with a series of more than fifty pictures of comic and sensational contemporary events reported in the *Postal News,* a newspaper published by Kumagaiya Shōshichi from April 1875 through the spring of 1876. The format of the prints was one used frequently by Yoshitoshi's teacher, Kuniyoshi, and other artists in the middle of the century: a squarish picture placed below a band containing an explanatory text alongside the series title. In this case the text seems to come from the issue of the newspaper given in the title cartouche.

Most Japanese writers assume that the "newspaper prints" were published as a kind of bonus for subscribers. Some were, but others like the *Postal News* prints seem simply to have been based on newspaper stories and sold commercially like other woodblock prints.

In this print an Italian and an Englishman, clerks in a French bank in Yokohama, embezzled funds but were overtaken by an English ship as they attempted to escape. They committed suicide rather than submit to capture and imprisonment. The text was written by Mitsumata Ryōfu.

11. Black Monster Attacking a Carpenter's Wife

c. August 1875

Series: *The Postal News (Yūbin hōchi shimbun),*
no. 663
Ōban
Signature: Taiso Yoshitoshi
Seal: Yoshitoshi
Publisher: Kinshōdō
Engraver: Horikō Gin

However violent the murders and however
imaginative the apparitions in Yoshitoshi's early
prints, they seldom seem as disturbing as his
illustrations of real, or supposedly real, events
taken from the daily newspapers. Previously
there had always been some distance between Yoshitoshi, his subjects, and his audience, but with the newspaper prints he built a
firm bridge across these gaps. Not all the
Postal News prints are as lurid and dramatic
as this one and catalog number 10, but they all
reveal a common touch.

In this print, "a certain carpenter's foreman" in
Fukudachō, a neighborhood in the Kanda district of Tokyo, looks on with horror as a ghostly
monster attacks his sickly wife. This was said
to have happened every night, and the wife
became increasingly ill until she left the carpenter to stay with relatives, whereupon the
visits from the monster ceased. The text was
written by Matsubayashi Hakuen.

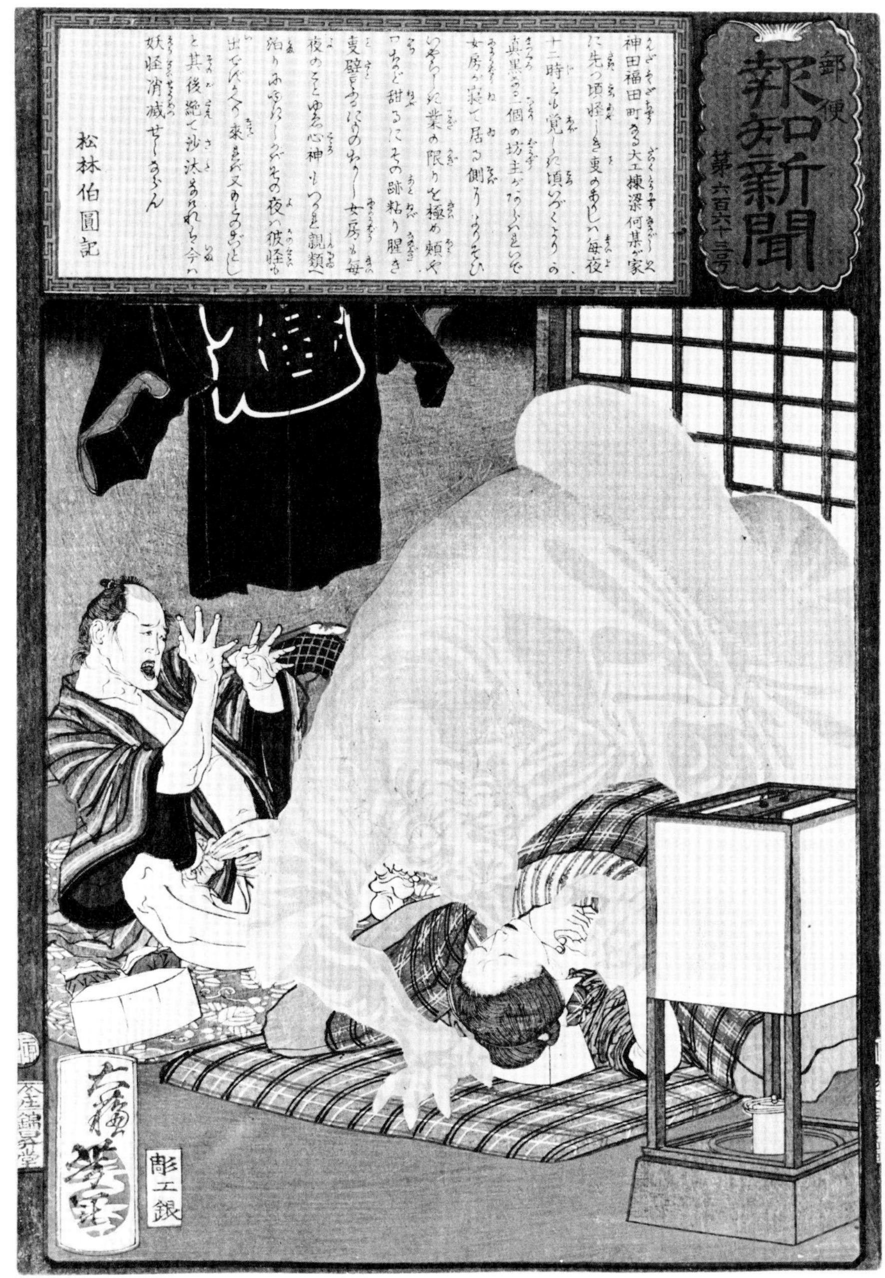

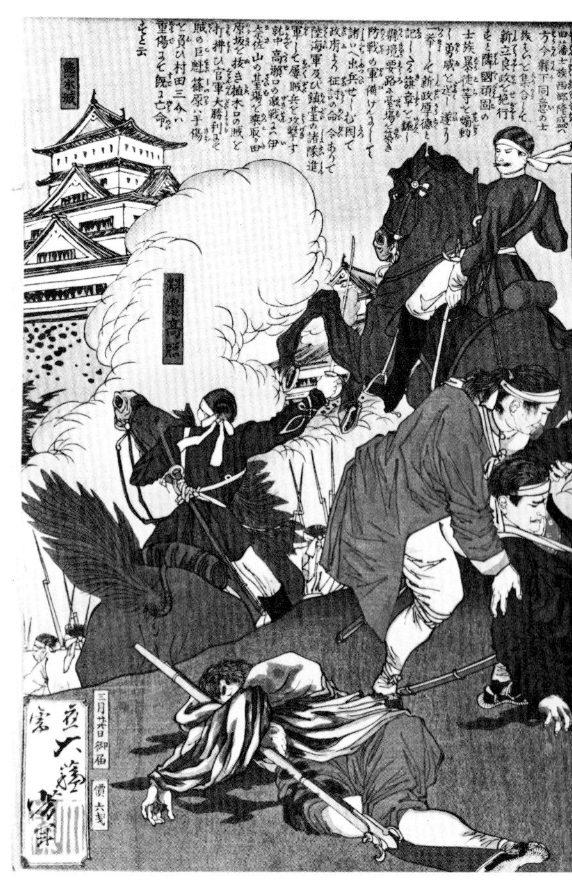

12. The Death of Murata Sansuke

March 26, 1877

Series: *From the Chronicles of the Conquest of Kagoshima in Satsuma Province (Sasshū kagoshima seitōki no uchi)*
Ōban triptych
Signature: Ōju Taiso Yoshitoshi
Seal: Yoshitoshi
Publisher: Funazu Chūjirō

Murata Sansuke was a follower of Saigō Takamori, a statesman and military leader who was largely responsible for the reunification of Japan after the emperor's restoration in 1868. In later years, Saigō became discontented with the direction taken by the new government, particularly its treatment of lower-level samurai. He retired to the feudal domain of Satsuma on the southern island of Kyushu, where dispossessed samurai gathered around him. In 1877 he led them in an insurrection, known as the Satsuma Rebellion, which government forces easily suppressed.

Saigō's defection was sensational news, and the Japanese avidly followed events of the short-lived insurrection. Enterprising publishers hired Ukiyo-e artists to design woodblock prints of important incidents and battles, and without exception the artists showed a sympathetic respect for the rebels' ideals and valor. With his facility for battle scenes and his active imagination, Yoshitoshi quickly became the foremost print designer of the war.

One pupil remembers that at this time the street in front of Yoshitoshi's house was "as busy as a marketplace."[2] Yoshitoshi never visited the battlefield, and his prints, with their Western-looking soldiers, are idealized and often fanciful. While few of his war prints are particularly beautiful or powerful, the popular success and financial security he achieved during this period were conditions that made his later work possible.

The rebel soldiers are all named on adjacent red boxes: the soldier in profile on horseback at the right is General Saigō; beside him on horseback is Kirino Toshiaki; before him with his arm in a sling is Ikegami Shirō; Murata Sansuke is the fallen figure in the center. In the background, the mustachioed Shinohara Kokkan rides toward Kumamoto Castle, as one soldier raises the flag of the Satsuma clan and the other a banner with the slogan of the revolt: "A new government of deep virtue" *(shinsei kōtoku)*. The inscription gives a general account of the uprising and ends with a remark on Murata's death.

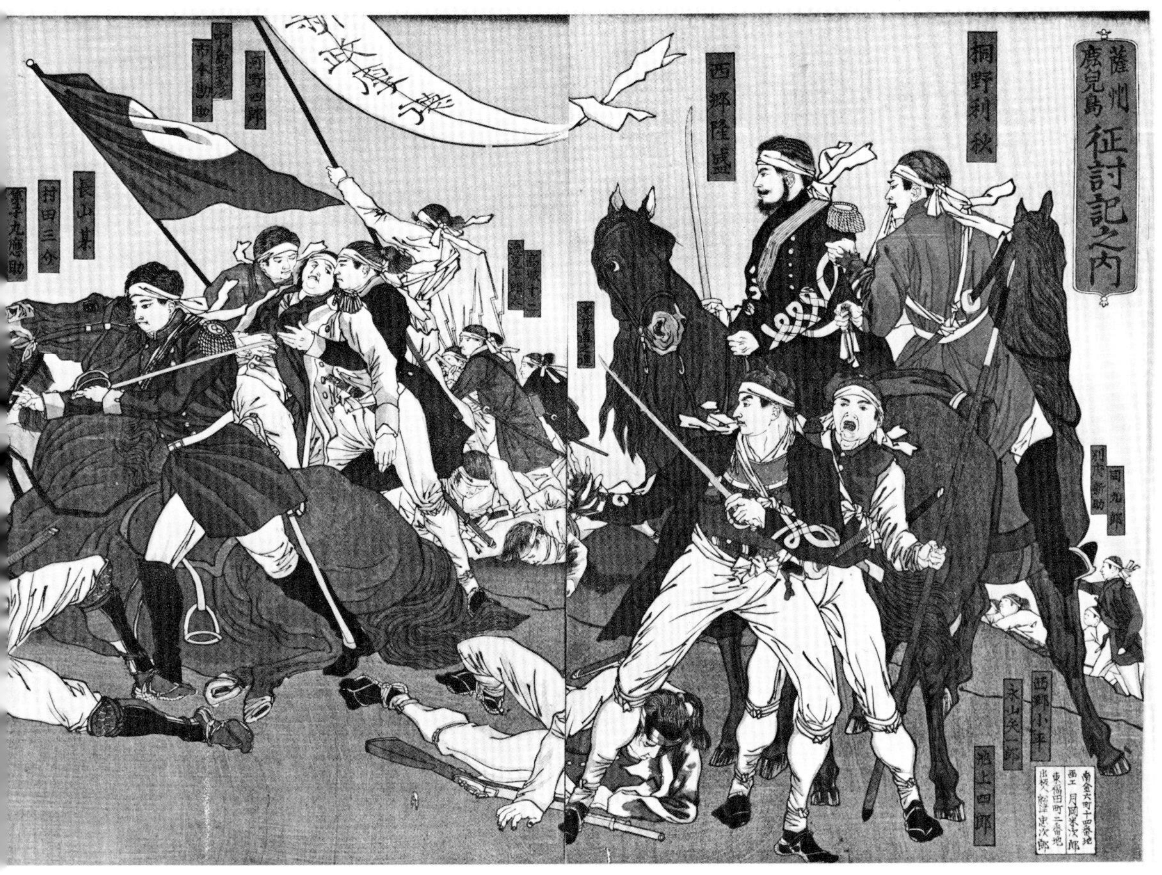

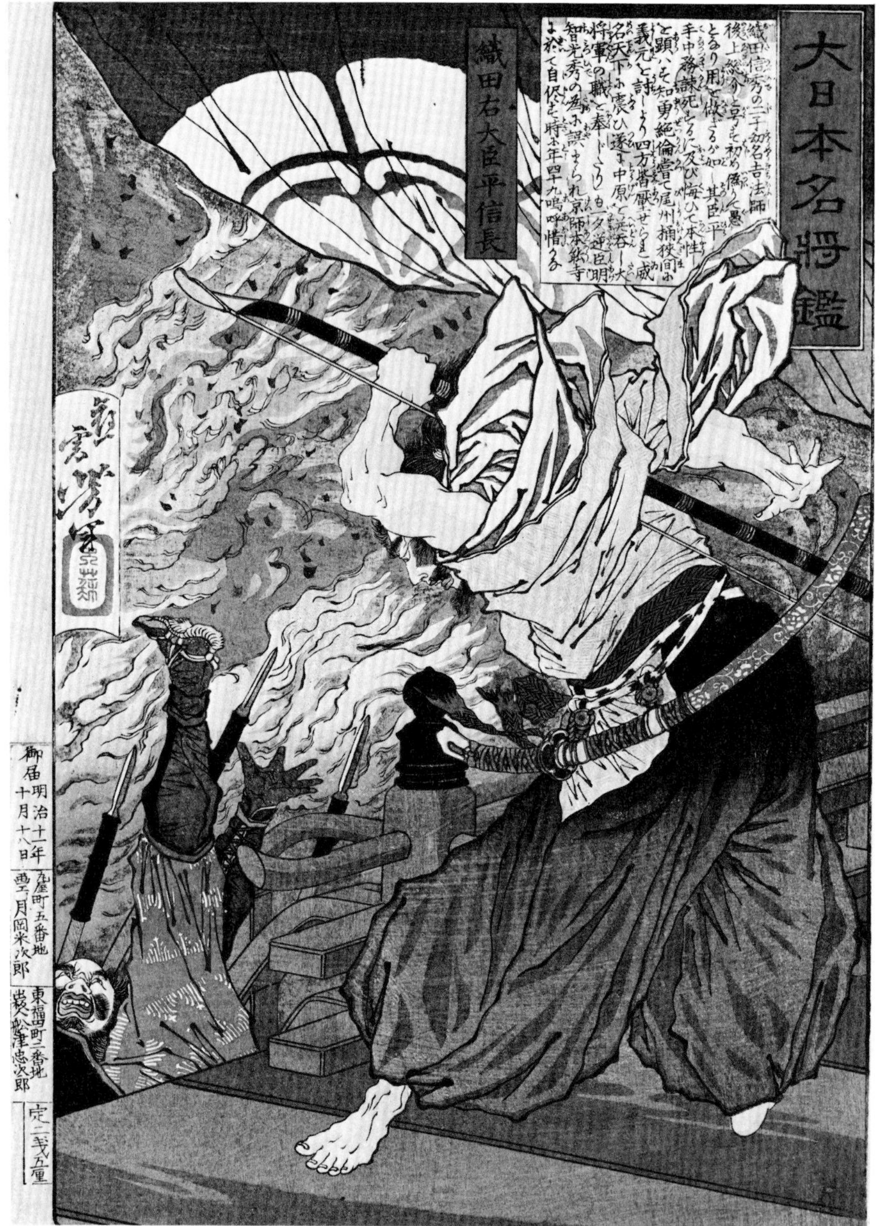

13. Oda Nobunaga Defending Himself at Honnōji Temple
October 18, 1878

Series: *A Mirror of Famous Generals of Japan (Dainippon meishō kagami)*
Ōban
Signature: Ōju Yoshitoshi
Seal: Taiso
Publisher: Funazu Chūjirō

Oda Nobunaga, the general who deposed the last Ashikaga shogun, waged relentless warfare against his many enemies toward the end of the sixteenth century with the motto, "Rule the empire by force!" He fell victim to treachery in 1582 when one of his own generals, Akechi Mitsuhide, betrayed him and attacked him at his residence in Honnō Temple in Kyoto. The temple was burned, and, although Nobunaga's troops furiously repelled the attack, they were defeated. Nobunaga was said to have committed suicide, but his body was not recovered after the temple burned.

The *Mirror of Famous Generals of Japan* was published at intervals over a period of several years, covering a total of fifty-one subjects. The series was published by Funazu Chūjirō, one of Tokyo's leading new publishers who had issued many of Yoshitoshi's Satsuma Rebellion prints. The prints were skillfully engraved and carefully printed, often with delicately colored borders, and sold for 2½ *sen,* a half *sen* more, it seems, than usual commercial prints during this period. The colors used in the series were varied, and it was in this set that Yoshitoshi first began to explore ways to use color to convey mood.

14. Musashibō Benkei Battling with Young Ushiwaka on Gojō Bridge

October 18, 1886

Series: *A Mirror of Famous Generals of Japan*
(Dainippon meishō kagami)
Ōban
Signature: Ōju Yoshitoshi
Seal: Taiso
Publisher: Funazu Chūjirō

After the Heian court depicted so elegantly in the *Tale of Genji* languished, Japan was plunged into civil wars in which the two most powerful factions were the Taira (Heike) and the Minamoto (Genji) clans. Taira no Kiyomori ruthlessly seized power in the mid-twelfth century. In an uncommon act of mercy he spared the children of his Minamoto adversaries, and when they became adults they led the campaigns that ended in the defeat of his clan.

These children were raised separately. One of them named Ushiwaka lived in a temple on Mt. Kurama northeast of Kyoto where, legend has it, he was taught the martial arts by goblins called *tengu*.[3] When his education was complete, he left the temple to seek his elder brother Yoritomo. On his way he crossed the Kamo River at Gojō Bridge in Kyoto, where he met Musashibō Benkei, a colossal priest who challenged him and demanded his sword. In the ensuing duel, the agile youth exhausted the older man, who swore to serve the victor. When Ushiwaka took the name Yoshitsune and began campaigning against the Taira forces, Benkei was one of his most faithful followers. The scene of their fight on Gojō Bridge has been depicted frequently in prints, paintings, and decorative arts. Yoshitoshi departs from convention by drawing their duel as a graceful dance. The silver ball behind the two men is the full moon.

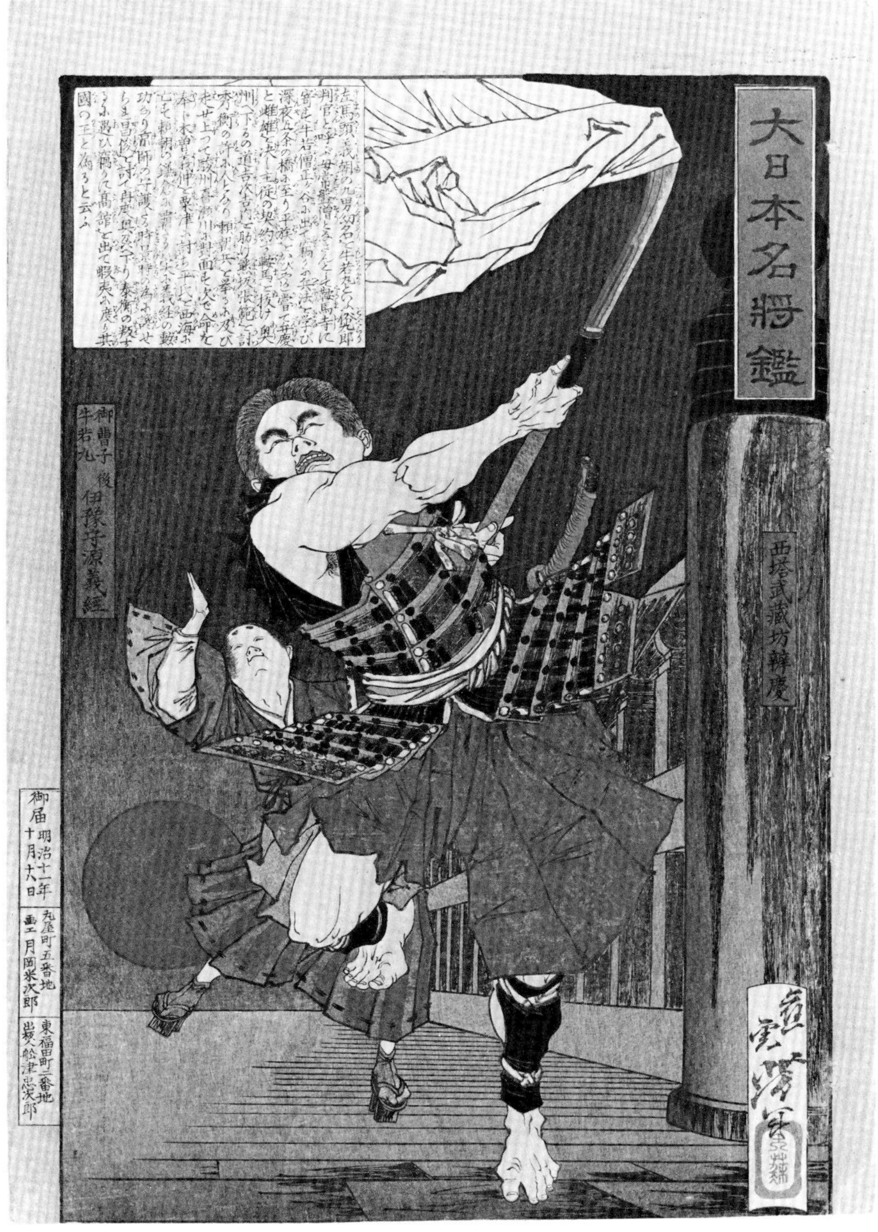

15. Gojō Bridge, an Episode from the _Life of Yoshitsune (Gikeiki gojōbashi no zu)_
1881

Ōban triptych
Signature: Taiso Yoshitoshi
Seal: Yoshitoshi
Publisher: Morimoto Junzaburō

Yoshitoshi was capable of the most extreme exaggeration as well as remarkable restraint. In this picture, the entire body of the warrior priest Benkei seems knotted with rage as he grapples with Ushiwaka's veil after the youth has leapt nimbly from his grasp. About this time the moon began to appear more and more frequently in Yoshitoshi's prints as a silent witness to the passionate and momentous affairs of men.

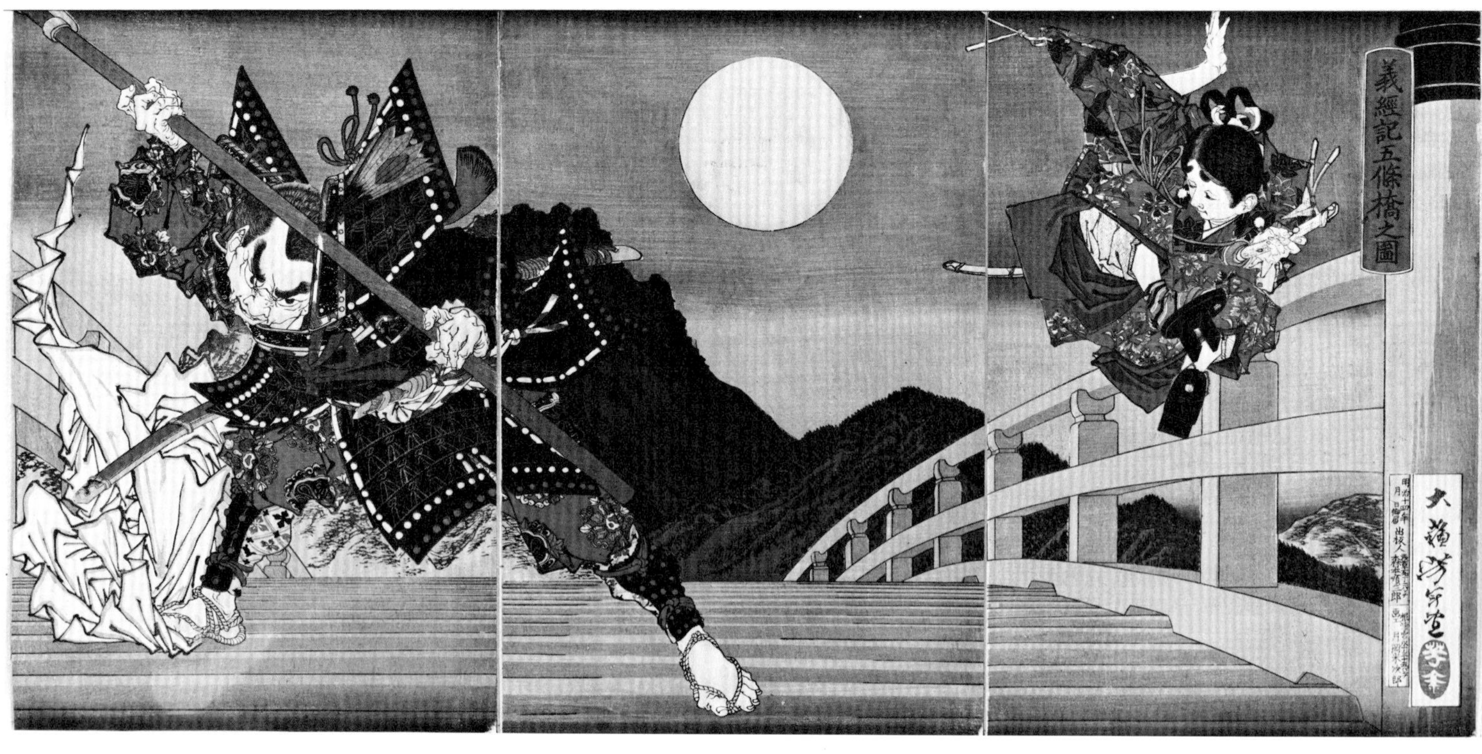

16. Karukaya Dōshin Refusing to Recognize Ishidōmaru

September 21, 1881

Series: *Twenty-four Accomplishments in Imperial Japan (Kōkoku nijūshikō)*
Ōban
Signature: Taiso Yoshitoshi ga
Seal: Taiso
Publisher: Tsuda Genshichi

The story of Katō Saemon Shigeuji, a wealthy lord in Kyushu during the Ashikaga period, was the subject of ballads, puppet plays, and Noh dramas. Returning home one night he saw his wife and a companion playing *gō,* a Japanese game similar to checkers. While they appeared quite friendly, their long hair was writhing like snakes, hissing and biting at each other. This sight so saddened him that he left his home the next morning and became a priest at Mount Kōya, taking the name of Karukaya. His wife searched for him for many years and finally reached the temple where he lived. Since women could not enter the temple precincts, she sent Ishidōmaru, her son, to make inquiries. He met his father unwittingly, but Karukaya refused to recognize his son, even when the boy recognized a mole over his father's eye which his mother said would identify him. Yoshitoshi touchingly conveys the pathos of this scene as the boy clutches his father's hand and the father turns away with a gesture of resignation.

The *Twenty-four Accomplishments* was begun in May 1881 and completed in 1887. Some of the prints first published in 1881 were reissued with different colors when the entire group was published as a set. The entire set was republished by Matsuki Heikichi between 1893 and 1895, after Yoshitoshi's death, with altered signatures and completely different, paler colors, sometimes with keyblock changes. This print and the next (cat. no. 17) are fine, fresh impressions of the earliest edition. The texts on the prints are by Ryūtei Tanehiko II, using the signature "Tentendōjin." His words are poetic and allusive, and they convey a verbal equivalent of the mood of Yoshitoshi's picture. The circumstances of the publication are unknown: it is not clear whether Tanehiko wrote for Yoshitoshi's picture, or if Yoshitoshi illustrated Tanehiko's text.

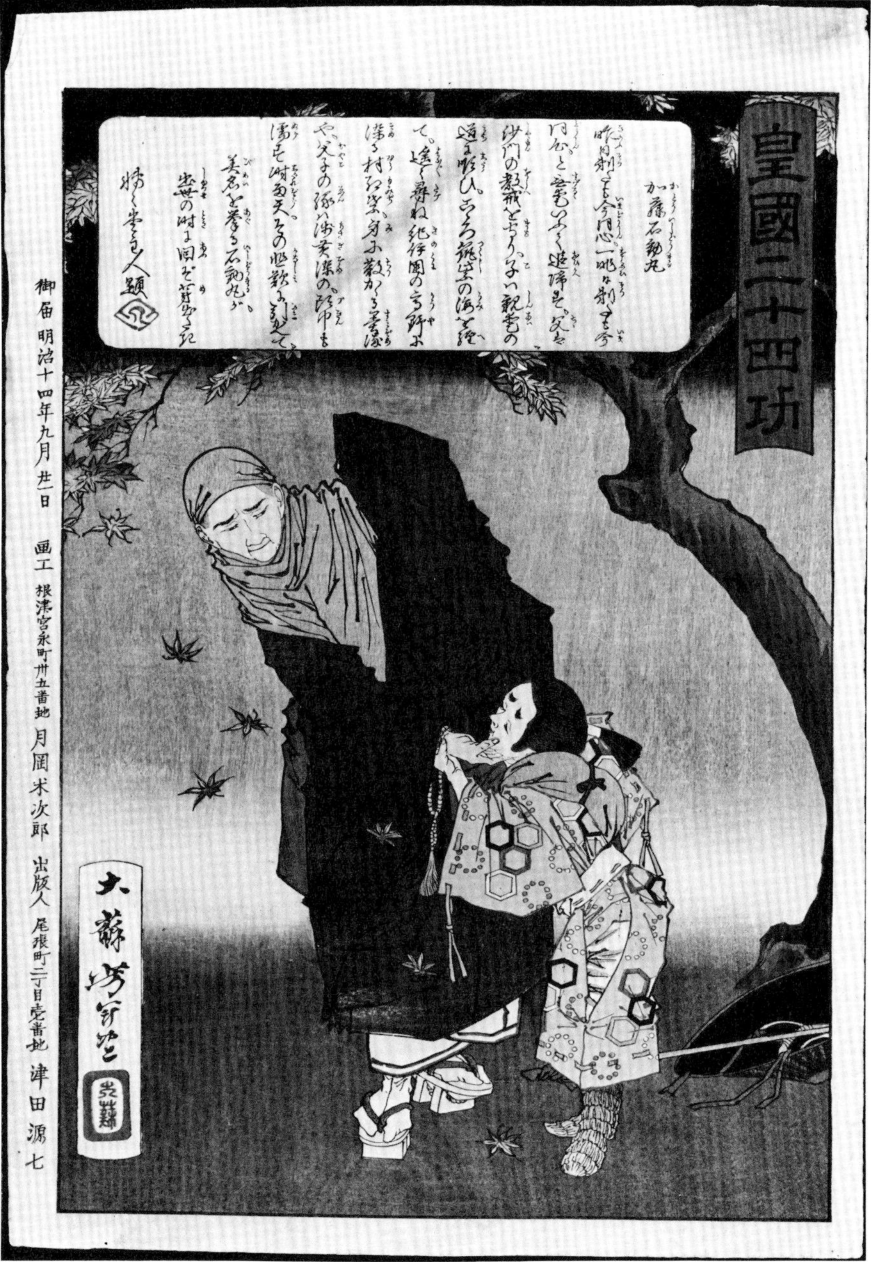

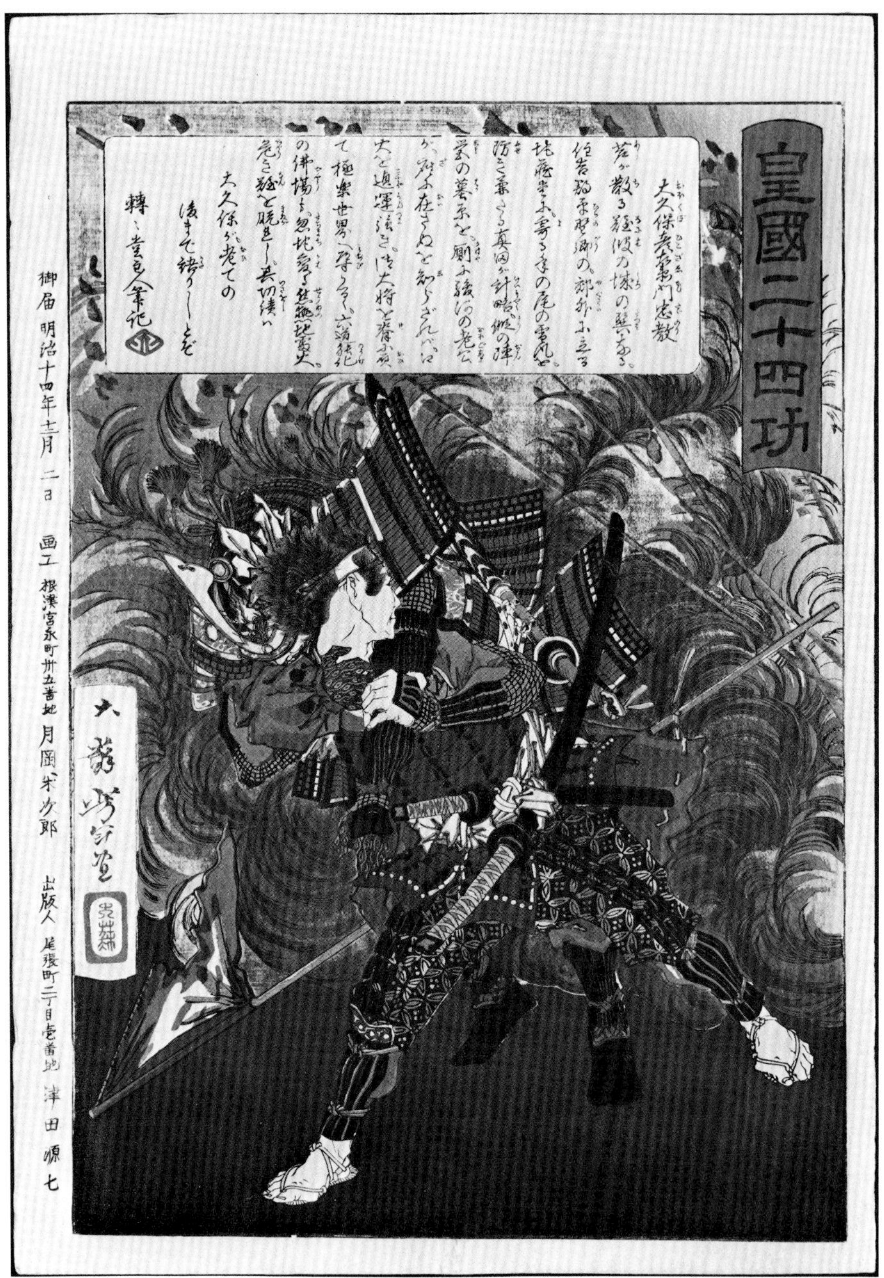

17. Ōkubo Hikozaemon Tadataka Rescuing Tokugawa Ieyasu

December 2, 1881

Series: *Twenty-four Accomplishments in Imperial Japan (Kōkoku nijūshikō)*
Ōban
Signature: Taiso Yoshitoshi ga
Seal: Taiso
Publisher: Tsuda Genshichi

Ōkubo Hikozaemon (1560–1639) was one of Tokugawa Ieyasu's trusted generals and advisers. The episode in Yoshitoshi's picture is not mentioned in the brief biographies of Ōkubo in standard history books,[4] but from the print's text by Ryūtei Tanehiko II it is clear that the incident took place soon after Ieyasu's successful seige of Osaka castle. A temporary encampment was set up in Hirano village near Sumiyoshi in a temple building dedicated to Bodhisattva Jizō. The building came under fire, and Ōkubo risked his own life to carry his general to safety. For a moment death seemed certain, and Ōkubo expected that he was carrying his lord to paradise, but suddenly the danger was past.

This print and catalog number 16 from the same series show Yoskitoshi's expressive range: he was equally at home in depicting explosive violence or delicate shades of melancholy and happiness.

18. Taira no Kiyomori Seeing Skulls in the Snowy Garden
May 10, 1882

Series: *A New Selection of Strange Events*
(*Shinyō rokkaisen*)
Ōban triptych
Signature: Ōju Yoshitoshi ga
Seal: Taiso
Publisher: Funazu Chūjirō
Engraver: Horikō Enkatsu

Taira no Kiyomori (1117–1181) was an ambitious and cruel man who seized power by force and guile and maintained it with a rule of terror. Unsatisfied as the military lord of half of Japan, he assumed prerogatives of the emperor. Retribution came in the form of mental illness. One winter's night, as Kiyomori stood on his balcony overlooking his peaceful garden, before his eyes the rocks and shrubs became the skulls of his victims. The hallucination persisted, and Kiyomori fell ill with a horrible fever from which he soon died (see cat. no. 19).

Gokensha Shujin, author of the brief biography on this print, seems to have seen Kiyomori's hubris, rather than his atrocities, as the cause of his downfall. His text has political overtones; perhaps it was intended as a warning to the arrogant clique which controlled the national government by the 1880s. Yoshitoshi, on the other hand, simply portrays the moral ruination of an individual without added satirical meaning.

The idea and composition of the *Skull Garden* seems to be taken from an unusual *ōban* triptych designed by Utagawa Hiroshige and published about 1850. Hiroshige's picture is far more balanced and geometrical than Yoshitoshi's: the wide garden is filled with skeletons and skulls, and Kiyomori is drawn without emotion or judgment as a noble lord poised between the warm interior of the palace and the cold, frightening hallucination in the snowy landscape. Yoshitoshi's Kiyomori, by contrast, is neither noble nor strong. His lined face looks weak and tired, his pose is hesitant, not resolute; his luxurious brocades hamper him and seem unfit for a lay priest and a warrior. His concubines tremble, and he seems to have been infected by their fear. Unlike Gokensha or Hiroshige, Yoshitoshi suggests that Kiyomori's debauchery left him powerless, vulnerable, and prey to terrifying visions and imaginings.

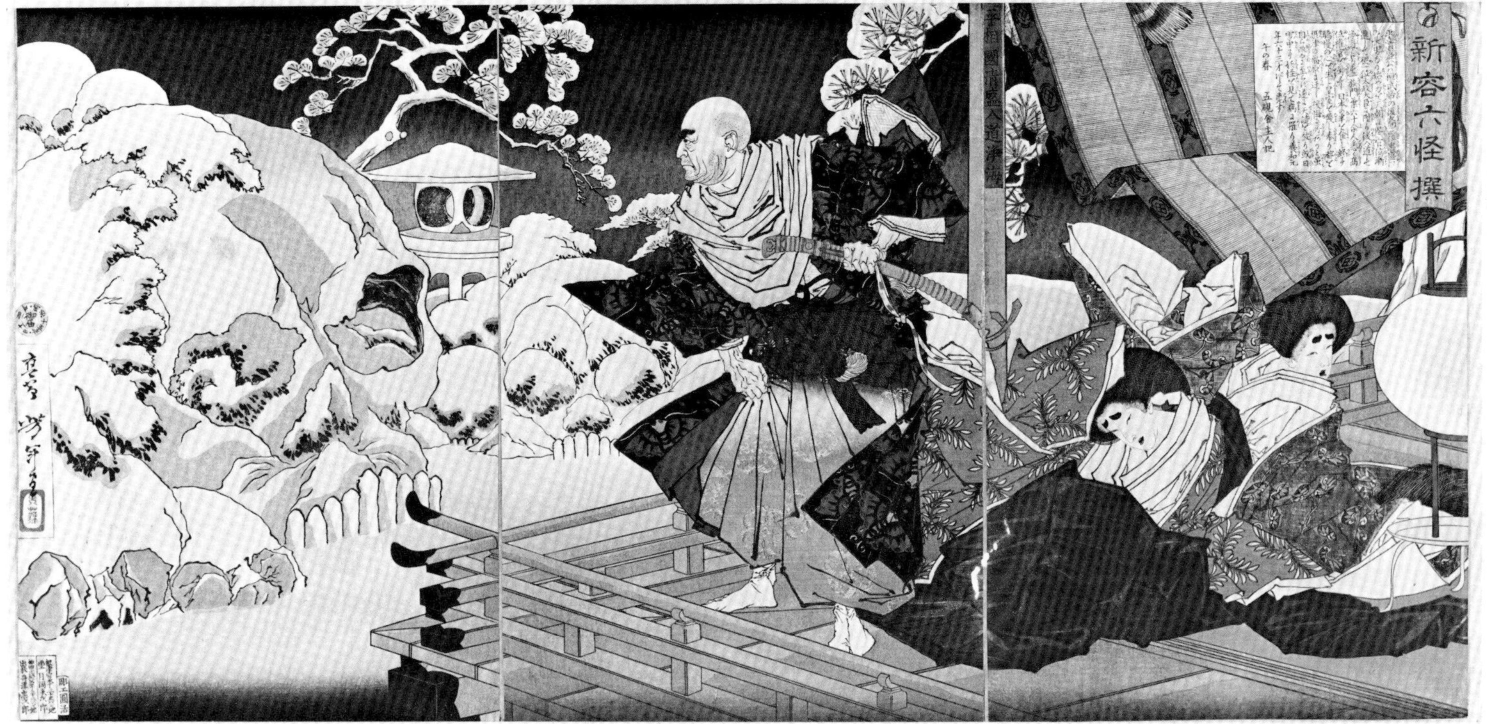

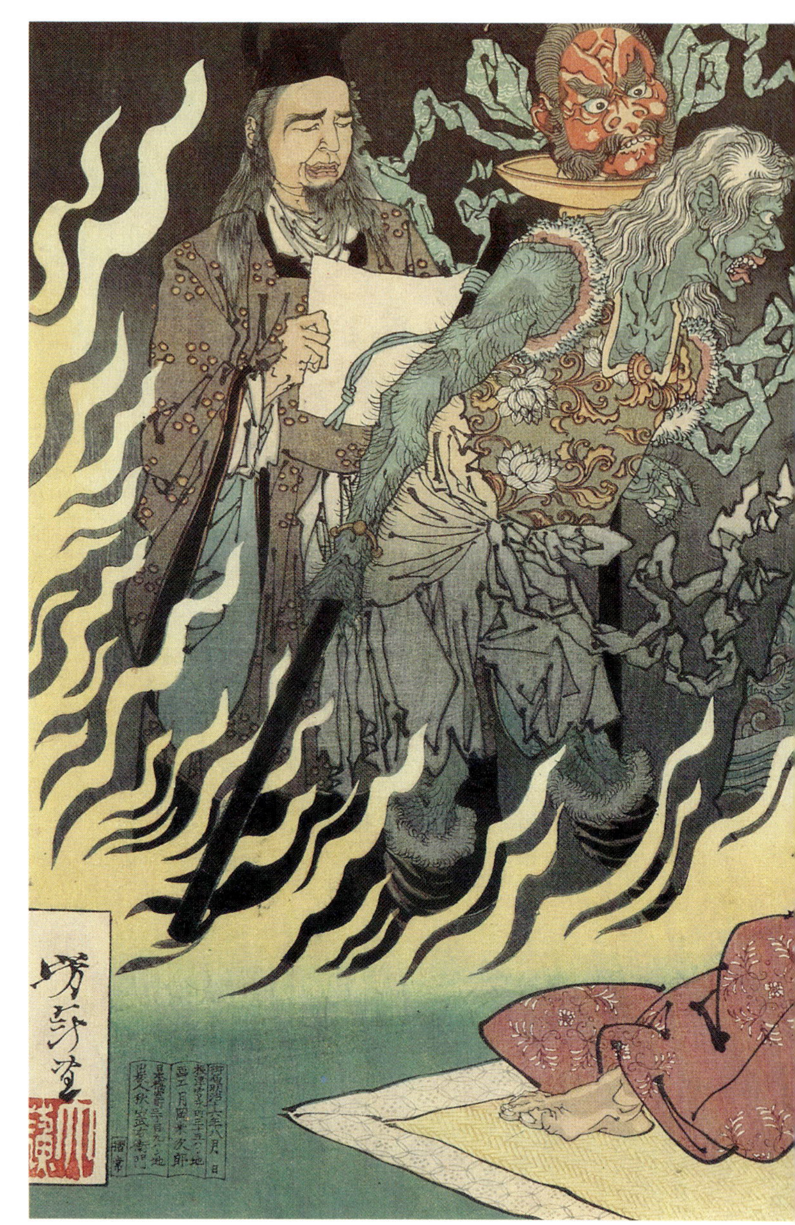

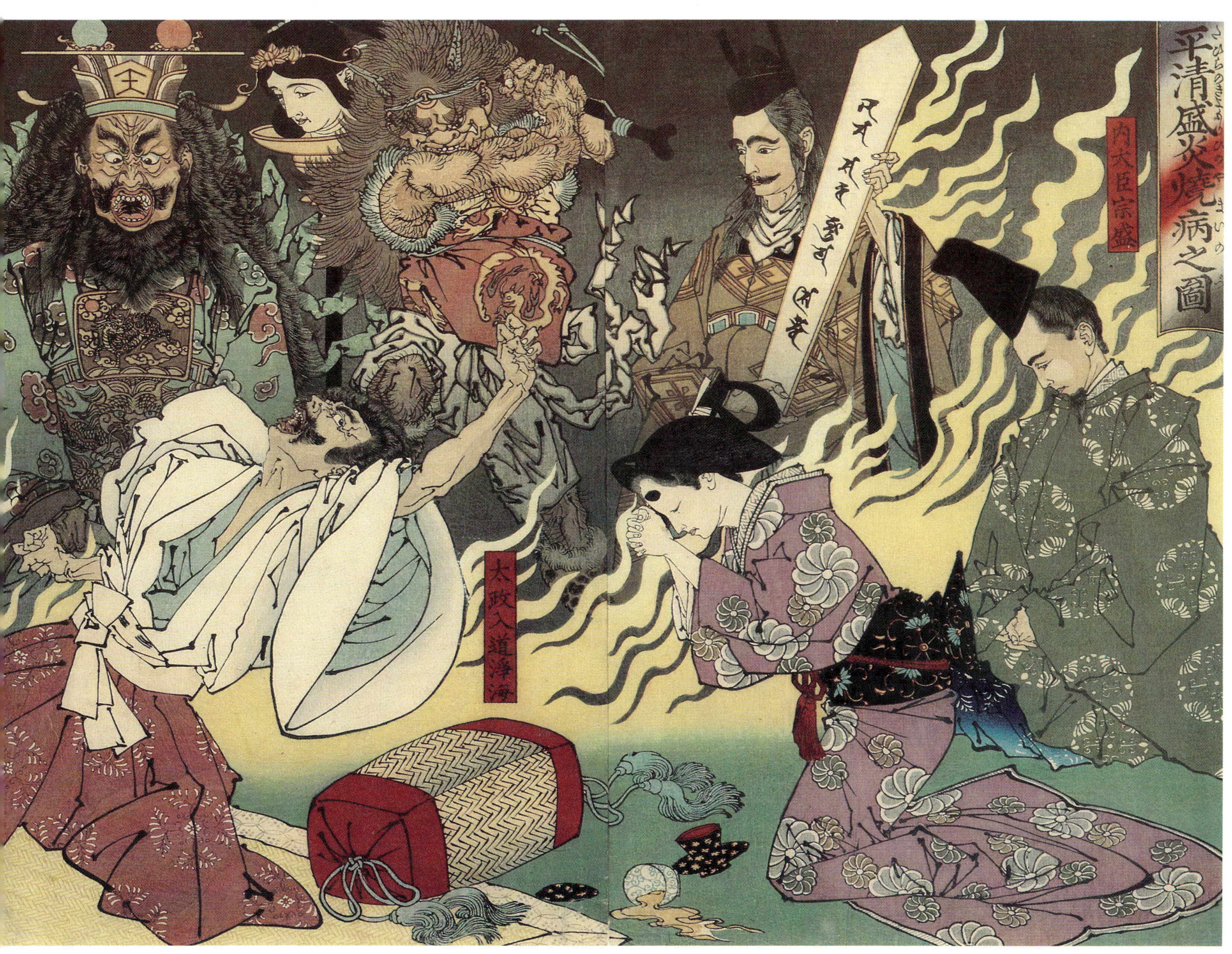
平清盛炎焼病之圖
内大臣宗盛
太政入道浄海

19. The Fever of Taira no Kiyomori
(Taira no kiyomori hi no yamai no zu),
August 1883

Ōban triptych
Signature: Yoshitoshi ga
Seal: Taiso
Publisher: Akiyama Buemon
Engraver: Yamamoto to
Printer: Tsune

The events preceding the death of Kiyomori
are related in the *Tales of the Heike Clan
(Heike monogatari)*, book six:

*His wife Niidono saw a horrible dream. A burning
carriage was drawn into the gate. Before and
behind were creatures with faces resembling
horses and cows. An iron plaque on the front
of the carriage bore the word* mu, *or nothing.
"Whence does this carriage come?" Niidono
asked. "From Ema, king of hell," was the
reply, "for Kiyomori." "And what is the iron
plaque?" she asked. "For his crime of burning
the Rushana Buddha he was sentenced to the
depth of the* mugen *hell. Half the name has
been inscribed, the other half not yet." Niidono
awoke sweating from her dream and everyone
to whom she told it felt his skin contract with
fear. Niidono prayed and made votive offerings
of gold, silver, porcelain, horses, arrows, bows,
and swords, but all in vain. His sons and
daughters gathered by his bed and prayed in
grief for a cure, but no cure came. On the second day of the second month of 1181, despite
his terrible fever, Niidono approached his
bedside, and said tearfully, "Sir, your condition
worsens every day. If there is anything you
would say, pray let me hear it now." On the
fourth day of the same month, suffering horribly
from fever, Kiyomori lay down on a board
soaked with water as a last resort. This brought
him no relief, and he died in torture. The sound
of the horses and carriages of condoling
visitors echoed to the sky and shook the great
earth.*[5]

In Yoshitoshi's picture, Niidono and her son
kneel silently by Kiyomori's bedside as he is
seized with painful convulsions. Behind him
rises a vision of hell. At the center is Ema, the
stern king of hell, flanked by the solemn figures
of people who may have been Kiyomori's
victims. In contrast to the usual portrayal of hell
with orange and red flames, Yoshitoshi has
chosen a strange combination of yellow, green,
and violet to emphasize the abnormality of the
scene and the terrible distortion of Kiyomori's
illness.

20. Hōjō Takatoki Tormented by Goblins
December 7, 1883

Series: *Yoshitoshi's Warriors Trembling with
Courage (Yoshitoshi mushaburui)*
Ōban
Signature: Taiso Yoshitoshi
Seal: Taiso
Engraver: Horikō Muneoka
Publisher: Kobayashi Tetsujirō

Hōjō Takatoki (1303–1333) was the ninth and
last of the Hōjō clan regents who ruled Japan
on behalf of the emperor during the Kamakura
period. Upon Takatoki's death, the Hōjō regents
were replaced by the first of the Ashikaga
shoguns. Takatoki, who had assumed office
at the age of eleven and had taken charge of
the government at the age of sixteen, was
feeble-minded, vicious, and debauched.
He surrounded himself with thirty-seven concubines, some two thousand actors, and a
kennel of five thousand fighting dogs with
which he staged extravagant dogfights every
month.[6]

At the height of this debauchery, his palace
was supposedly infested with *tengu,* the long-
nosed goblins shown in Yoshitoshi's print, who
mocked and attacked him. When the Ashikaga
forces led by Nitta Yoshisada attacked Kamakura, Takatoki was completely unprepared.
His palace was burned, and he retired to Tōshō
Temple with 870 vassals and relatives, all of
whom committed suicide on a single day in 1333.

The *Warriors Trembling with Courage* was
Yoshitoshi's last, most intense, and in many
ways finest set of evocations of the historical
past. The goblins swarming about Takatoki's
head seem almost an embodiment of the
man's mental confusion, like the creatures in
Goya's etching *The Sleep of Reason Produces
Monsters* for *Los Caprichos.*

21. Matsunaga Hisahide before His Suicide
December 7, 1883

Series: *Yoshitoshi's Warriors Trembling with
Courage (Yoshitoshi mushaburui)*
Ōban
Signature: Taiso Yoshitoshi ga
Seal: Taiso
Engraver: Horikō Muneoka
Publisher: Kobayashi Tetsujirō

Yoshitoshi's Warriors Trembling with Courage
is the transitional series from the clamor of
Yoshitoshi's early prints—with their astonishing
range of design and tone—to the silence of
the *One Hundred Aspects of the Moon* prints,
which convey intense, single moods. Many of
the subjects in the *Warriors* are agitated or
violent, but every element of drawing, composition, shading, and color is contrived to deepen
a single mood, in this case the angry defiance
of the aged warrior who hurls the clay cup
against the pillar just before committing ritual
suicide.

Matsunaga Hisahide (1507–1577) was the
chief minister of the shogun Ashikaga Yoshiteru, whom he forced to commit suicide in
1565. Later, Yoshiteru's younger brother Yoshiaki,
the last of the Ashikaga shoguns, appealed
to Matsunaga for help against Oda Nobunaga,
the warlord who had usurped the shogun's
powers. In 1573 Nobunaga and his son Nobutada led an attack against Kyoto and drove
out Yoshiaku. Nobutada defeated Matsunaga
and forced him to commit suicide in 1577.[7]

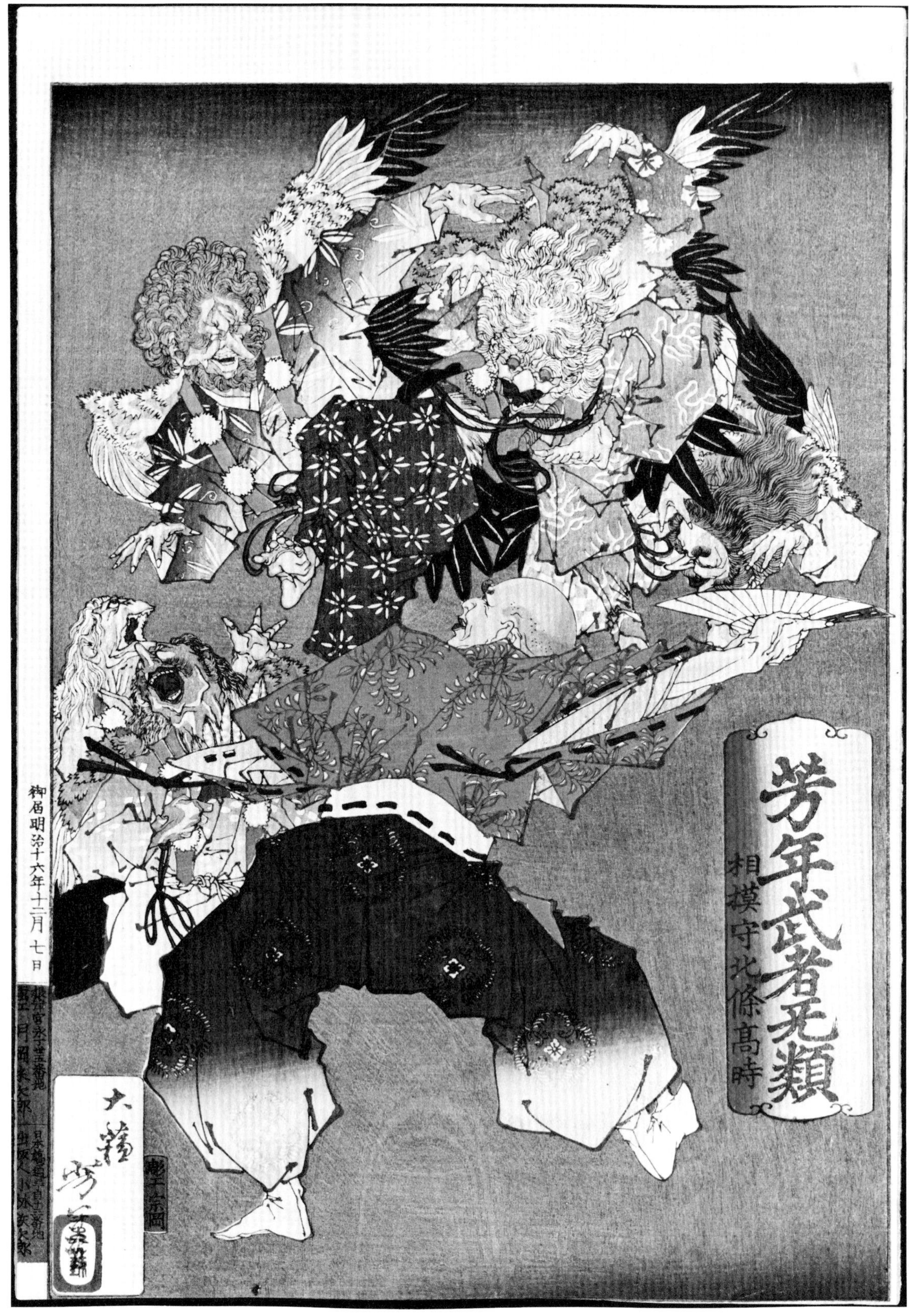
芳年武者无類
相模守北條髙時
御届明治十六年十二月 七日
大蘇
芳年

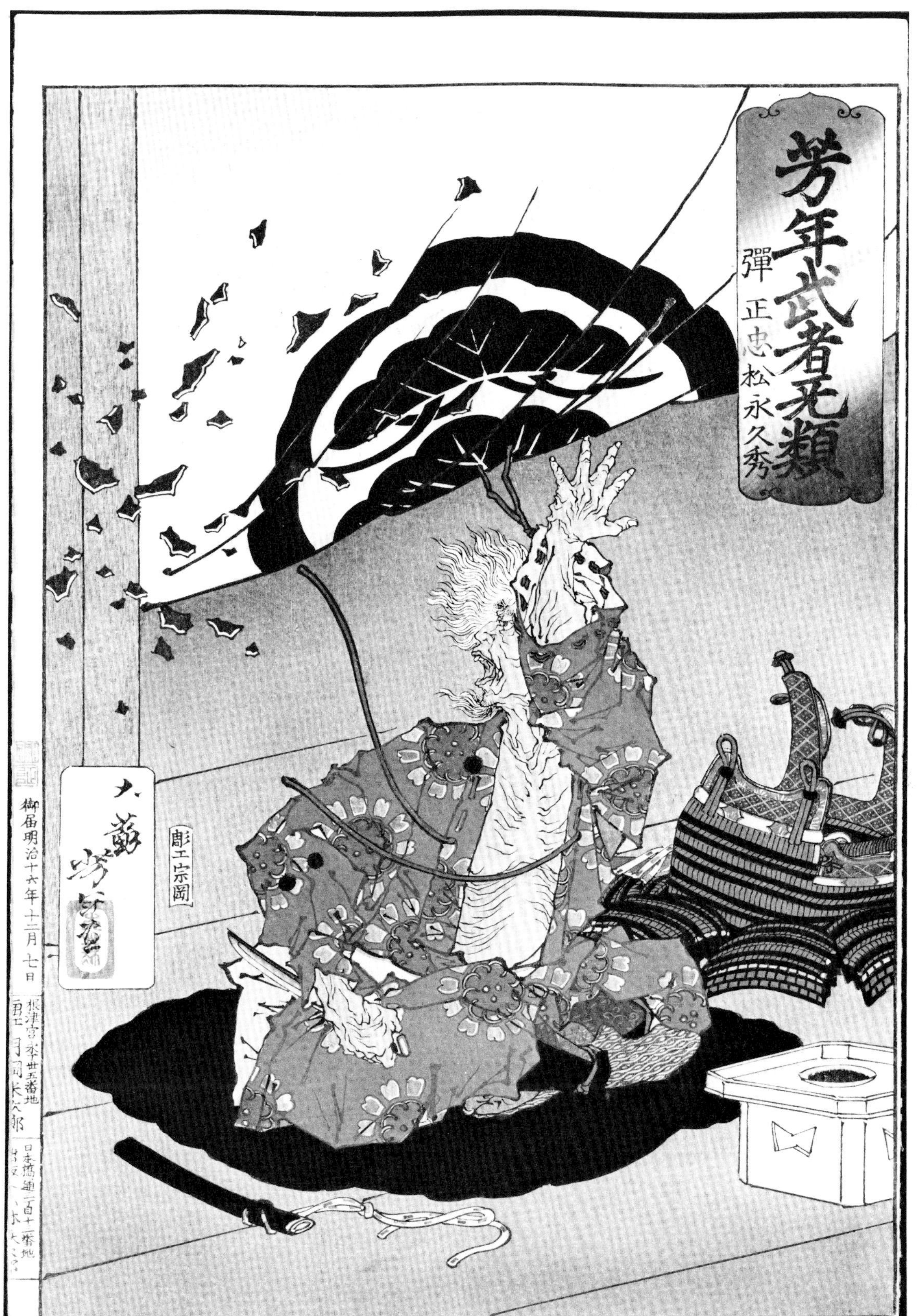
芳年武者无類
彈正忠松永久秀
大蘇
芳年
彫工宗岡

22. Summer: Women Bathing at the Daishōrō

(Natsu nezu hanayashiki daishōrō),
September 1883

Series: *The Four Seasons at their Height
(Zensei shiki)*
Ōban triptych
Signature: Ōju Yoshitoshi ga
Seal: Taiso
Publisher: Akiyama Buemon
Engraver: Yamamoto tō

After he moved to Nezu, Yoshitoshi was a frequent visitor to the elegant brothel of Daishōrō where he was intimate with the courtesan Maboroshidayū, known as The Phantom, whose portrait appears in the winter subject of the *Four Seasons*. The triptychs in this set are among the few prints of women that Yoshitoshi designed during his sojourn in Nezu. Like the women in Yoshitoshi's prints from the end of the 1870s, the women in the bathhouse are openly seductive and sexual, but they are drawn with far more sensitivity and respect, without the harsh and vulgar aniline pigments of the earlier prints. The four women in the foreground are identified from right to left as Kagetsu, Yoneju, Nakagawa, and Shingaku. The calligraphy panel over the window at the right reads "beware of fire" *(hi no yōjin)*. Akiyama Buemon, the publisher, was several years older than Yoshitoshi and became one of his closest friends during the last decade of his life. The engraver of the print, Yamamoto, lived in Shiba, a district south of the Nihonbashi district of central Tokyo where Akiyama had his shop.

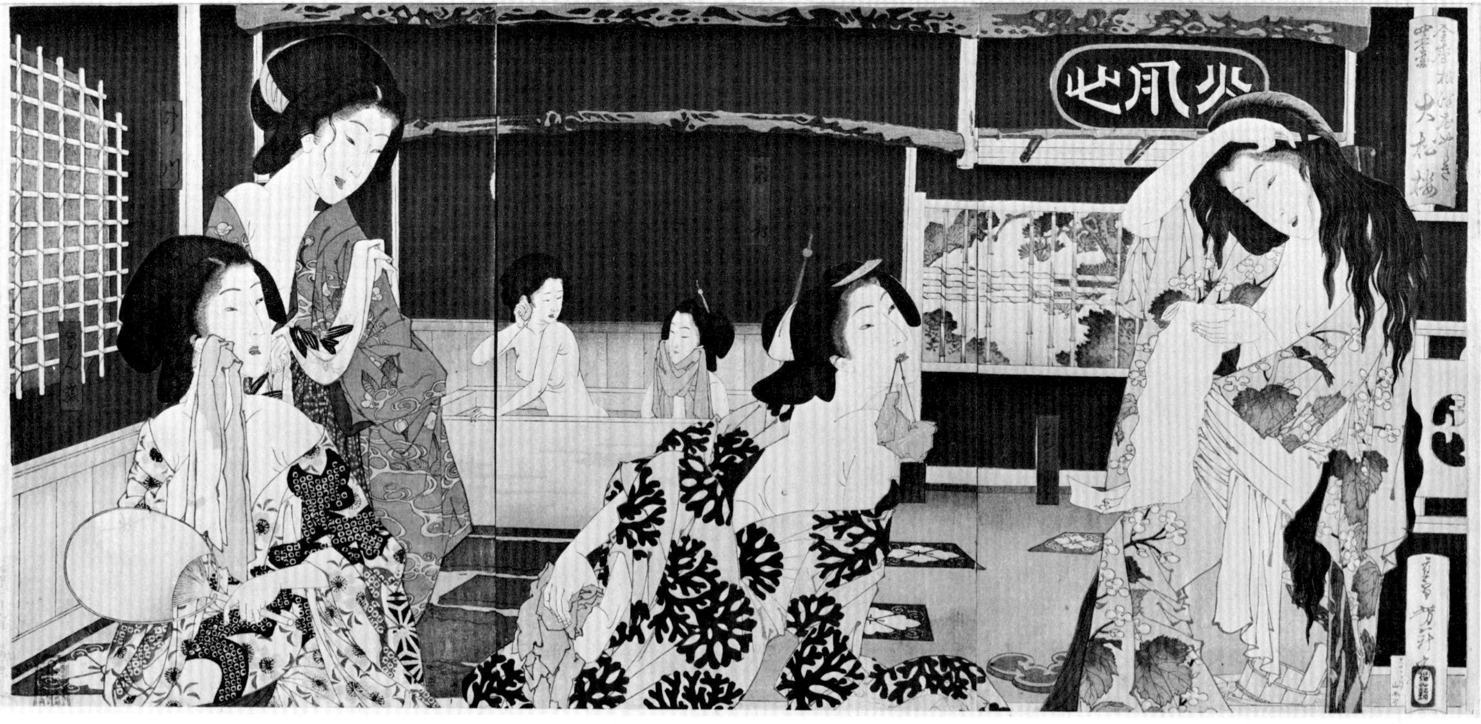

23. Famous Places in the East: The Ancient Incident of Umewaka and the Child Seller beside the Sumida River

(Azuma meisho sumidagawa umewaka no furugoto), July 1883

Ōban triptych
Signature: Taiso Yoshitoshi
Seal: Yoshitoshi no in
Publisher: Akiyama Buemon
Engraver: Yamamoto tō
Printer: Suri Tsune

During the wars and disorders that marked the medieval period in Japan, the members of a Kyoto family named Yoshida were separated. The twelve-year-old son, Umewaka, wandered eastward to the Sumida River which runs through the present city of Tokyo. Exhausted and ill from his travels, the boy died after composing a touching poem addressed to the gulls, asking if the dew on the riverbank would vanish. The boy was buried by the river, and a temple sprang up at his tomb; the temple, called Mokuboji, exists to this day. With the passage of time, the legend changed and grew. In one story the boy, a brilliant student at the Getsurin Temple on Mt. Hiei, ran away after failing in competition with another youth named Matsuwaka. On the shores of Lake Biwa near Ōtsu he was seized by a slave dealer named Nobuo Tōda, who led him as far as the Sumida River before the child perished. *The Sumida River,* a Noh play based on this legend, presents the overwhelming grief of Umewaka's mother, who searches the country for him and eventually comes upon his grave. The Noh play was also adapted for the puppet theater and later for the Kabuki stage. The story is popular to this day.

In literature Umewaka is always presented as a helpless victim, and his death as a tragedy. Yoshitoshi's print seems more ambiguous. Umewaka is dressed in the attractive, feminine clothes of a temple page. He has a girlish beauty, and the expression on his face as he looks toward his captor does not seem to be one of simple exhaustion, illness, or fatigue. Does the man approach the boy with menace or concern? Is the boy seductive or frightened? What tension rises in the fullness of the moon, in the falling rain, in the fullness of the cherry blossom whose petals have just begun to flutter down, just past their peak?

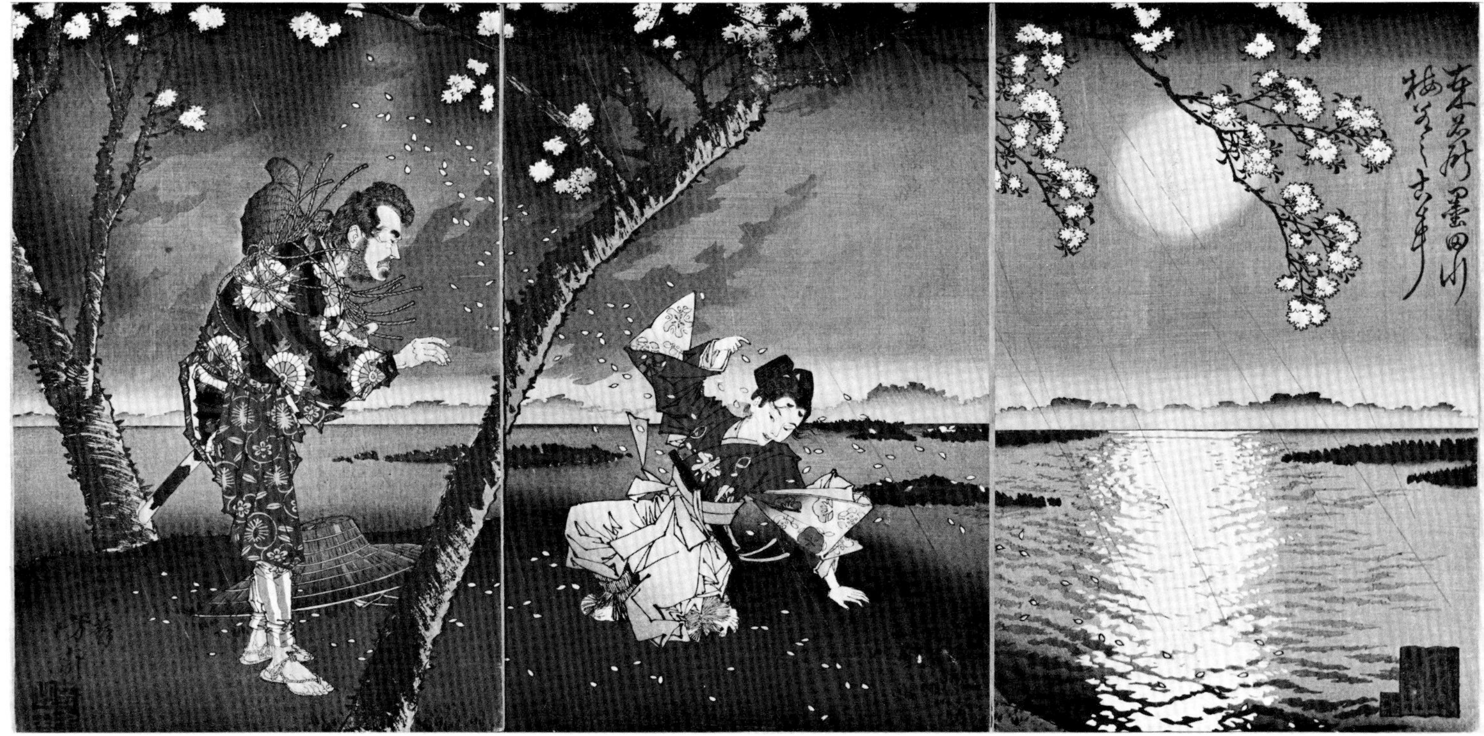

**24. Fujiwara no Yasumasa Playing the Flute
by Moonlight**
(Fujiwara no yasumasa gekka roteki zu),
February 12, 1883

Ōban triptych
Signature: Ōju Taiso Yoshitoshi sha
Seals: Taiso Yoshitoshi
Publisher: Akiyama Buemon

Fujiwara no Yasumasa (958–1036) was a celebrated poet and flautist in the Heian court.[8]
He apparently was the second husband of the poet Izumi Shikibu and at one point served as the governor of Tango province, near Kyoto.[9]
At this time the Heian court was in decline, and banditry and disorder were increasing in the countryside.

Legend has it that one moonlit night, as Yasumasa was strolling along the roadway on the lonely moor of Ichiharano, the bandit Hakamadare Yasusuke lay in wait, determined to kill him. As Yasumasa drew closer, the sound of his flute enchanted the highwayman, who was unable so much as to draw his sword. Entirely charmed by the power of music, he followed Yasumasa to his home, where the flautist took notice of the docile brigand and presented him with a suit of clothing. The story became the subject of a pantomime dance first performed by Onoe Kikugorō III and Ichikawa Danjūrō VII at the Ichimura Theater in Edo in 1822. It was performed again in Edo at the Morita Theater in 1862, when Yoshitoshi was designing many woodblock prints of the Kabuki stage.

Yoshitoshi used the image of the bandit and the courtier fluting by moonlight in the vignette accompanying a portrait of the female entertainer Otake in a series of half-length portraits of women matched with warriors published in December 1879. He used it as a separate subject in one of the three paintings he chose to exhibit when he was invited to join the first government-sponsored exhibition of modern Japanese painting in the autumn of 1882. He won no prize or formal recognition for the painting, but his publisher Akiyama decided to issue the picture as a print, and the following spring, when it was published as a triptych, it was immediately recognized as one of the artist's masterpieces. The next month the Kabuki actor Ichikawa Danjūrō IX staged a two-part dance pantomime during regular performances at the Shintomi Theater, entitled *The Willow and the Cherry Tree in Color Woodblock Prints (Yanagizakura azuma nishiki-e).* The first half was a re-creation, based on Yoshitoshi's print, of the dance first performed in 1882. The play was an enormous success, and in June Yoshitoshi used the tableau for a float in the Sannō Festival procession for the Hie Shrine, an important and popular annual event. Two plasterers made life-size models of the figures; Yoshitoshi painted their faces and hands; and Ichikawa Danjūrō IX lent costumes to clothe them. The men accompanying the float wore kimonos painted by Yoshitoshi to look like feathered robes, and Yoshitoshi and some of his favorite pupils rode in the prow. The entire production was satirized in Yoshitoshi's own newspaper, the *Eiri jiyū shimbun (Illustrated Free Newspaper).*

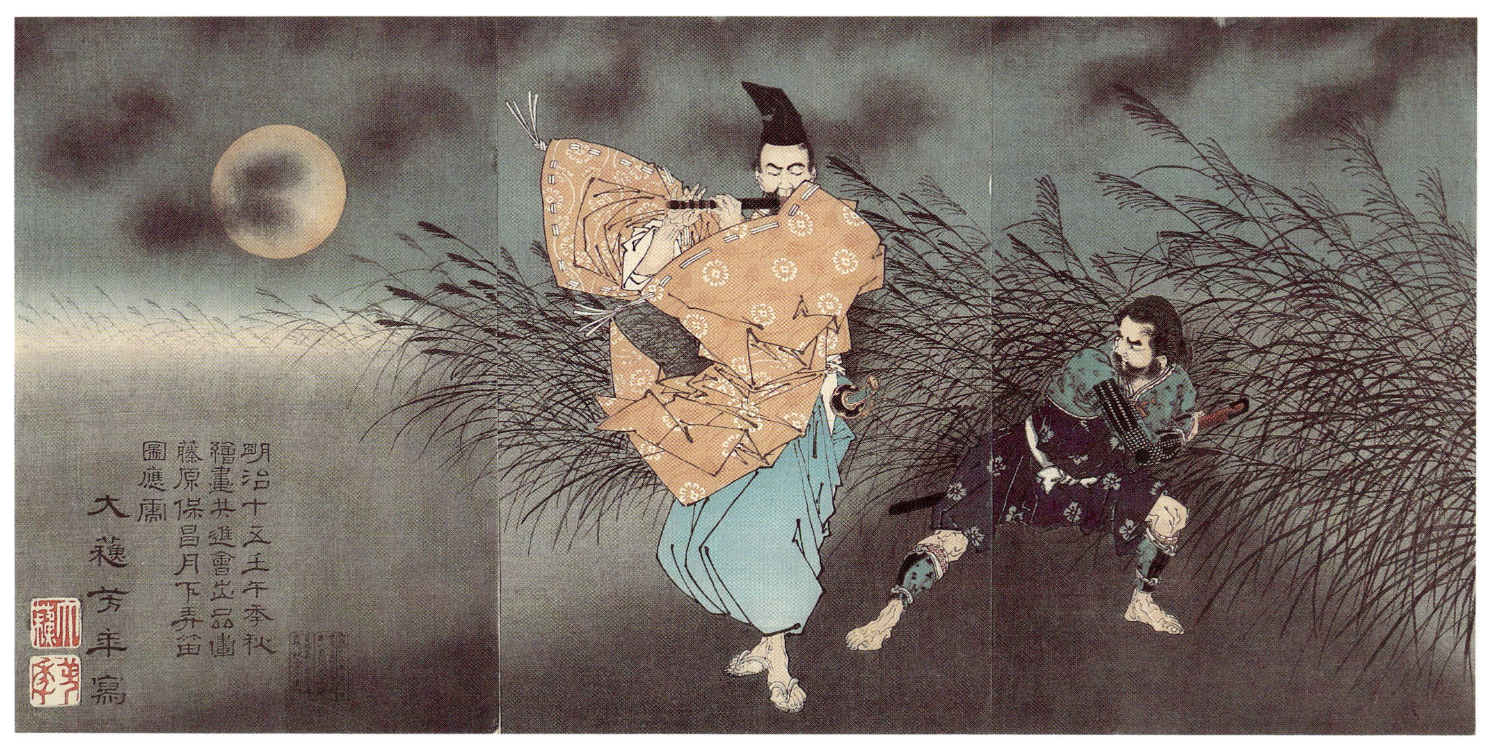
明治十五壬午季秋
繪畫共進會出品畫
藤原保昌月下弄笛
圖應需
大蘇芳年寫

25. Demons of Illness and Poverty Stalking the Lucky Gods
(Hōnen songa), 1884

Ōban triptych
Signature: Ōju Yoshitoshi ga
Seal: Taiso Yoshitoshi
Publisher: Akiyama Buemon
Engraver: Yamomoto tō

Yoshitoshi was trained as an Ukiyo-e artist, and most of his prints are conceived in that style—that is to say, the figures have sharp, clear outlines, stand out distinctly against their backgrounds, and display an overall emphasis on rich color, pattern, and detail. There were other schools of painting in Japan, however, which emphasized pale, monochrome washes and individual brushstrokes, and many Ukiyo-e artists including Yoshitoshi adapted this style for the backgrounds of their prints to make their central figures stand out even more brilliantly and dramatically. Occasionally artists designed prints like this one of the demons of illness and poverty entirely in the "painterly" style. Most frequently during the late nineteenth century these prints were satires or caricatures, and there is an element of coarse humor in the figures of Ebisu and Daikoku, two of the seven Lucky Gods, hiding under the cloth sack of rice. But the drawing of the demons at the left is quite serious. The engraver has exerted himself to reproduce the rough, ragged quality of Yoshitoshi's brushstrokes, and the painter has used his skills to reproduce the delicate washes of color on the figures and the gradations of texture on the background.

The first two characters of the four-character title are the artist's name, Yoshitoshi. The second pair, *songa,* is an unorthodox combination meaning a picture for thought. The Japanese, however, appreciate puns and wordplay. If Yoshitoshi's name is pronounced in Chinese style, as *hōnen,* it is a homonym for an "abundant year," and *songa* is a homonym for a picture of defeat or loss. The note before the poem by Yoshitoshi's friend Keika says that the verse is based on an understanding of the artist's intention; it reads: "Don't confuse the demons of illness and poverty with beauties like Komachi and Seishi. Look how frightened the gods of fortune are!" *(Jaki kyūki seishi komachi to machigae na kokoro no fuku no kowagaru o mite).*

There seems to have been an economic recession in 1883–84, and, although Yoshitoshi's personal affairs prospered, he seems to have felt the specters of famine and misery stalking the land. The gods seem as jovial and unconcerned beneath their full rice sack as a pair of children playing hide-and-seek, and perhaps the print was conceived as a warning that prosperity was a fragile condition.

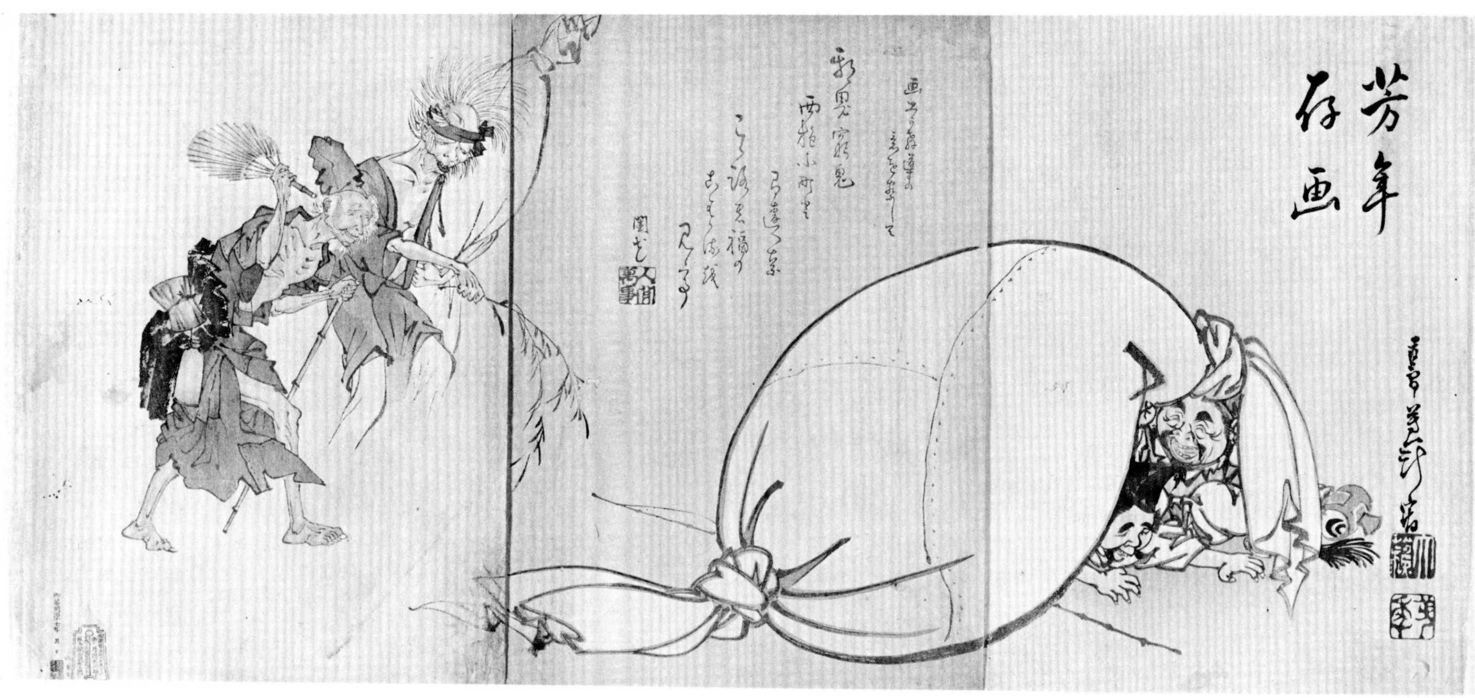

26. Fudō Threatening Yūten with His Sword
May 1885

Ōban triptych
Signature: Yoshitoshi
Seal: Taiso
Publisher: Akiyama Buemon
Engraver: Horikō Enkatsu

In 1656, a young novice at Zōjōji Temple of the Jōdo sect was praying one night, chanting a sutra, before the image of the god Fudō. Suddenly the statue came to life, seized him by the arm, and raised his sword as if to slay him. The boy fainted. When he revived, the statue was motionless, but beside him on the ground lay a replica of the god's sword. He went to his superior to ask what this terrifying event might mean. His superior told him that he had been chosen for great work and asked him to leave the sword with him and to forget what had happened until such time as he needed to

remember. The novice was given the name Yūten, and when he grew older he was recognized by the shogun and traveled throughout the country establishing temples. Eventually he became abbot of Zōjōji Temple and then retired to a country village near Edo where he lived quietly until his death in 1718. The childhood incident is described in a biography of Yūten published in 1808. A six-volume popular illustrated biography published in 1803 and 1804 may have contained an illustration which inspired Yoshitoshi's print.[10]

Yūten was born in 1637, so he would have been nineteen at the time of the incident; in Yoshitoshi's print the boy is far younger. It is interesting that Yoshitoshi, who was precocious as a child, should have been so sympathetic to children. The figures to the right and left are acolytes of the god. This is one of the few individual prints that Yoshitoshi did not give a title.

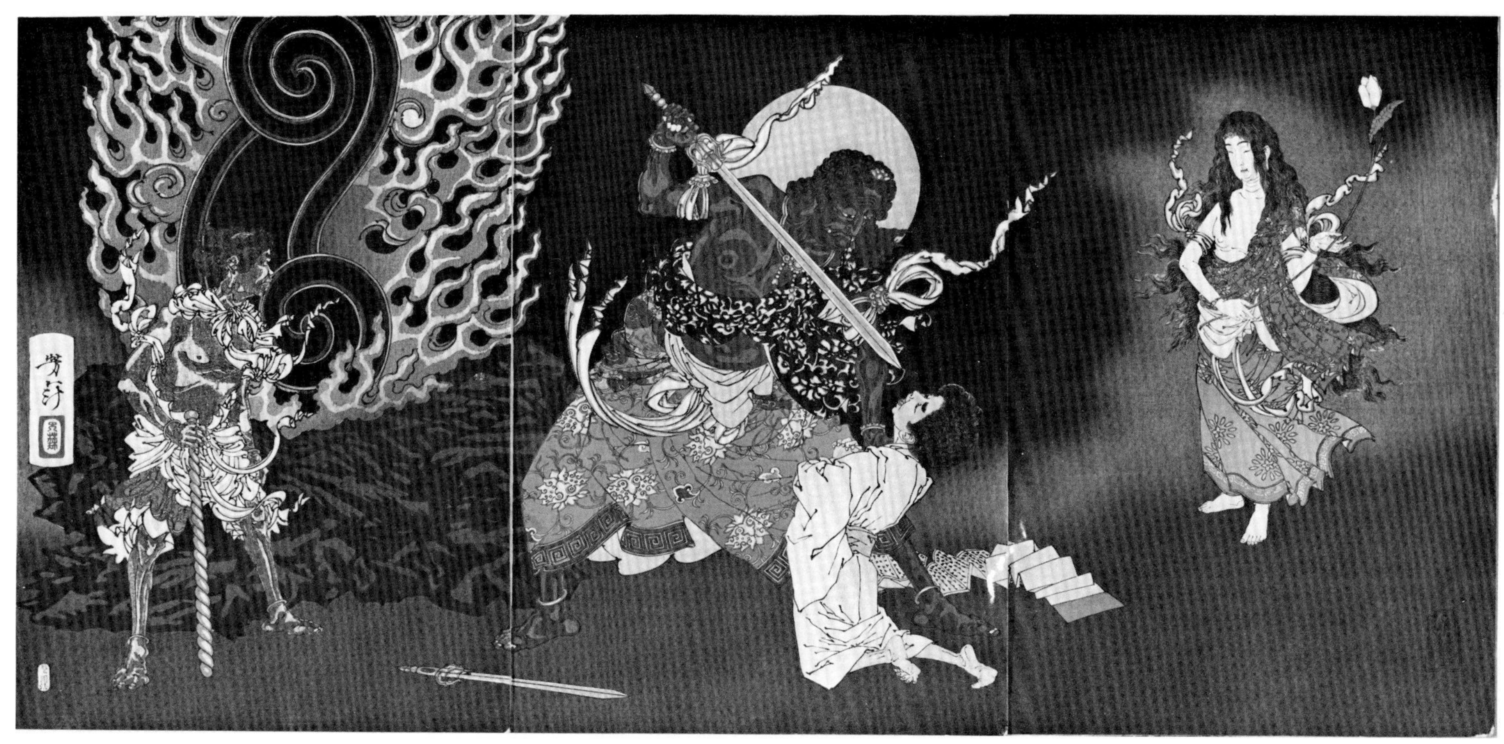

**27. Chang Shun, the White Stripe in the
Waves, Wrestling with Li K'uei, the Black
Whirlwind, in the Ching Yang River**
*(Rōrihakuchō chōjun kokusempū riki kōchū ni
tatakau no zu)*, c. 1887

Vertical *ōban* diptych
Signature: Ōju Yoshitoshi ga
Seal: Taiso

Chang Shun and Li K'uei, nicknamed the White
Stripe in the Waves and the Black Whirlwind,
respectively, were among the 108 outlaw-
heroes of the thirteenth-century Chinese novel
Tales of the Water Margin (Shui hu chuan). The
book was translated into Japanese at the beginning of the nineteenth century as the *Suikoden,* and its Robin Hood-like heroes became
immensely popular in literature and art.

In the incident portrayed here, Li K'uei, a rois-
terous, undisciplined bully, was dining with two
companions on the banks of the Ching Yang
River. When the food ran out, Li forcibly attempted to steal the nearby fisherman's catch.
He succeeded only in creating confusion and
in losing most of the catch. A fair stranger
suddenly appeared and challenged Li, who
hurled him to the ground and beat him until the
two were forced to separate. The stranger
proved to be Chang Shun, the owner of the fish
market. Challenging Li again, he offered him "a
drink of water." While Chang Shun could walk

under water for ten miles and live underwater
for seven nights and days, Li K'uei could
hardly swim. The fight progressed before hundreds of onlookers until one of Li's companions
separated them and Chang was invited to join
the outlaw band.

The first edition of the *Suikoden* was illustrated
by Hokusai, and the tales became popular
subjects for artists. The first to design full-size
color woodblock prints of the outlaw-heroes
was Yoshitoshi's teacher Ichiyūsai Kuniyoshi.
His first set of *Suikoden* prints, published in the
late 1820s, offered a powerful new vision of
nobility and heroic action which established
Kuniyoshi's reputation with the Edo public. It
also made a deep impression on Yoshitoshi,
who designed many *Suikoden* prints at the
beginning of his career. One of Kuniyoshi's
original designs appears to be the inspiration
for this print. The two figures in Kuniyoshi's
print are confined to one upright panel; there
is a rock at the lower right; and, although two
fish swim off to the left, there are no water
weeds or octopus at the bottom of the print. In
Kuniyoshi's print, the fair, tattooed hero wears
a sword about his waist and is identified as
Gen Shōgo grappling with an enemy soldier.
Yoshitoshi has used this same scenery and
poses in portraying a more famous episode
from the novel, the story of Chang Shun and
Li K'uei.

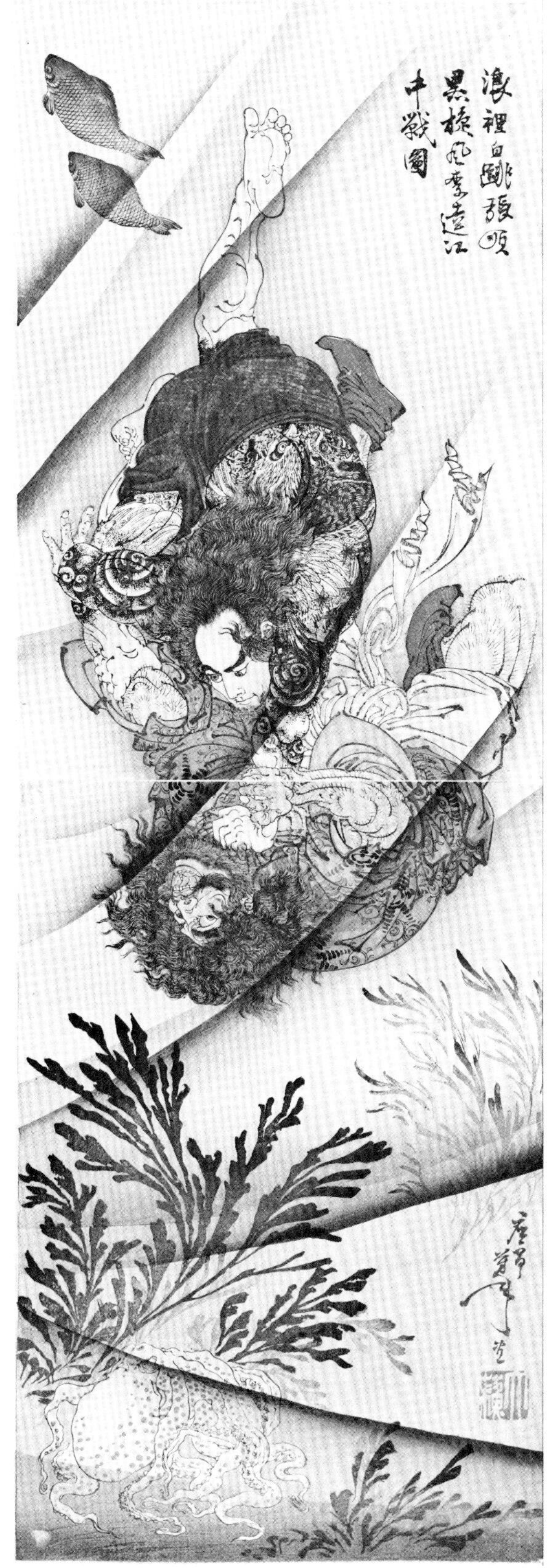

浪裡白跳張順
黒旋風李逵江
中戰圖

28. Two Heroes Fighting atop Hōryūkaku
(Hōryūkaku ryōyū dōzuru), October 1885

Vertical *ōban* diptych
Signature: Ōju Yoshitoshi ga
Seal: Taiso
Publisher: Matsui Eikichi
Engraver: Chokuzan

These two heroes are characters in *The Story of Eight Dogs of the Satomi Clan,* the fifty-three-volume novel written by Takizawa Bakin between 1814 and 1841. In the novel, the Lord of Satomi offers his daughter Fusehime in marriage to any warrior who can take a castle he is beseiging. A dog takes up the challenge and succeeds. The father at first refuses but then honors his promise. Soon afterward the daughter finds herself pregnant and disembowels herself to prevent the mortification of bearing the dog's children. As she dies, eight jewels spring from her womb, each inscribed with the name of a Confucian virtue. The jewels fly out into space and come to rest in eight different women, each of whose children is born clutching one of the jewels. Most of the book describes the meetings and eventual recognitions between the brothers, and the end describes their adventures as a group "punishing evil and rewarding virtue" throughout Japan.

One of the most famous episodes in the novel is the duel between Inuzuka Shino and Inukai Gempachi on the roof of the Hōryūkaku Tower of Koga Castle beside the Tone River. Gempachi is searching for a sword which has been entrusted to Shino, who is unaware that it has been stolen from him. Completely unaware of their relationship, the two brothers stage a magnificent fight; both slip off the roof and fall unconscious into a boat which carries them downstream to other adventures.

In the autumn of 1852 Ichiyūsai Kuniyoshi designed an upright panel print of the battle, which Yoshitoshi used as the inspiration for his print. In Kuniyoshi's print the viewer looks at the scene from below: the nearer figure is smaller, the building is foreshortened, and there is a full moon in the sky and geese instead of the plump birds in Yoshitoshi's print. The red in this diptych is an aniline dye that is very susceptible to light and moisture. The print has never been exposed to light, and the colors are fresh and brilliant. The slight change in color on the roof in the lower panel was caused by water.

29. The Lonely House on Adachi Moor in Northern Japan
(Ōshū adachigahara hitotsuya no zu),
September 1885

Vertical *ōban diptych*
Signature: Ōju Yoshitoshi ga
Seal: Yoshitoshi
Publisher: Matsui Eikichi
Engraver: Chokuzan chōkoku

This horrifying but strangely fascinating print portrays the hag of Adachi Moor, a legendary figure who murdered pregnant women and drank the blood of their unborn children.

Late in his life Yoshitoshi seems to have returned over and over again to images that impressed him during his youth in Kuniyoshi's studio. About 1840 Kuniyoshi designed his first print of a subject similar to this one: the miracle of Bodhisattva Kannon on Asaji Moor near Edo. A wicked woman, living in an isolated hut with her kind daughter, lured travelers to spend the night there. Offering them a stone pillow, the woman murdered them during the night and then stole their possessions. The daughter was horrified and prayed to Bodhisattva Kannon for help. Soon afterward Kannon appeared at their door as a handsome young traveler, with whom the daughter fell in love. That night she arranged for the youth to sleep safely while she lay down on the stone pillow. Her mother came out brandishing a knife but recognized her daughter just before she brought it down. Suddenly aware of her misdeeds, she was maddened with remorse and flung herself into a nearby pond.

This subject apparently appealed to Kuniyoshi, for he went on to design several more prints and an enormous votive painting on the same theme. The later prints all contain elements that appear in Yoshitoshi's print: the broken walls, the flowers outside, the thatched divider, the wrinkled old woman. One of Kuniyoshi's diptychs is deliberately mistitled *The Lonely House on Adachi Moor* to increase its suggestion of horror and sexual violence, although the figure of Kannon in the background identifies it clearly as the story of Asaji Moor. It is the sensuality of this last print, so unusual for Kuniyoshi, that suffuses Yoshitoshi's work.

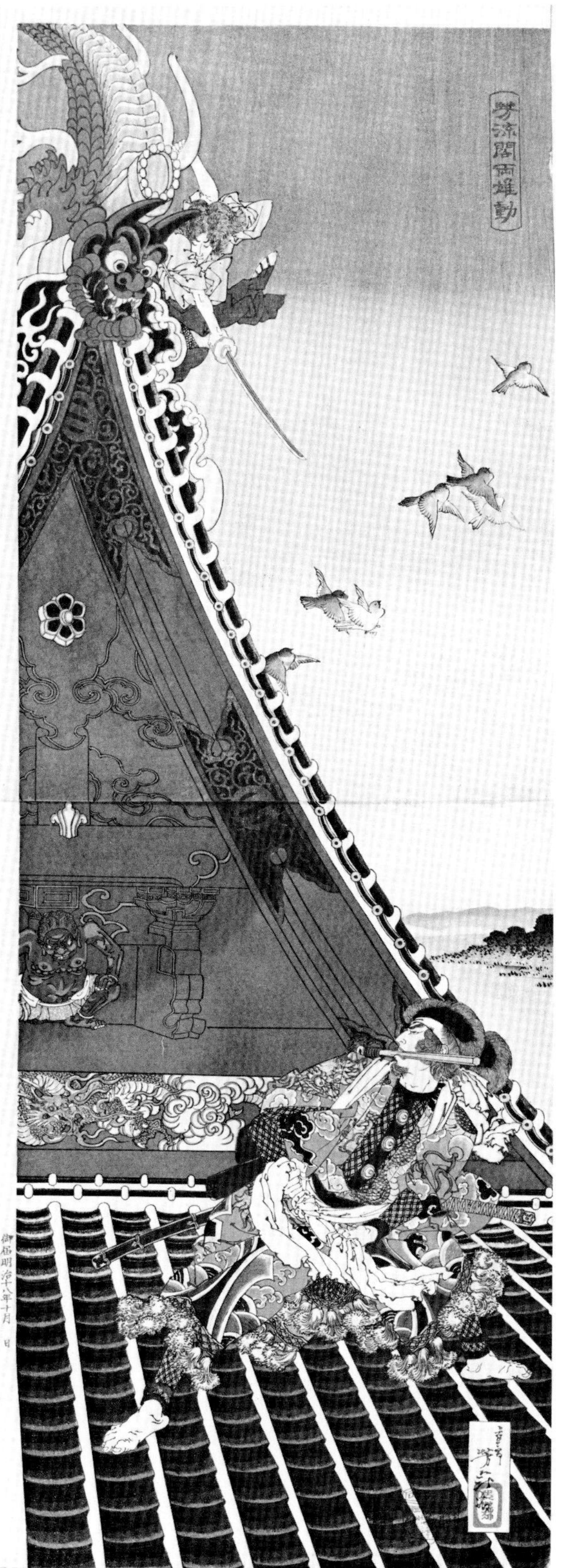

芳流閣両雄動

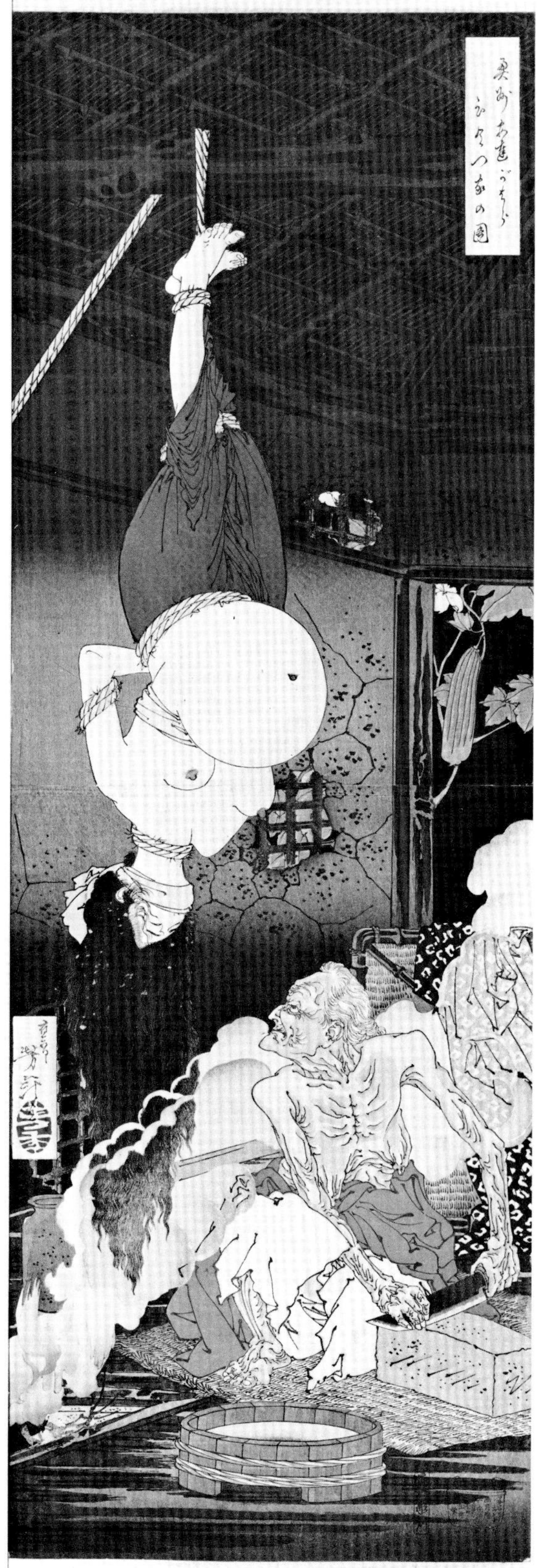

英勇あら達ぐれべし
ぶんごつ女の圖

30. The Story of Otomi and Yosaburō

(Otomi yosaburō no hanashi),
December 14, 1885

Series: *A New Selection of Eastern Color Prints
(Shinsen azuma nishiki-e)*
Ōban diptych
Signature: Yoshitoshi
Seal: Yoshitoshi
Publisher: Tsunashima Kamekichi

In the Kabuki version of this story, Izuya Yosaburō was an extremely handsome man who fell in love with Otomi, a geisha who had become the mistress of a gang leader. When their affair was discovered, Otomi escaped, flung herself into the sea, and was presumed drowned. Yosaburō was tortured and his face mutilated by the gang leader in revenge. In the years that followed, Yosaburō became a blackmailer and a petty thief. Unbeknownst to him, Otomi had been saved from drowning by a man whom she did not recognize as her brother and had been taken to the Genyadana district of Edo to live innocently with him. Yosaburō's confederate Yasu, called The Bat because of a tattoo on his cheek, met Otomi and guessed some scandal that he and Yosaburō could profit from. The two approached the gateway to the district at night, and Yasu pointed out the house to Yosaburō, whose face was covered to conceal his scars. Later the lovers recognized one another, but, before they could be reunited, Yosaburō was captured by the police and sent into exile.

This print has come to be considered one of the artist's masterpieces. Yoshitoshi himself expected it to be popular, and when the publisher informed him that it was not selling, he replied "They're all blind then" *(Mekura sennin).*[11] The whimsical spotted dog curled up beside the water tank (a protection against fire, as the sign just above it indicates) is similar to a cat that appears in many prints by Yoshitoshi's teacher Kuniyoshi, whose studio was in Genyadana. The hazy clouds also appear frequently in Kuniyoshi's landscape prints. Yoshitoshi's personal servant, Toshimasa, is said to have posed for the figure of Yasu The Bat, and an old paper merchant who knew Yoshitoshi in his youth said that in those days the artist was the very image of Yosaburō, "a handsome young man with his sash tied tight and low around his waist."[12] Perhaps the paper merchant was thinking of the Yosaburō in Yoshitoshi's print.

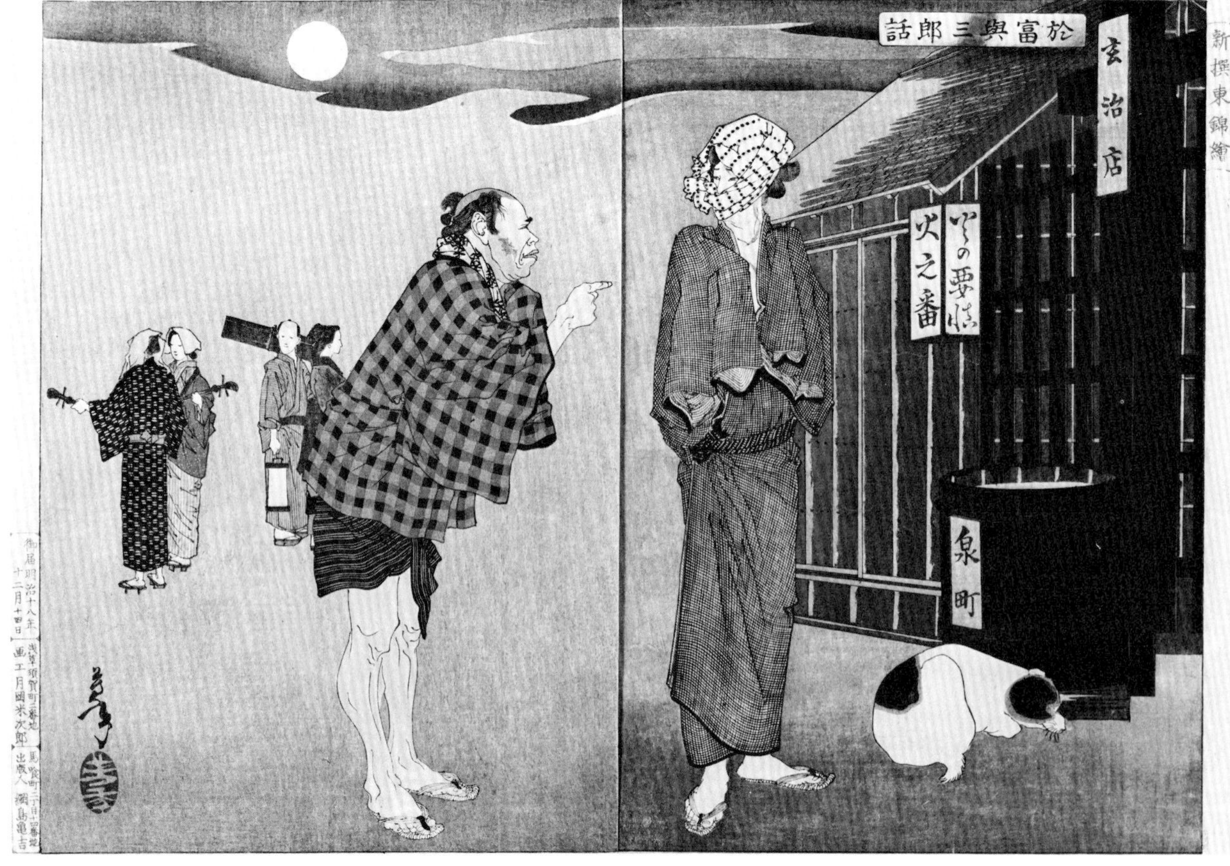

64

31. Chōan Killing His Younger Brother at Fudanotsuji

(Chōan fudanotsuji nite otōto o satsugai no zu),
February 1, 1885

Series: *A New Selection of Eastern Color Prints
(Shinsen azuma nishiki-e)*
Ōban diptych
Signature: Yoshitoshi
Seal: Taiso
Publisher: Tsunajima Kamekichi
Engraver: Enkatsu tō

Yoshitoshi usually found a way to avoid the obvious in his designs: if the subject matter was well known, he portrayed the action in an unusual manner; if the action was clear, the subject was an unfamiliar one. This print is one of the latter.

Chōan is a character in a Kabuki drama, but synopses of the plays do not mention his murdering a brother. In the play, Murai Chōan forces his sister to separate from her lover and then torments her until she kills him. Her lover commits suicide, and the three are arraigned before the king of hell. When Chōan's misdeeds are discovered, the lovers are allowed to enter paradise together. We can only assume that the character in this play is the same Chōan of Yoshitoshi's print.

There is no doubt, however, about the furious violence of the scene, the tormented trees, the sulfurous sky, and the flashes of lightning reflecting at once the victim's terror and the brother's murderous intent. The background is engraved to imitate splashes of ink and is conceived with a bold, abstract freedom. A similar technique was used very effectively in Kiyochika's stunning triptychs of the Sino- and Russo-Japanese wars in 1893 and 1904, which were a bridge between traditional Ukiyo-e and the modern Japanese woodblock print.

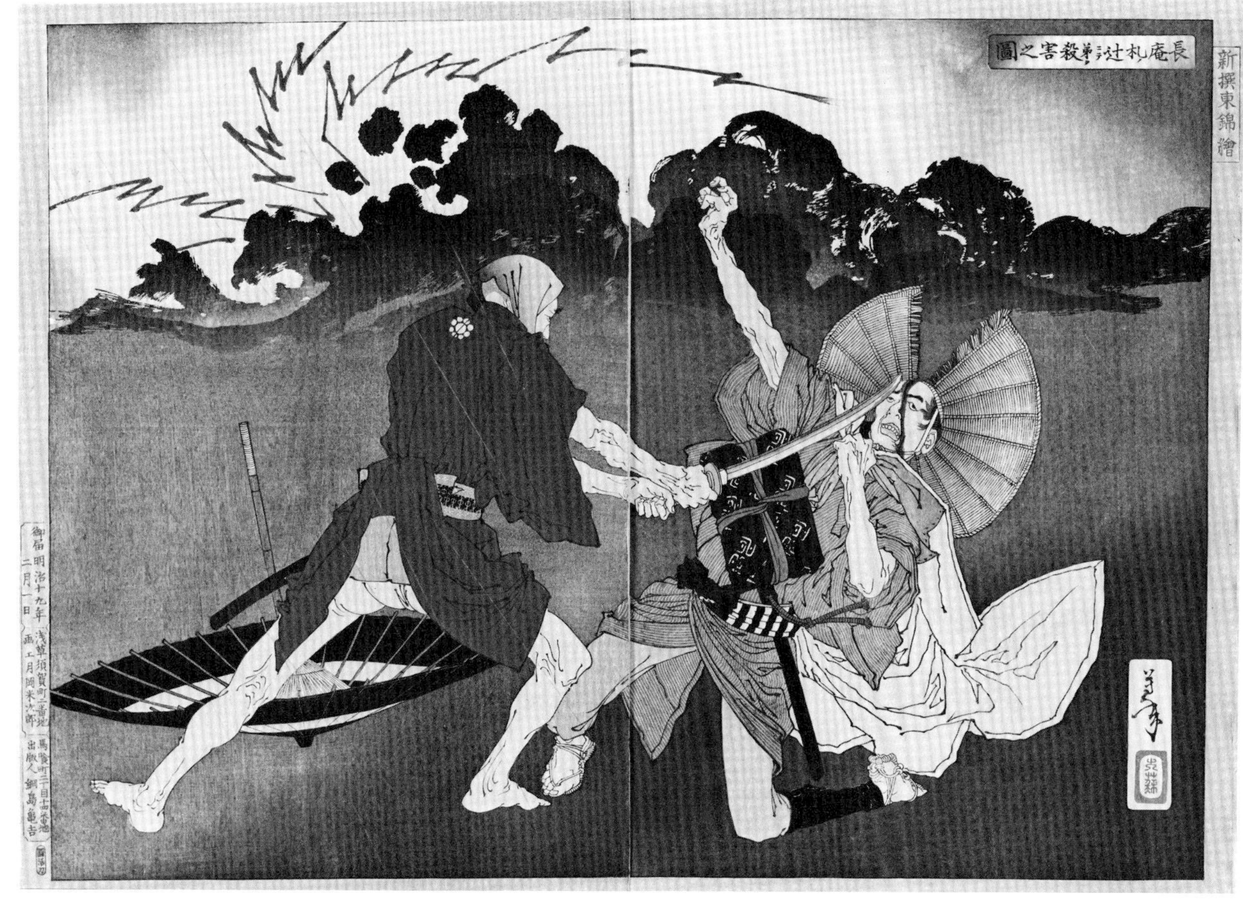

32. The Story of Sano Jirōzaemon
(Sano jirōzaemon no hanashi), February 1,
1886

Series: *A New Selection of Eastern Color Prints
(Shinsen azuma nishiki-e)*
Ōban diptych
Signature: Yoshitoshi
Seal: Taiso
Publisher: Tsunajima Kamekichi
Engraver: Hori Yata

Jirōzaemon was a farmer from the village of
Sano, in the province of Shimotsuke, who
journeyed to Edo in the 1720s. He visited the
Yoshiwara district and conceived a passion for
the courtesan Yatsuhashi of the Daihyōgoya
brothel. Yatsuhashi at that time was engaged
with a client and kept putting off Jirōzaemon.
One day he chanced to meet Yatsuhashi and
her lover together and finally realized why she
had been refusing his advances. That night he
hid himself by the gate to the Yoshiwara. As
Yatsuhashi and her lover were about to part, he
leapt out without a word, murdered them, and
ran amok, wounding several people before he
was captured. The story was adapted for the
Kabuki stage in 1850.

In Yoshitoshi's picture, the unattractive farmer
with his pock-marked face has already killed
Yatsuhashi's lover and has pursued the courtesan into a building. As she falls, the swirling
drapery of her robe, the intense red of her un-
dergarments, and the sheets of tissue paper
which scatter from her bosom as she falls
create an atmosphere which only intensifies
Jirōzaemon's fury and heat.

The *New Selection* series was Yoshitoshi's
homage to the city of his birth. Much of his earlier work had been based on national history,
ancient legend, and fantasy, but in this set he
turned to the urban folklore and legends of
Tokugawa Edo. In twenty prints executed between the end of 1885 and the beginning of
1887, he presented the elegance, passion,
violence, and excitement of life in the capital.
The prints were designed as diptychs and had
yellow borders with the series title and publication information printed in the margins as
though the pictures were album paintings. The
engraving and printing of the earliest impressions is extraordinarily accomplished, although
coarse late impressions of many subjects
show that they were popular and that many
were printed without the same painstaking
care. The prints took time to produce and were
published in groups between 1885 and 1889.
This is one of seven in the second group
published in February 1886.

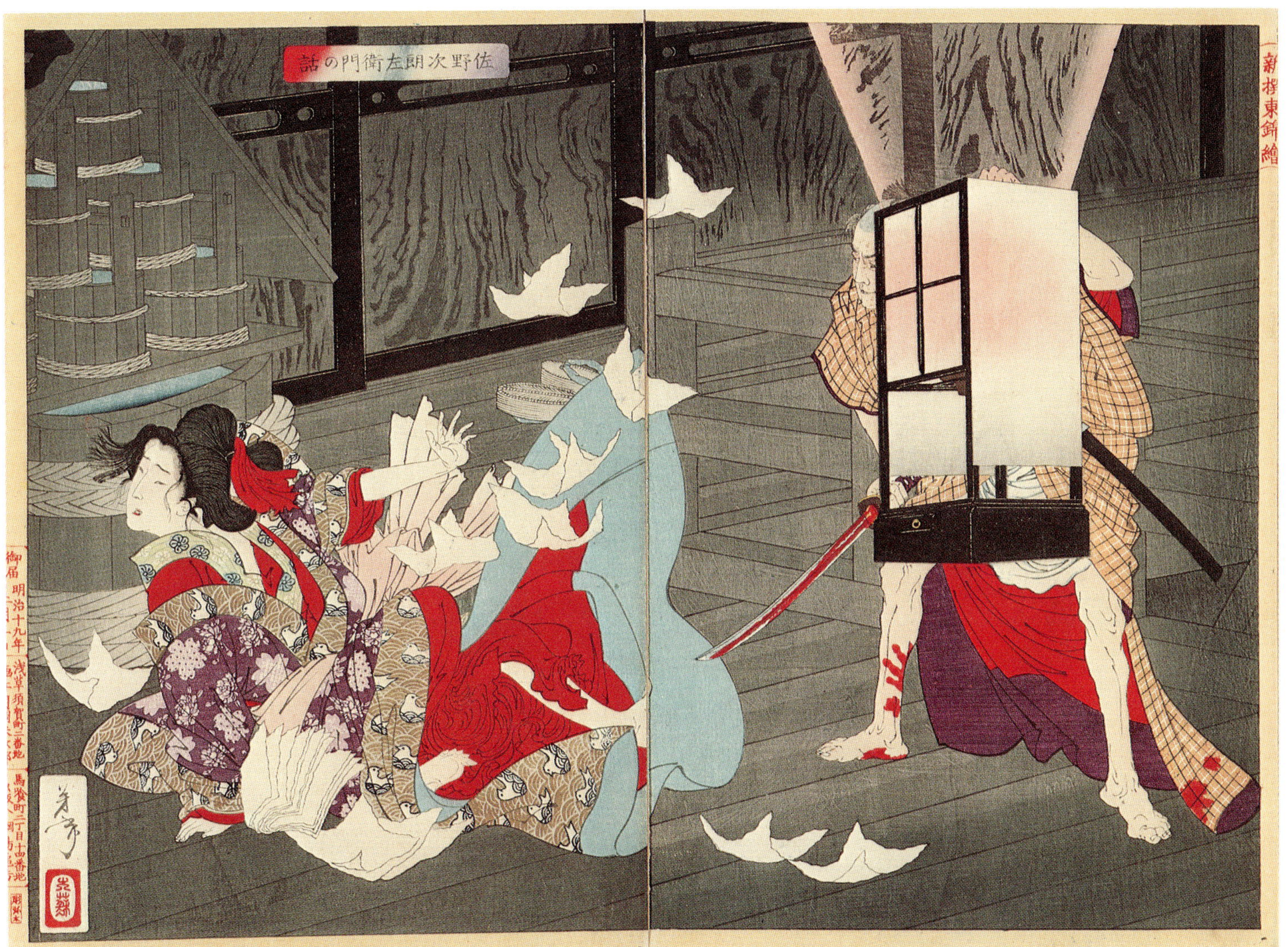

新撰東錦絵
佐野次朗左衛門の話

33. The Battle of the Wrestlers and the Firemen at Shimmei Shrine
(Shimmei sumō tōsō no zu), March 22, 1886

Series: *A New Selection of Eastern Color Prints*
(Shinsen azuma nishiki-e)
Oban diptych
Signature: Yoshitoshi
Seal: Taiso
Publisher: Tsunajima Kamekichi
Engraver: Enkatsu tō

During the second month of 1805, while several sumō wrestlers were demonstrating their strength on the precincts of the Shimmei Shrine in the Shiba district of Edo, they were attacked by a gang of firemen. A bloody battle ensued and later became the subject of a series of popular Kabuki plays. Yoshitoshi's print shows the wrestler Yotsuguruma Daijin defending himself against Kotengu Heisuke, one of the firemen of the *Me* company, while a companion holds the rest of the firemen at bay. The figure of the wrestler seems to be based on a print from Kuniyoshi's *Kisokaidō* series published about 1852.

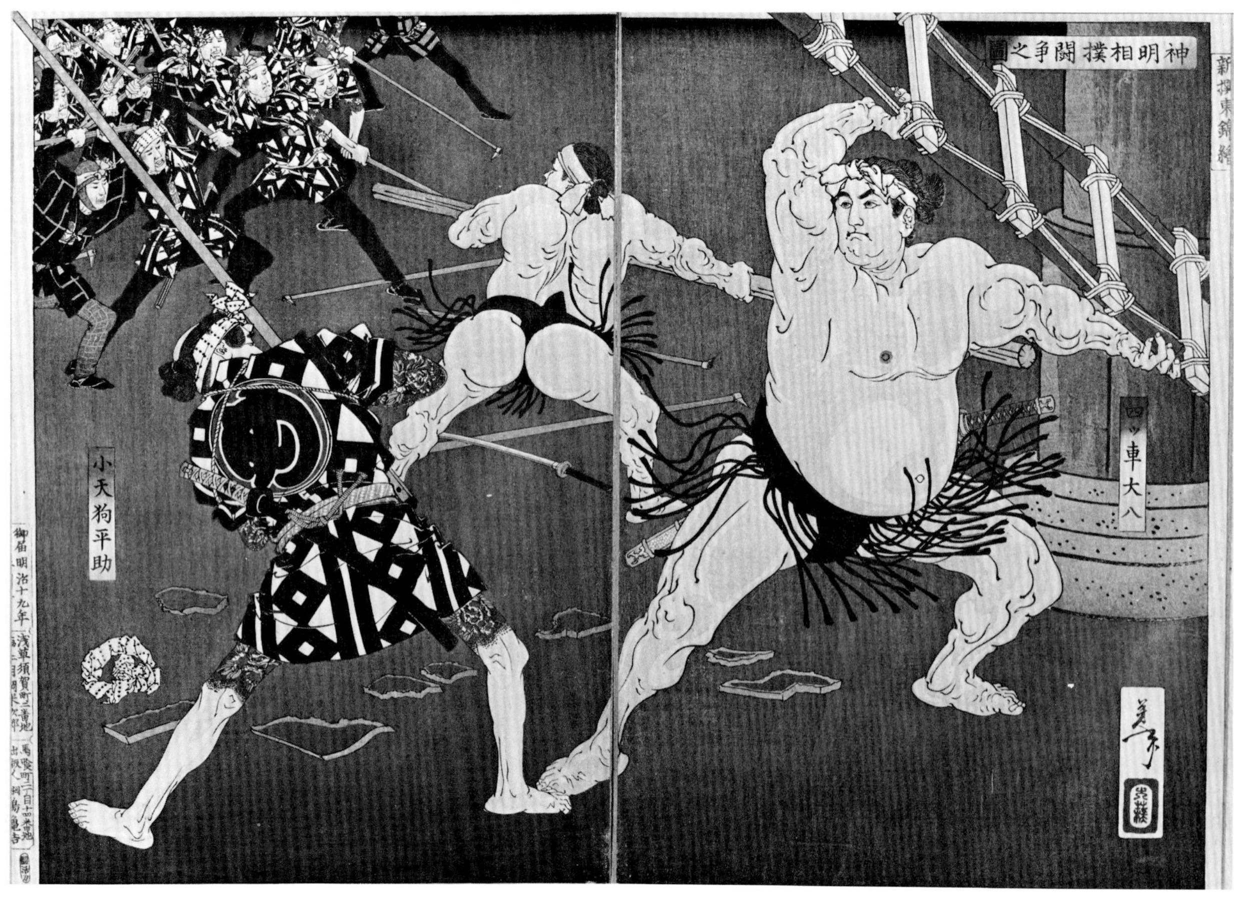

34. A Woman Saving the Nation: A Chronicle of Great Peace

(Gokoku onna taiheiki), 1886

Ōban triptych
Signature: *Ōju Yoshitoshi ga*
Seal: *Yoshitoshi*
Publisher: *Akiyama Buemon*
Engraver: *Enkatsu tō*

Tsunayoshi (1646–1709), the fifth Tokugawa shogun who presided over the great flowering of Japanese culture in the Genroku period, was a man of considerable taste, learning, and literary accomplishment. At the beginning of his career he earnestly studied Confucianism and actively patronized the arts. Later he dissipated himself, neglected his duties as a ruler, and left much power and great wealth to his minister, Yanagisawa Yoshiyasu, who popularly was accused of corrupting Tsunayoshi and pandering to his weaknesses. Historically, Yanagisawa outlived the shogun and comfortably retired after Tsunayoshi's death. Yet, in the manuscript accounts of the period on which a

Kabuki play eventually was based, Yanagisawa overstepped himself when he began to work curses on Tsunayoshi and planned to poison him. A loyal councillor discovered the plot and warned the shogun, who refused to listen. The councillor therefore confided in Osamenokata, the shogun's wife, who stabbed Yanagisawa to protect her husband, thus "saving the nation," and then killed herself.

Part of the power of Yoshitoshi's print is in its ambiguity. Tsunayoshi dozes and dreams of a lover. As if in a dream, the girl is closer to us than the shogun, larger than life, more vivid, and more intense. Beside him, wide awake, his wife waits for Yanagisawa to come. At the same time she seems to guard her husband jealously, ready to kill the suspected dream rival. The colors were originally more brilliant, and in areas where moisture was present the red and purple have run and slightly faded. This strange, remarkable picture is engraved with an almost decadent refinement that suits the mood of the tale.

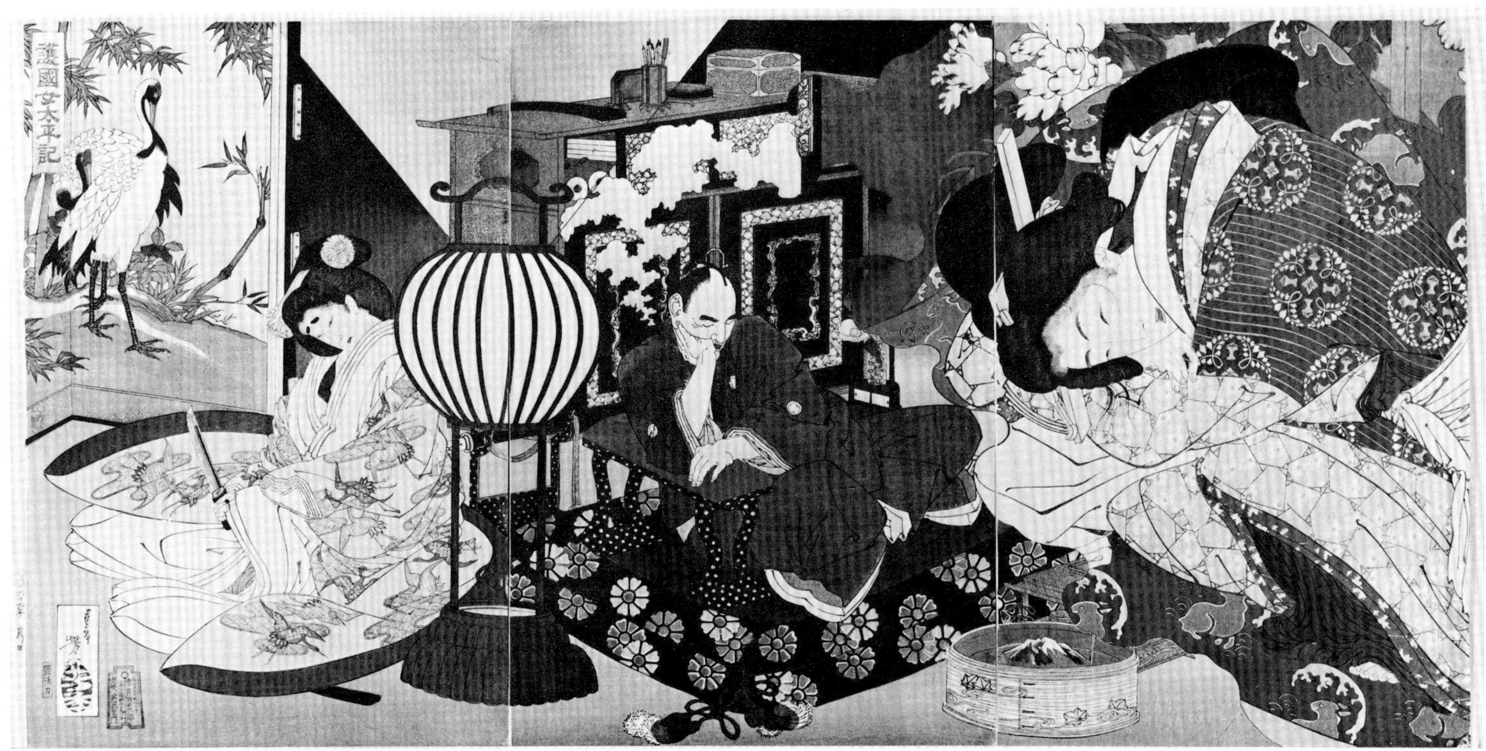

35. Shunkan Watching Enviously from Kikai Island as Yasuyori Is Unexpectedly Pardoned and Returns to the Capital
(Shunkan sōzu kikaigashima ni oite tamatama yasuyori no shamen sembō kito no zu),
May 1886

Vertical *ōban* diptych
Signature: Yoshitoshi
Seal: Taiso
Publisher: Matsui Eikichi
Engraver: Horikō Negishi Chokuzan

Shunkan, the abbot of the Zen temple Hōshōji in Kyoto, was exiled to the barren island of Kikaigashima off the coast of Kyūshū in the summer of 1177 with two confederates, Naritsune and Yasuyori, for conspiring against the military ruler Taira no Kiyomori. The following year Kiyomori granted a general amnesty to many political prisoners as an offering to the gods for the safe delivery of his consort's child. A messenger arrived at the island with a pardon for Naritsune and Yasuyori, but no word for Shunkan. As the two courtiers boarded the boat, Shunkan stood on the shore, pleading and beseeching until the ship was out of sight. The story was used for a Noh play and eventually became part of the Kabuki repertoire. Shunkan's grief on stage is pathetic and almost unbearably sad. There is grief in Yoshitoshi's print, but also hatred and anger, as Shunkan's hopes scatter like sea spray or a flock of gulls.

36. The Depravity of Seigen
(Seigen daraku no zu), 1889

Vertical *ōban* diptych
Signature: Yoshitoshi
Seal: Yoshitoshi
Publisher: Hasegawa Tsunejirō

In some versions of this popular tale, the priest Seigen was the abbot of Kiyomizu Temple in Kyoto, and Sakurahime was the beautiful, proper daughter of a well-to-do family in that city. One spring day when Sakurahime visited the temple to view the cherry blossoms, she and Seigen saw one another, and from that moment they behaved as though possessed. The two contrived to meet, had sexual relations, and could not bear to be parted. Seigen broke his vows, was expelled from his temple, and Sakurahime left her home to be with him. In one version of the story Seigen died, but his ghost continued to haunt Sakurahime. In the version portrayed in this print, she has died but her spirit still possesses the priest, who embraces her robes as if she were there.

In the mid-1880s Yoshitoshi designed fifteen or sixteen vertical diptychs, including some of his finest prints. Most, perhaps all of them were originally published by Matsui Eikichi. Many were republished in the late 1880s by Hasagawa Tsunejirō, the publisher of this print. The red seal in the upper left corner reads, "Reproduction not allowed."

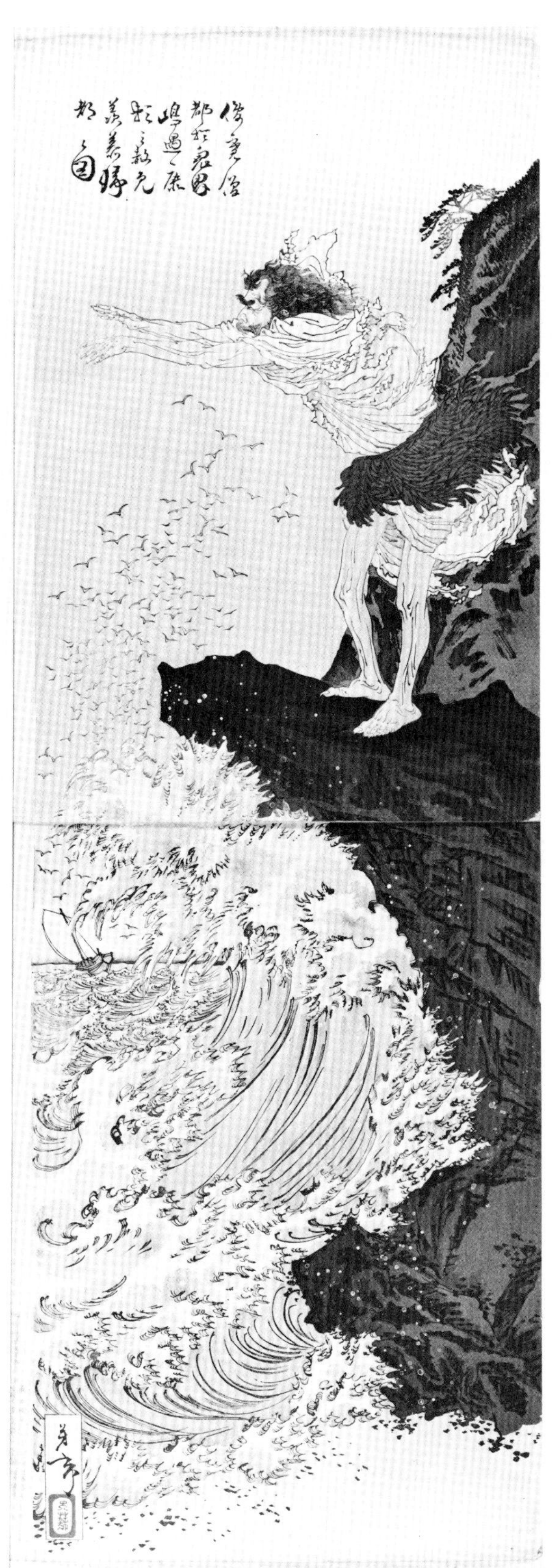

耀々美暈

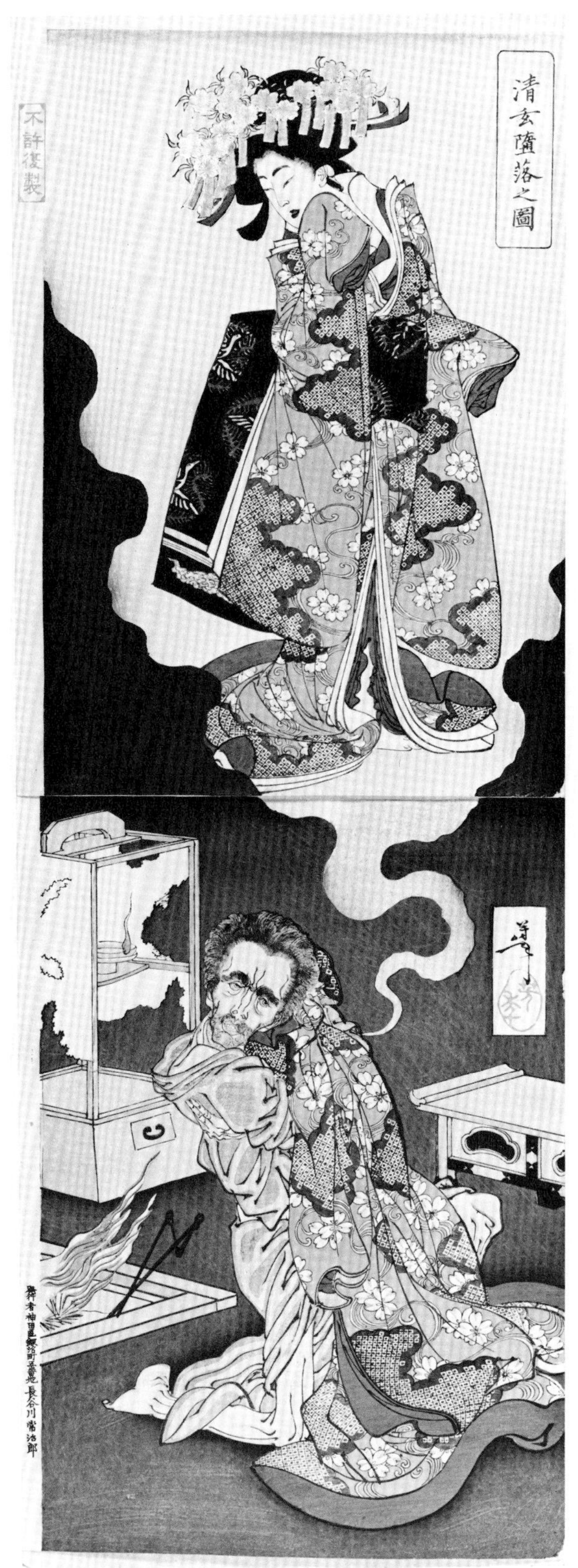

清玄墮落之圖
不許復製

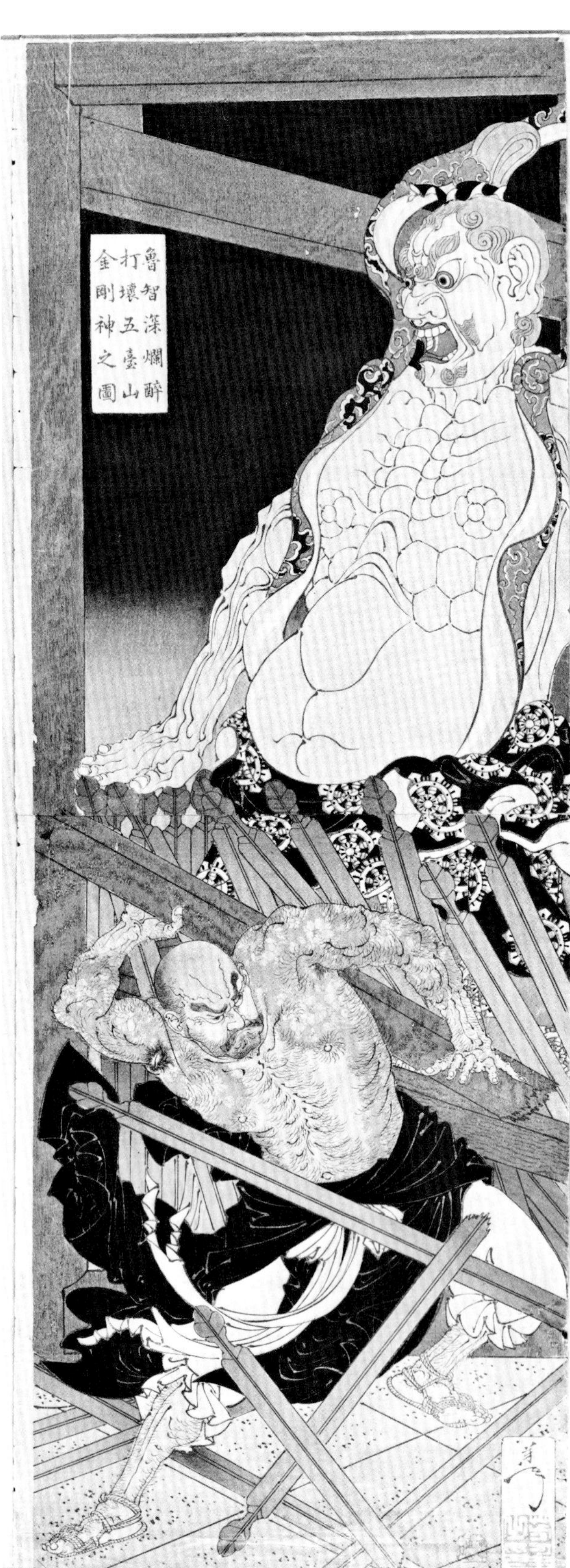

37. Lu Chi Shen in a Drunken Rage Smashing the Guardian Figure at the Temple on the Five-Crested Mountain

(Rochishin ransui godaizan kongōjin o uchikowasu no zu), September 1, 1887

Vertical *ōban* diptych
Signature: Yoshitoshi
Seal: Yoshitoshi no in
Publisher: Matsui Eikichi
Engraver: Negishi Chokuzan tō

Lu Ta, a captain of imperial soldiers in the Chinese military court, accidentally killed a man in a fit of anger. To escape the death penalty he decided to become a priest, and he made his way to the temple on the Five-Crested Mountain. The abbot received him, cut his hair, and renamed him Lu Chi Shen, Lu of Deep Wisdom. Before many days had passed, it was obvious that Lu was incorrigible. He had no concept of discipline, disregarded his priestly vows, and because of his violent temper and prodigious strength could not be punished. One night he staggered back drunk to the temple and decided to do some exercises beside the gate of the temple to make sure he had not become weak. The first swing of his fist shattered one of the gate columns; a second blow shattered another. Surprised at the crashing lumber, Lu looked up and saw one of the wooden guardian figures on the gate looming over him. In his stupor the figure seemed to be mocking him, and he attacked it, as well as the second guardian figure on the gate. He then smashed the door and broke into the middle of the main hall of the temple where hundreds of priests were sitting in meditation. Lu flailed about in his drunken rage until out of his robe fell a roasted dog's leg, showing that he also had committed the crime of eating meat. The abbot was summoned, and he dismissed Lu with a letter of safekeeping and four scrolls which he commanded him to preserve and to obey their teachings. Lu had many more adventures and was finally recorded as The Lone Star Among the Stars of Heaven, or The Tattooed Priest, one of the 108 heroes of the *Suikoden* (see cat. no. 27). This is the earliest state of the print with the date and publisher's address in the lower left margin.

**38. Ichikawa Danjūrō IX as Musashibō
Benkei in _Kanjinchō_**
1887 or 1890

Ōban triptych
Signature: Ōju Yoshitoshi ga
Seal: Yoshitoshi no in
Publisher: Akiyama Buemon
Engraver: Hori Yū

After defeating the Taira clan, Minamoto no
Yoshitsune returned to Kamakura to pledge
fealty to his elder half-brother Yoritomo who had
assumed control of the government. Yoritomo
refused to trust his brother's sincerity and or-
dered Yoshitsune captured and his forces dis-
persed. Yoshitsune escaped by land and sea,
traveling far westward and then doubling back
along the coast of the Japan Sea in the hope
of reaching Hiraizumi in northern Japan, where
he felt he would be secure. His followers, including Benkei, disguised themselves as itinerant
priests raising funds for a temple, and at the
barrier of Ataka their identity was challenged.

This episode is often performed on the Kabuki
stage under the title _The Subscription Record
(Kanjinchō),_ and the play was brought to its
present form and popularity by Ichikawa Danjūrō IX, the actor portrayed in Yoshitoshi's print.
At the climax of the play, the suspicious warden at the government barrier requires Benkei
to read the subscription list. The warrior-priest
draws out an empty scroll and improvises a
convincing series of donors and amounts; the
warden finally accepts this as proof, allowing
the group to pass safely onward.

In the print, Benkei, dressed as a traveling
priest, seems to be about to unroll his scroll.
The seventeen-syllable poem at the right, written by Yoshitoshi's friend Keika, reads "The
flowers and their fragrance like traveler's robes
are wet with dew" _(Hana mo ka mo tsuyukeki
mono yo tabigoromo)._ The seal "Humanity: all
things" _(Ningen banji)_ is the poet's motto.

The Cole print is undated, but an impression in
a Japanese collection seems to have the date
April 1, 1887, stamped or printed beside the
signature.[13] If this date is correct, Yoshitoshi
may have produced the design in anticipation
of the first Kabuki play ever witnessed by an
emperor, a performance of _Kanjinchō,_ with
Danjūrō in the lead role, presented in the mansion of the foreign minister Baron Inoue on
April 27, 1887. The 1887 date for the print is
questionable, though, for the print is similar
in style to Yoshitoshi's portrait of another
friend which also has a poem by Keika, was
engraved by Hori Yū, and was published
by Akiyama in January 1890.

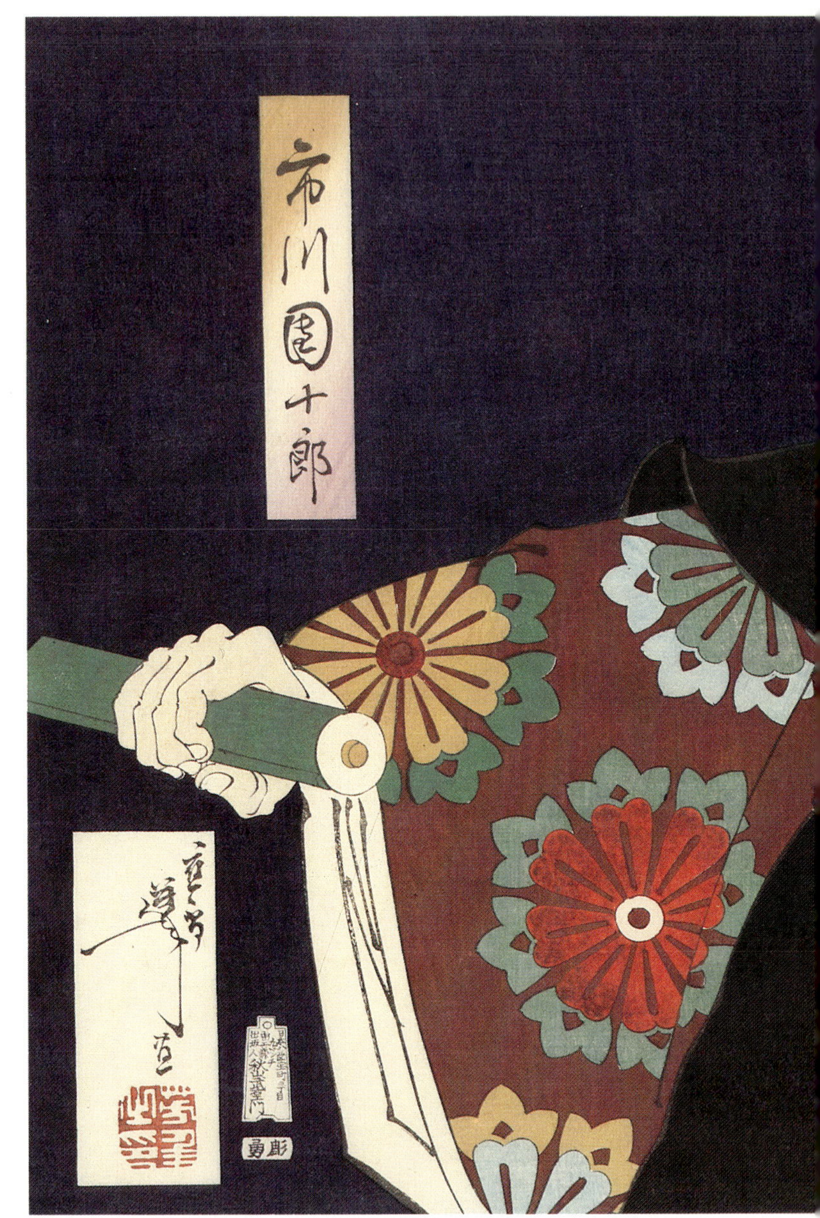

市川團十郎

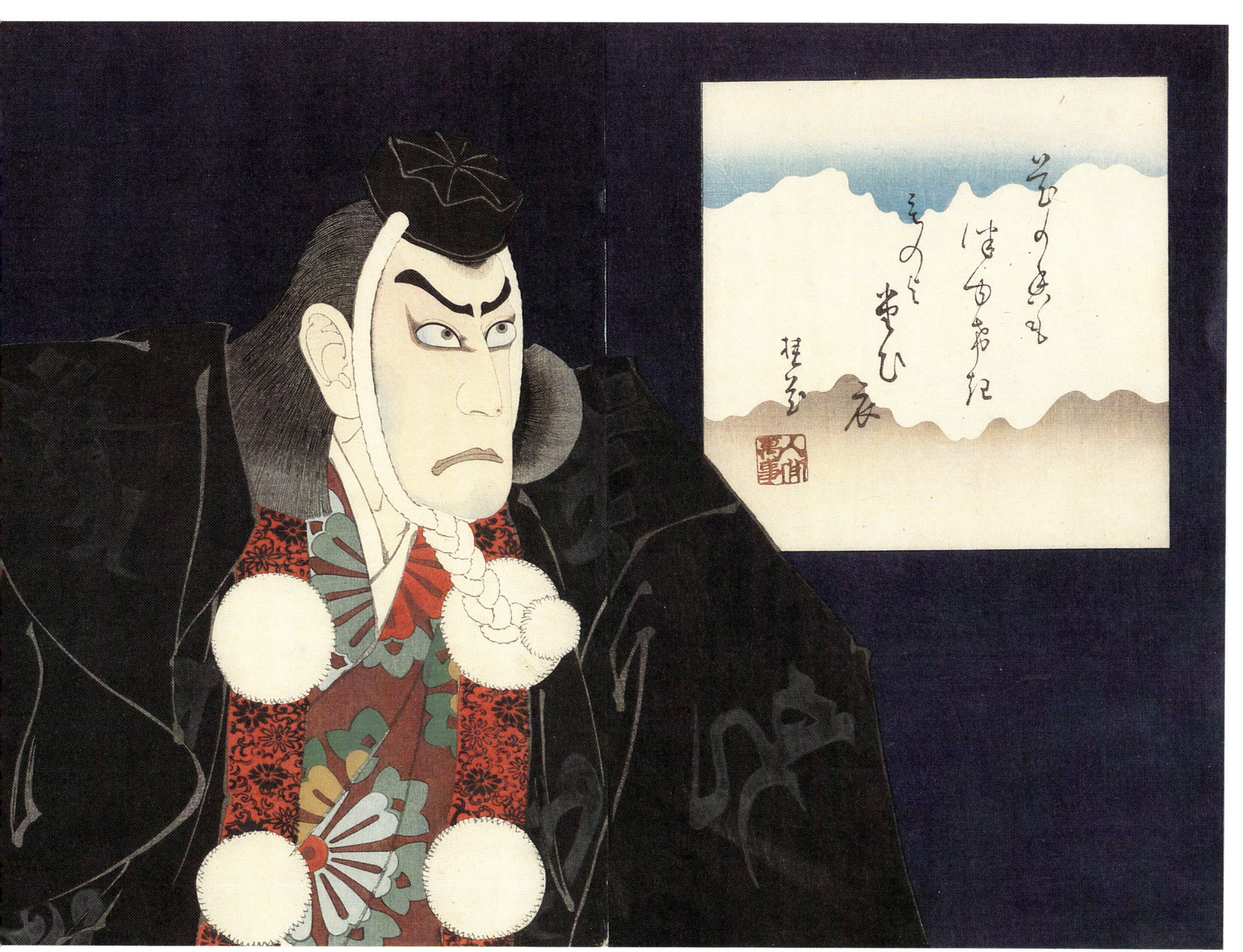

39a. Hanai Oume Killing Kamekichi

August 20, 1887
Series: *Lives of Modern People (Kinsei jimbutsu shi)*
Ōban
Signature: Yoshitoshi
Seal: Taiso
Publisher: The Yamato Newspaper Company

Hanai Oume, who formerly had been a geisha under other names, was the owner of the Suigetsu restaurant in Tokyo. The night of June 9, 1887, she killed a man named Kamekichi on the banks of the Sumida River and afterward was arrested and charged with murder. Oume pled in court that she had been refusing Kamekichi's advances for some time, that he had attacked her in the dark with a knife, and that she had killed him in self-defense. The prosecution charged that the couple had been lovers, that Oume was a woman with a violent temperament, that Kamekichi had become increasingly parasitic, and that she had premeditated the murder. Oume was sentenced by the court to life imprisonment. The trial made her a celebrity, and a play and a novel were written about her. She was paroled from prison in 1903 and from that time supported herself through public recitations of her story.

Yoshitoshi's print was published about two months after the murder as the eleventh in a series of twenty pictures of contemporary figures, issued as supplements by the *Yamato Newspaper*. This was Yoshitoshi's last set of "newspaper prints" (see cat. nos. 10, 11). The text at the top of the print presents a brief biography of Oume and a resume of the two theories of her guilt, concluding that one way or another, "she was certainly an extraordinary woman." Details in the figure's presentation show that Yoshitoshi was clearly convinced that the murder was in self-defense. Oume could neither have concealed nor held a knife before the meeting: she has dropped from her hands the umbrella and the lantern bearing the name of her restaurant, and a folded piece of cloth has fallen from the only place she could conceal a weapon, the pocket formed by the overlap of her robe across her chest. Also, the lantern is slashed indicating that she held it up to protect herself. How she tore the knife from her assailant the artist left us to guess, but he obviously sympathized with her cool determination to finish off the hapless Kamekichi once and for all rather than risk a later attack.

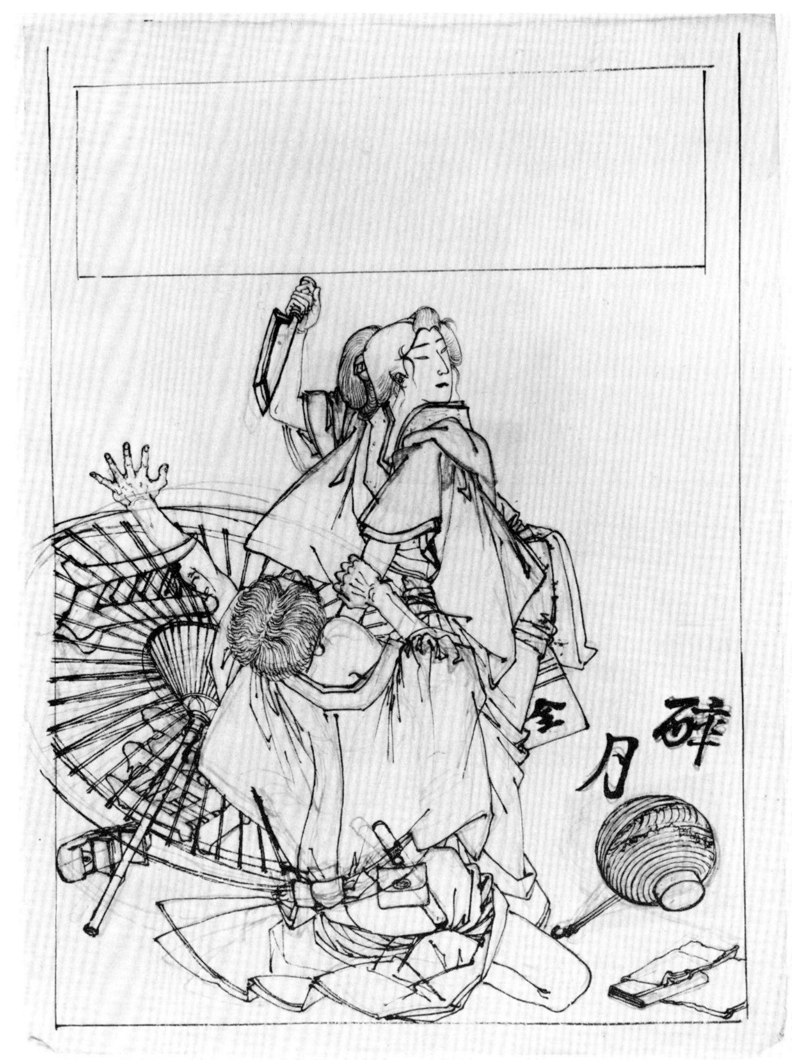

39b. Preparatory drawing in red and black ink, August 1887, unsigned

Yoshitoshi began this preparatory drawing with a sheet of paper roughly the size of a standard published print. He ruled the borderlines and the position of the text at the top of the print and then began to sketch the design quickly in light red ink. He first drew the naked bodies of the figures and, once they were positioned, began sketching in their clothing and placing the objects on the ground beside them, adjusting their placement to fit the rest of the picture as it developed. The Japanese characters for Oume's restaurant are reversed in the picture because they are seen through the translucent paper of the umbrella. The artist had some difficulty seeing them in his mind and wrote them out in their ordinary form at the right. Yoshitoshi seems to have sought more ways to demonstrate Oume's innocence as the drawing progressed. The umbrella was drawn hastily at the start and extends beyond the picture's tentative border. Originally the lantern seems to have been collapsed flat on the ground. He added Oume's final alibi, the folded cloth in the lower right hand corner which she carried at her breast leaving no room for the murderous knife. Then he took a thin sheet of paper, pasted it over the lantern he had originally drawn, and drew another falling open along Kamekichi's gash. There was one more correction on Oume's shoulder, and the picture was finished and ready to be copied for the engraver. It was probably then that he inscribed, on Oume's sash, the character *zen,* complete, which does not appear on the print.

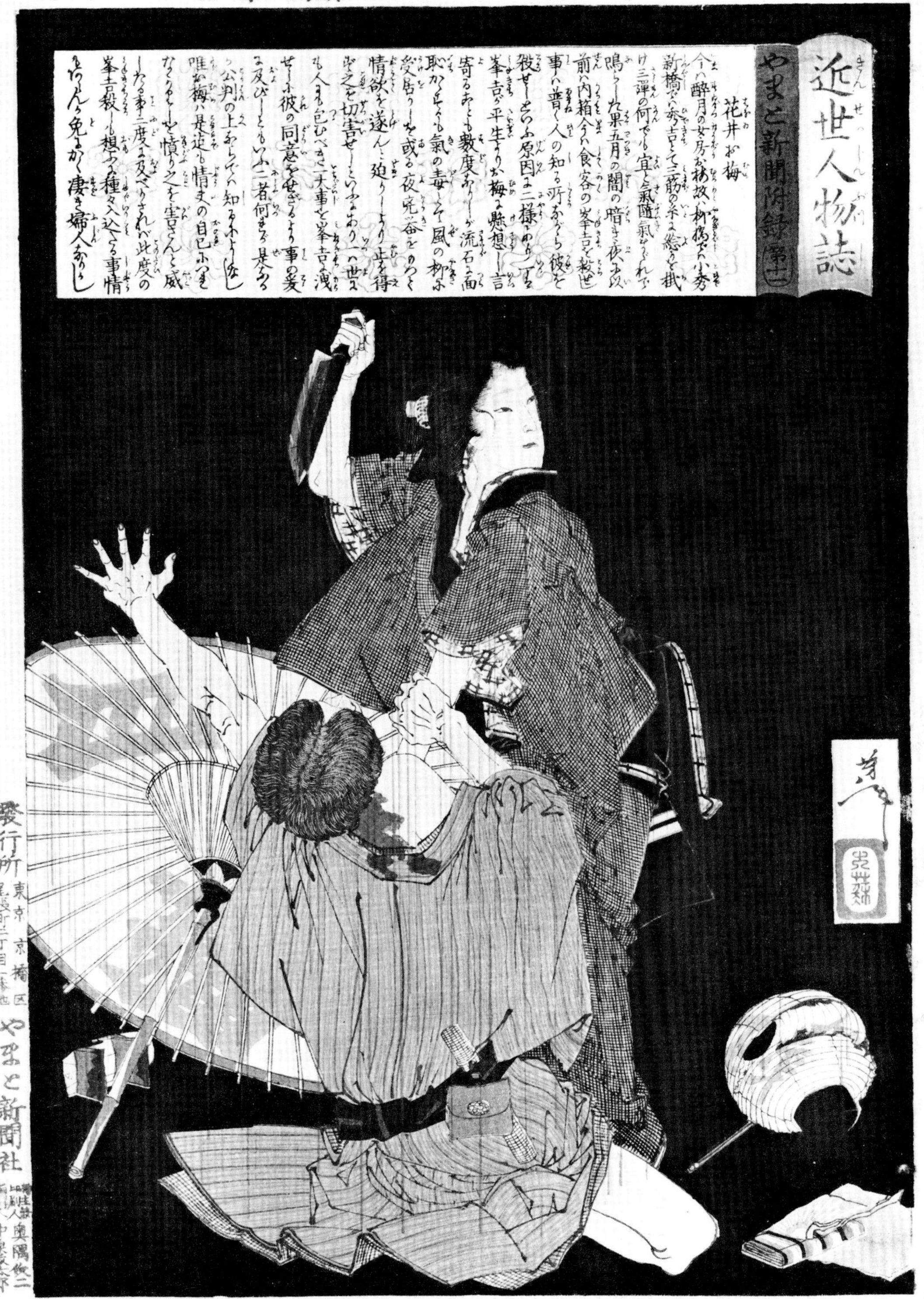

發行所　東京京橋区尾張町三丁目一番地　やまと新聞社
編輯人　奥隅敬二
印刷人　中泉藪太郎

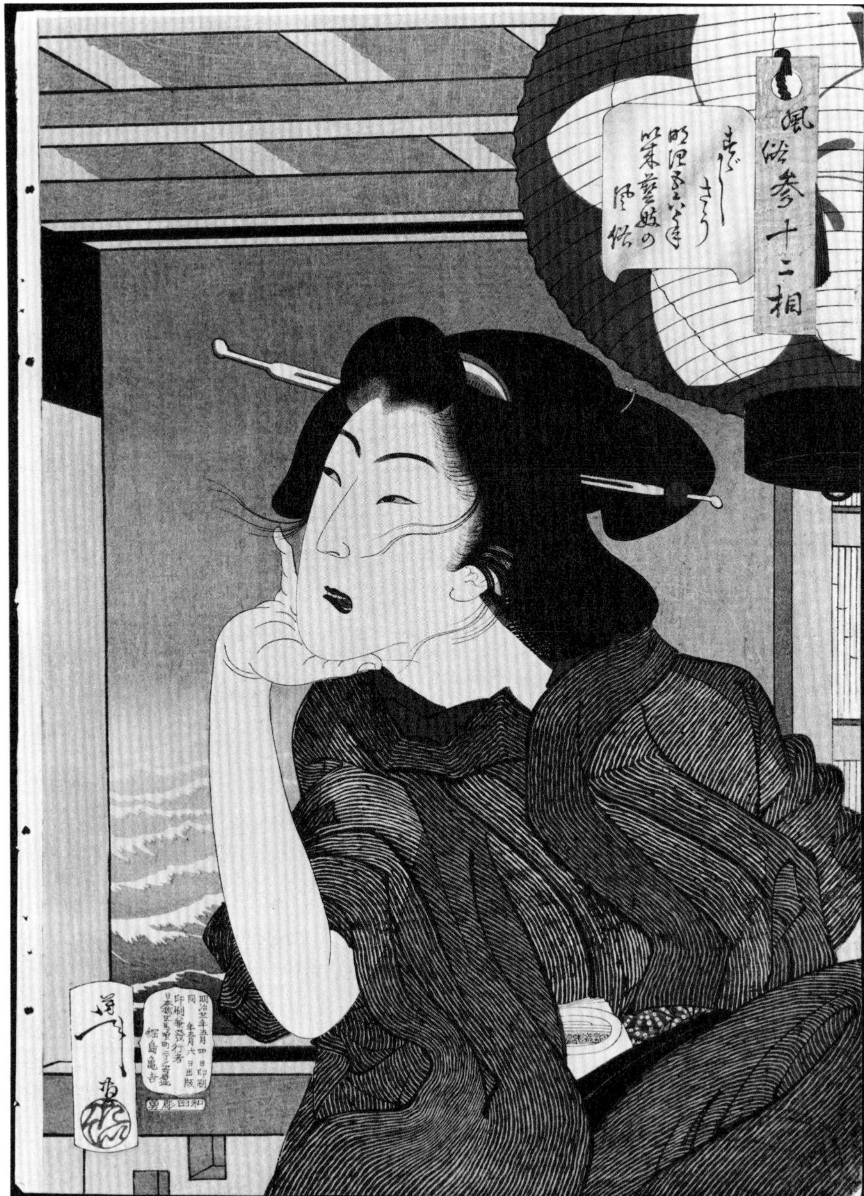

40. Cool: The Fashion of a Geisha in the Early 1870s

(Suzushi sō meiji go roku nen irai geigi no fūzoku), May 4, 1888

Series: *Thirty-two Aspects of Women (Fūzoku sanjūnisō)*
Ōban
Signature: Yoshitoshi ga
Seal: Taiso
Publisher: Tsunashima Kamekichi
Engraver: Wada Hori Yū

After his liaison with the geisha Oraku in the late 1870s, and the harsh, vulgar pictures of women he designed during that period, Yoshitoshi made few portraits of women until the *Thirty-Two Aspects of Women* set published in 1888. "Aspects," or *sō*, a technical term used by physiognomists, had been popularized by Utamaro, who designed many sets of female aspects, or types, during his career. The physiognomists believed that character was revealed not just by features, but also by gesture, clothing, carriage, manner, and speech. The idea of exploring a range of female types gave Yoshitoshi a valuable initial detachment from his subject, and he created even further detachment by presenting the *Thirty-two Aspects* in chronological sequence as a history of fashions *(fūzoku)* in the late Tokugawa period. The largest number of the prints portray women from the 1850s to the 1880s, the period for which the artist felt the most attraction. Nevertheless, the historical and sociological aspect of the set allowed Yoshitoshi momentarily to suspend his ambivalence toward women, and the set includes some fine prints. They seem to have been popular in their own day, because many were printed until the blocks were virtually worn out (see cat. no. 41). To enjoy the *Thirty-two Aspects* it is important to see them in fine, early impressions, as in this print of a geisha in a pleasure boat on the Sumida River. The delicate outlines and strands of hair are crisp and distinct, the gradations of color subtle, the colors fresh and unfaded. The woman's body seems almost to breathe sensuality through her transparent kimono.

Illustrated in color on first page.

41. Preparing to Take a Stroll:
A Married Woman in the Meiji Period

(Yūho ga shita sō meiji nenkan saikun no fūzoku), June 22, 1888

Series: *Thirty-two Aspects of Women*
(Fūzoku sanjūnisō)
Ōban
Signature: Yoshitoshi ga
Seal: Taiso
Publisher: Tsunashima Kamekichi
Engraver: Horikō Wada tō

Yoshitoshi, who refused to use modern oil lamps and scolded his students for wearing Western underwear, remained quite aloof from the Westernization of Japan which presented such a fertile field for other Ukiyo-e artists of Meiji period. In the early 1860s he designed a few prints of foreigners at Yokohama and, in the early 1870s, a few Western-style pictures of horse races, bridges, and railroads in an unsuccessful bid for popularity. During the Satsuma Rebellion he drew dozens of pictures of soldiers in smart Western-style uniforms (see cat. no. 12). In comic prints of the early 1880s he caricatured the affectations of the modernizing Japanese. This extremely popular print marks one of the few occasions on which he overcame his prejudice and designed a print of a modern woman in Western dress. This is the commoner of the two versions of the print and is almost always seen, as here, in a rather late impression showing wear on the outline block. (For an early impression of another print from the set, see cat. no. 40.) The second version is later, bears the name of the same publisher but of a different engraver—Toku—and was probably published before the end of the nineteenth century. This later version was printed from a different set of blocks, suggesting that the publisher had the popular print re-engraved when the original blocks wore out.

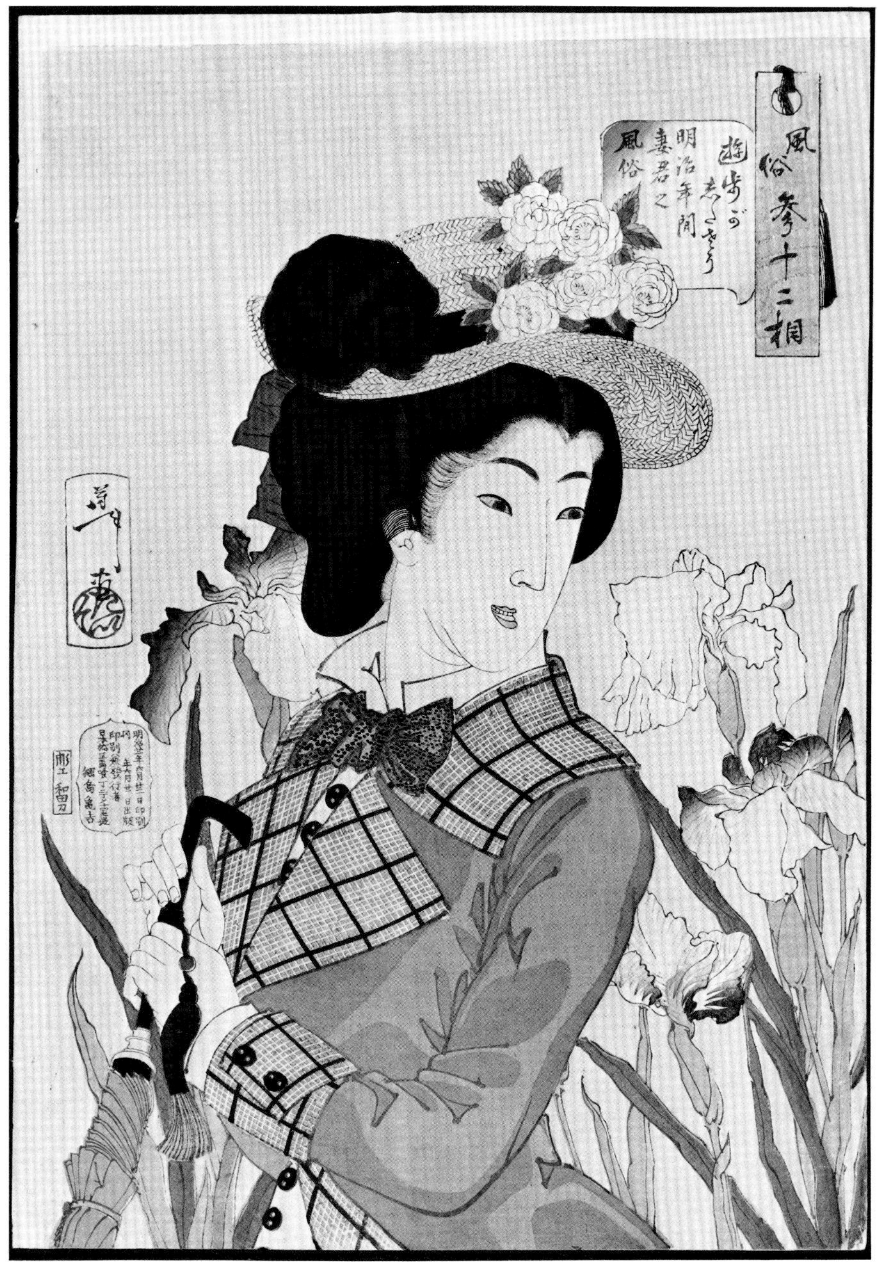

42. Oniwaka Observing the Great Carp in the Pond

(Oniwakamaru chichū ni rigyo o ukagau),
October 20, 1889

Series: *New Forms of Thirty-six Ghosts*
(Shinkei sanjūrokkaisen)
Ōban
Signature: Yoshitoshi
Seal: Yoshitoshi
Publisher: Sasaki Toyokichi
Engraver: Hori Yū

Many Japanese heroes were said to have begun their exploits during childhood. Musashibō Benkei, the warrior-priest who was the lifelong companion of Yoshitsune (see cat. no. 14), was born to a blacksmith's daughter in the mid-twelfth century. As a child, he was so obstreperous that he was given the nickname Oniwaka, The Little Devil. At the age of eight he heard that his father was one of the carved guardian figures outside the main gate at Kumano Shrine, and he made his way there to determine which one. The priests were amused and took him into the temple. They made him an acolyte and dressed him in finery, but they pestered him so much that he finally left. While at the temple he also learned that a great carp had devoured his mother, and so he went to the pond to kill the carp in revenge.

In the mid-1840s Kuniyoshi had designed a powerful triptych of Oniwaka standing on an outcrop of rock looking down at a carp that is ten times his size and extends across all three panels of the print. In the early 1870s Yoshitoshi had designed a single-sheet print of Oniwaka holding onto the carp as it swims to-ward the depths of the pool, and he repeated this treatment of the subject in a vertical diptych published in 1885. In his last print of the subject, seen here, he returned to Kuniyoshi's version, although his attention is focused more on the boy and the rock than on the fish.

Yoshitoshi was ill during this period, and it is well documented that he was assisted on the *Thirty-six Ghosts* series by two of his students, Toshikata and Toshihide (see cat. no. 9).[14] A drawing of Oniwaka is known which is directly related to this print. It is not by Yoshitoshi and suggests that one of the pupils may have drawn the figure for the print. The first character in the series title may be pronounced *shinkei* or *shingata;* both mean "new forms," but *shinkei* includes a pun on "nervous." The borderline of these prints is drawn unevenly to imitate wormholes as though the pictures were an ancient group of paintings. Japanese writers have interpreted these borders as a sign of Yoshitoshi's increasing disorientation; however, the identical borders appear on the thirty-one unpublished drawings for the set of ghost prints that Yoshitoshi began to design shortly after he moved to Nezu in 1880, the beginning of his most successful and productive period.[15]

The *Thirty-six Ghosts* were originally published by Sasaki Toyokichi between 1889 and 1892, with the last three prints in the set appearing shortly after Yoshitoshi's death. In 1902 the prints were republished in different colors by Matsuki Heikichi, and it may have been Matsuki who issued the table of contents for the set.

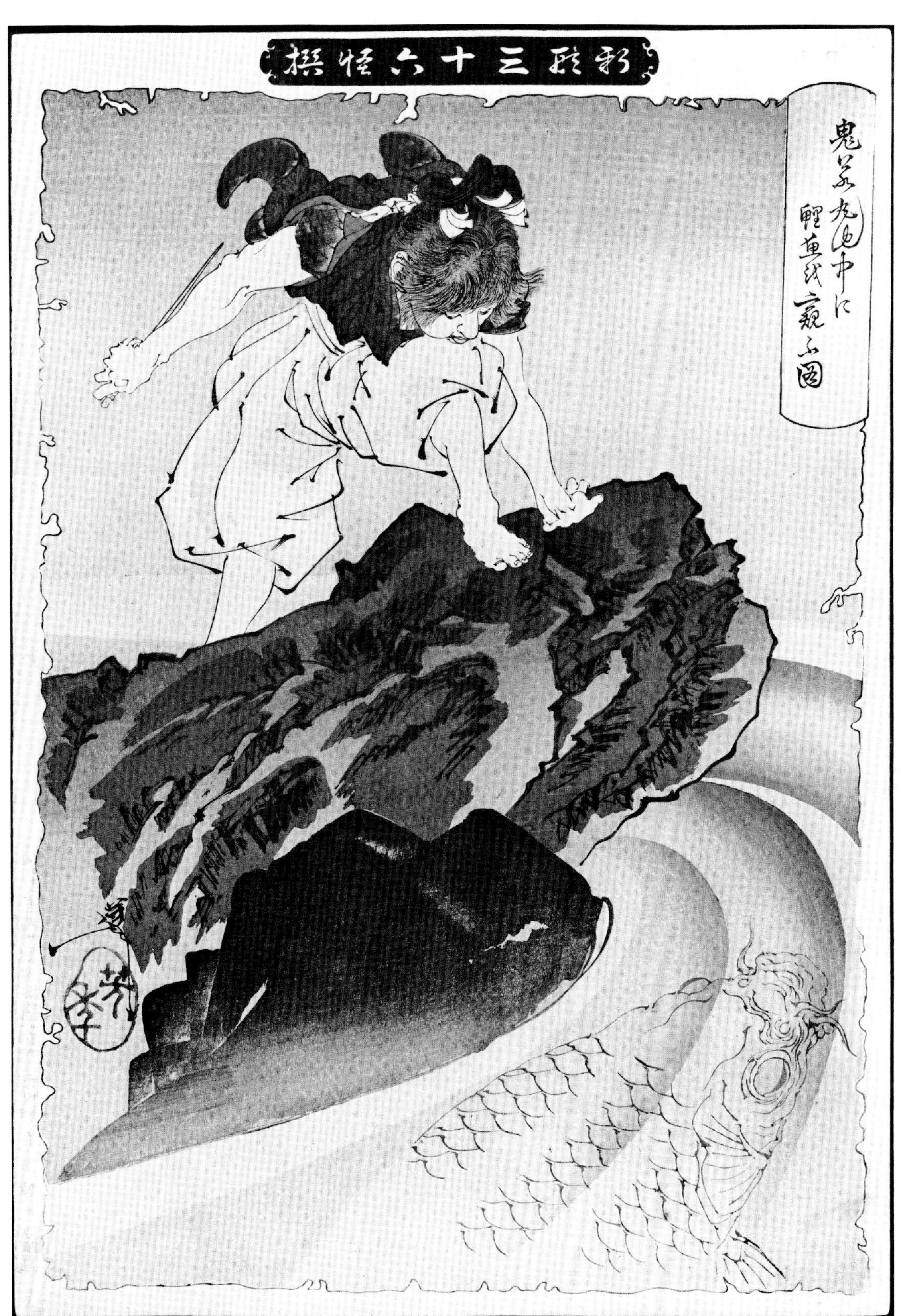
新形三十六怪撰
鬼若丸池中に
鯉魚を窺ふ圖

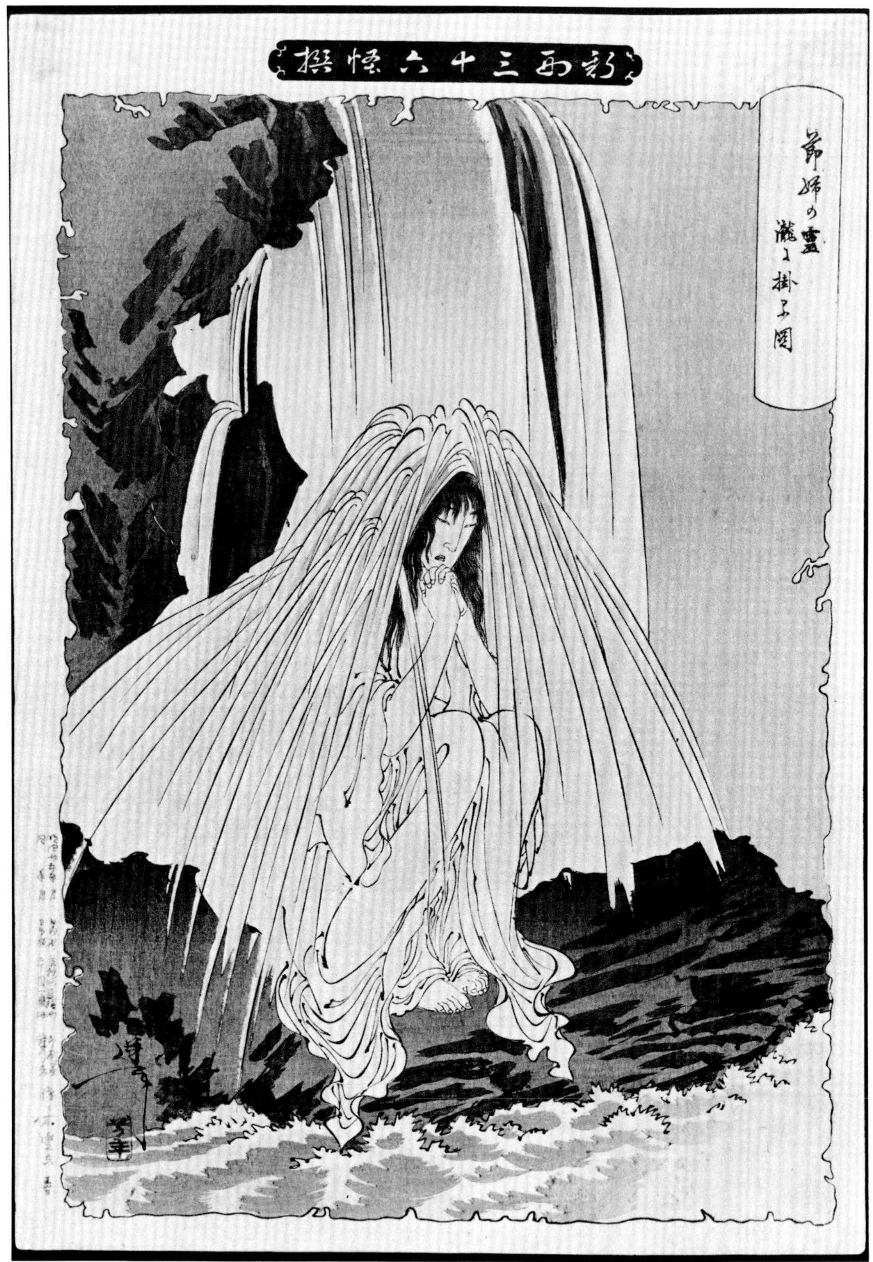

43. The Virtuous Woman's Spirit Praying under the Waterfall

(Seppu no rei taki ni kakaru zu), 1892

Series: *New Forms of Thirty-six Ghosts
(Shinkei sanjūrokkaisen)*
Ōban
Signature: Yoshitoshi
Seal: Yoshitoshi
Publisher: Sasaki Toyokichi
Engraver: Chokuzan

Tamiya Gempachirō, a fencing master from the Ikoma clan in Sanuki Province, was put to death in 1624 by a rival. His wife was pregnant and after his death bore a child named Bōtarō, whose only thought in his youth was to avenge his father's death. He realized his goal in 1641 and committed suicide himself immediately afterward as the law required. In Kabuki versions of the story, Bōtarō's enemy arranged to have him exiled to a remote temple while still a child and schemed to have him killed there. His loyal nurse Otsuji, aware of the danger to the child but powerless to intervene, kept a vigil and offered prayers to the god Kompira, finally killing herself with the prayer that the child be spared and her life accepted in exchange. Her prayer was answered, and the day she died young Bōtarō was released from captivity.

Several artists designed woodblock prints of the devoted nurse praying in the waterfall. A half-length portrait by Kunichika published in the early Meiji period even shows her cutting her throat to commit suicide. Yoshitoshi's print seems to be based on the left panel of a diptych by Kunisada published in 1885.[16]

44. Kobayakawa Takakage Debating with the Goblin Priest on Mount Hiko

(Kobayakawa takakage hikosan no tengu mondō no zu), 1892

Series: *New Forms of Thirty-six Ghosts
(Shinkei sanjūrokkaisen)*
Ōban
Signature: Yoshitoshi
Publisher: Sasaki Toyokichi
Engraver: Chokuzan

Kobayakawa Takakage (1553–1597) was a vassal of Toyotomi Hideyoshi who led several successful military campaigns in the second half of the sixteenth century in western and central Japan and became Hideyoshi's chief minister at the end of his life. During the conquest of northern Kyushu in the 1580s he camped on the slopes of the sacred Mount Hiko. Legend has it that a wind suddenly arose and before him appeared a long-nosed goblin dressed in the garb of a *yamabushi*, a type of itinerant priest who engaged in religious practices in the mountains. Here, as the wind parts the mist, we see Takakage's followers overcome with fear and astonishment as the general and the goblin begin their dialogue.

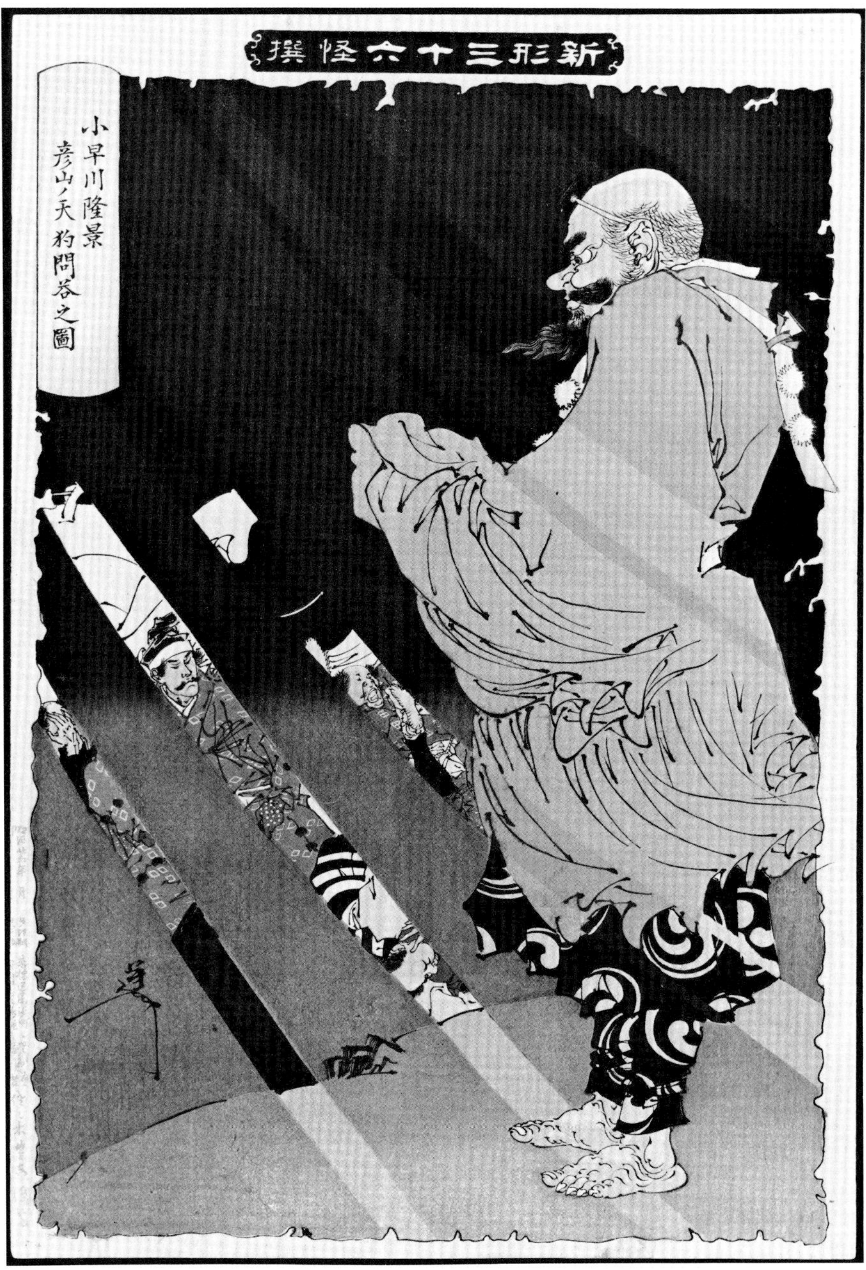

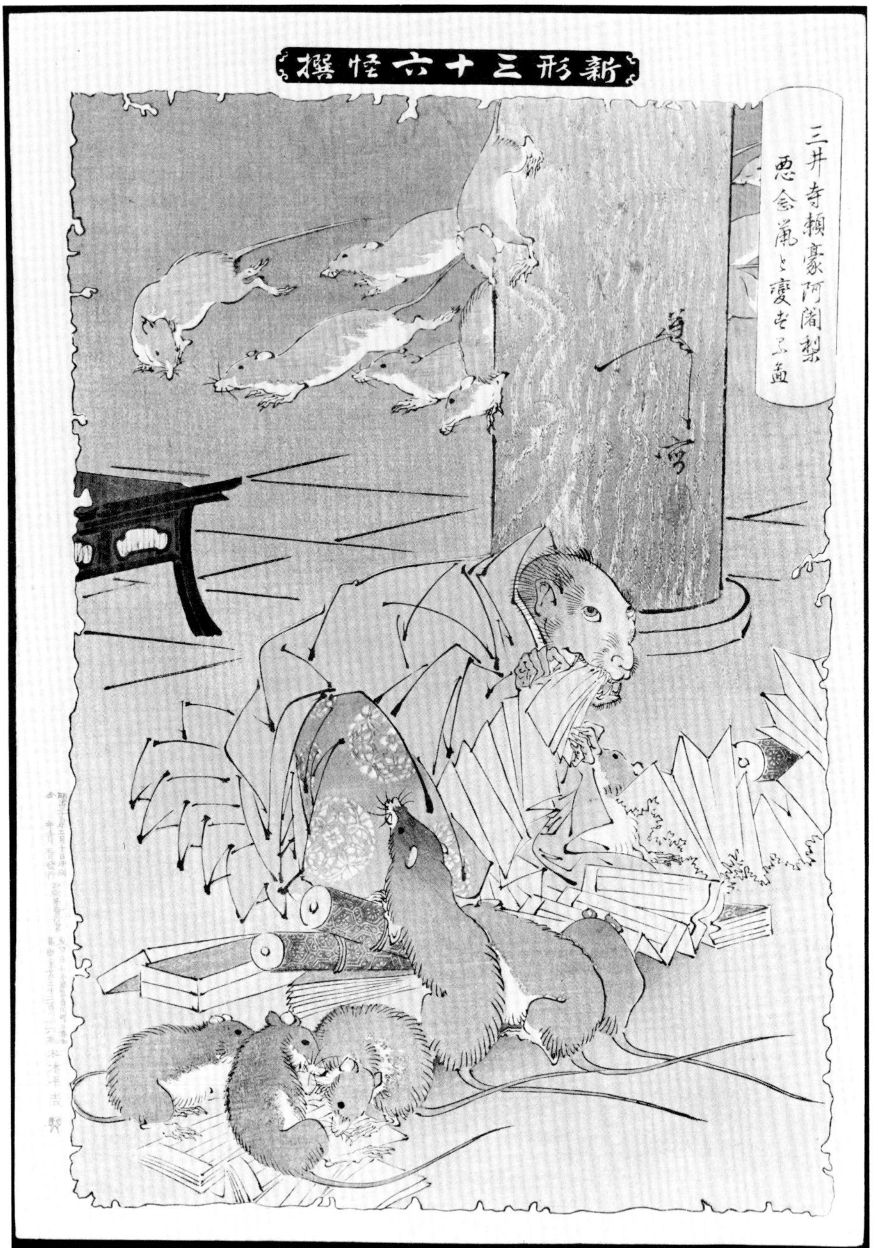

45. The Wicked Thoughts of the Priest Raigō Turning Him into a Rat at Mii Temple

(Miidera raigō ajari no akunen nezumi to henzuru zu), February 10, 1902

Series: *New Forms of Thirty-six Ghosts (Shinkei sanjūrokkaisen)*
Ōban
Signature: Yoshitoshi sha
Seal: Undeciphered
Publisher: Matsuki Heikichi

Raigō Ajari was the son of Ariie, Lord of Iga, grandson of Fujiwara no Mitsuke, and a spiritual adviser to the Emperor Shirakawa (1053–1129).[17] He was responsible for the discipline of the monks at Mii Temple. Shirakawa longed for a male heir, and his prayer was at last granted through Raigō's intervention. Overjoyed, the emperor promised Raigō anything he wished as a reward. The priest replied that his only wish was for a raised platform at his temple for prayer offerings. The raised platform was the prerogative of the powerful temples on Mt. Hiei, and the emperor fearfully refused to grant the favor. Raigō was consumed with anger; he refused to speak, appear, or eat, and he eventually died of starvation. Soon after his death in 1084, the baby prince also died. Afterward Raigō's wrathful spirit reportedly haunted Mii Temple in the form of a thousand rats who destroyed the priests' robes and sacred scriptures.

46. The Ghost of Akugenta Yoshihira Attacking Namba Jirō at Nunobiki Waterfall

(Nunobikinotaki akugenta yoshihira no rei namba jirō o utsu), December 12, 1889

Series: *New Forms of Thirty-six Ghosts (Shinkei sanjūrokkaisen)*
Ōban
Signature: Yoshitoshi
Seal: Yoshitoshi no in
Publisher: Sasaki Toyokichi
Engraver: Wada tō

The eldest son of Yoshitomo, Minamoto no Yoshihira (1140–1160), was a powerful young man sent at fifteen to defeat the armies of his uncle Yoshikata. He accomplished this with such ruthlessness and cruelty that he was given the nickname Wicked Genta. When his father was murdered in 1159, Yoshihira disguised himself as a peasant and entered Kyoto to seek revenge. He was recognized, however, and sentenced to be executed beside Nunobiki Waterfall near the modern city of Kobe. Legend says that the moment he was killed, his body sprang into the air and assumed the form of the Thunder God, and that Namba Jirō, his executioner, was killed by a terrifying flash of lightning.

Yoshitoshi shows the wrathful spirit of Yoshihira riding the clouds, his hand outstretched to fling a lightning bolt at his unfortunate executioner. The figure is taken from the top panel of a recently discovered print of the scene published in 1868, Yoshitoshi's only known vertical triptych.[18] The execution and revenge of Yoshihira was a popular story in the mid-nineteenth century and the subject of prints by many of Kuniyoshi's pupils.

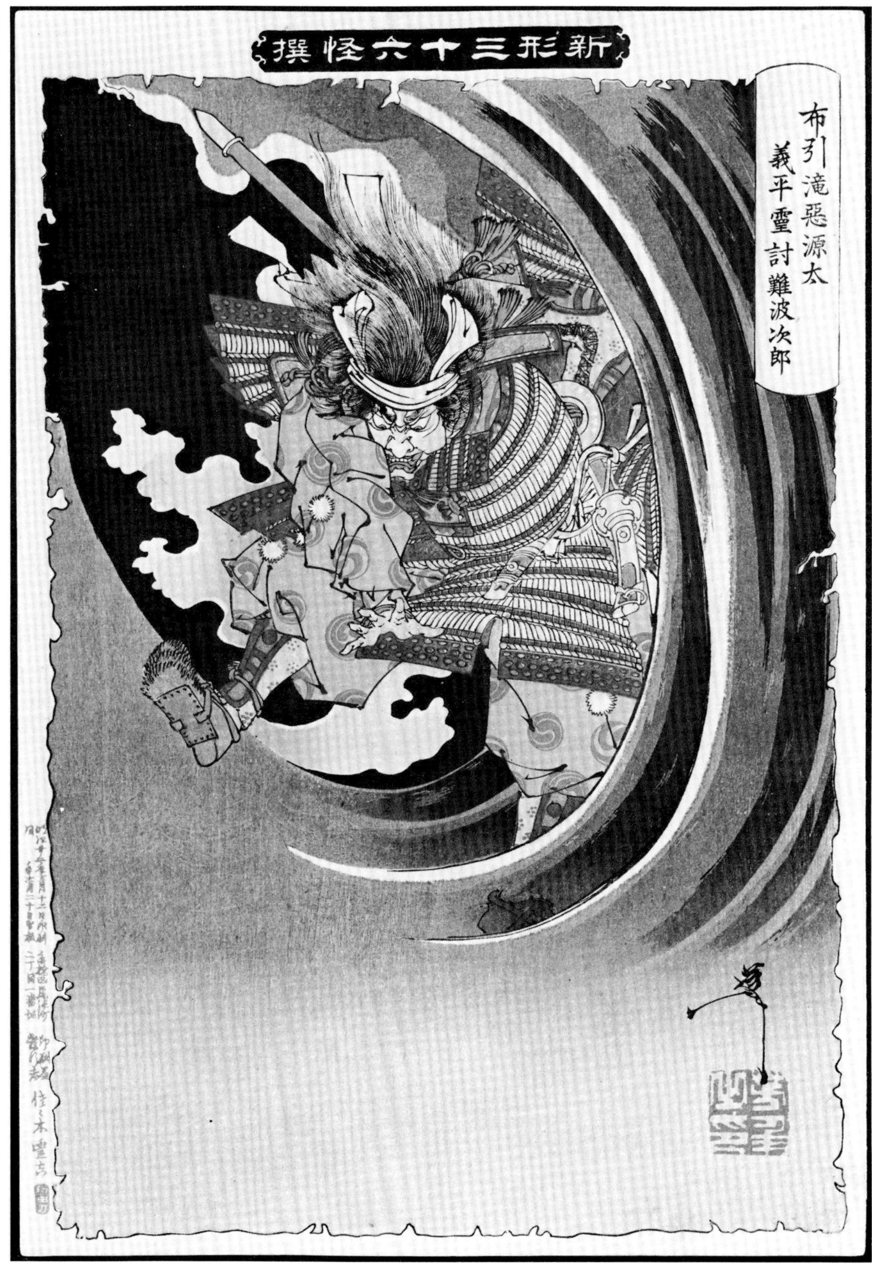

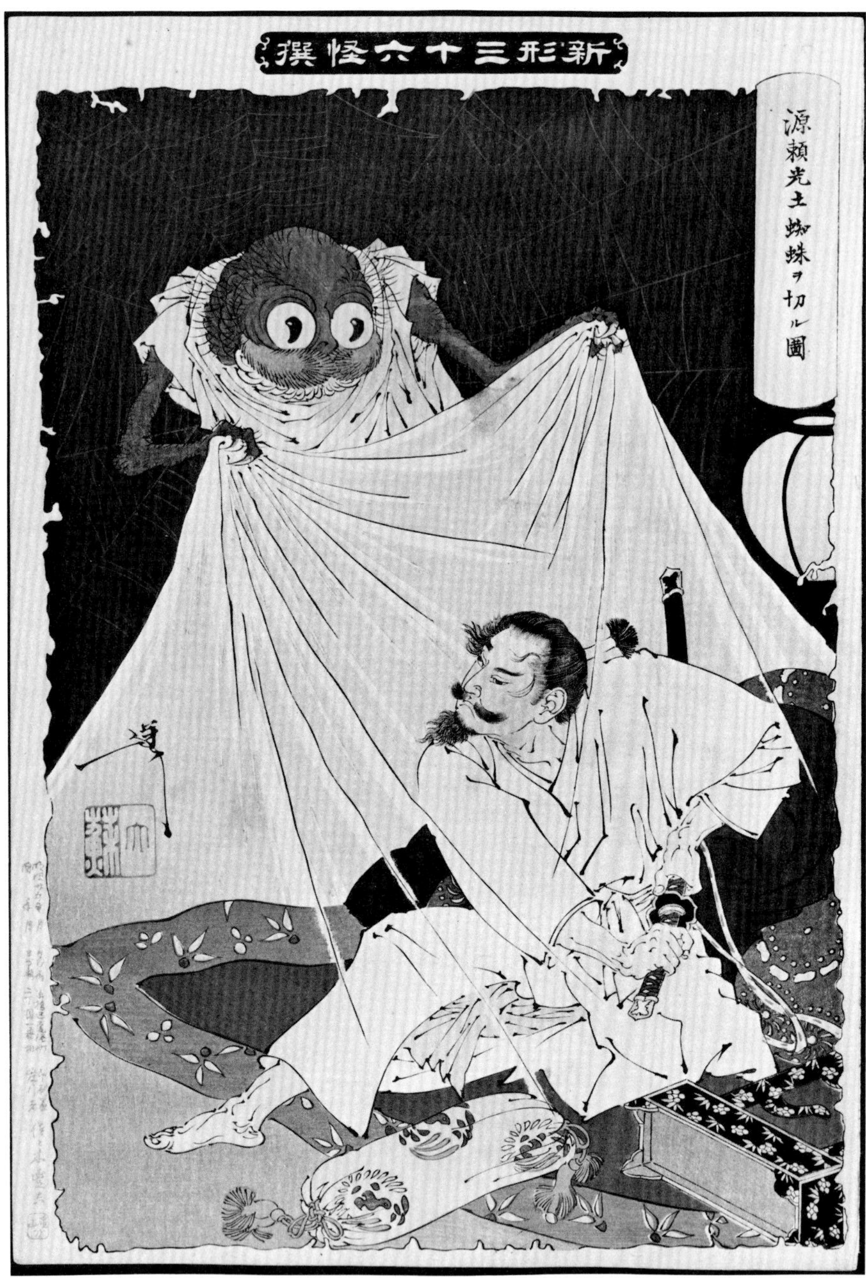

47. Minamoto no Yorimitsu Preparing to Kill the Earth Spider

(Minamoto no yorimitsu tsuchigumo o kiru zu), 1892

Series: *New Forms of Thirty-six Ghosts (Shinkei sanjūrokkaisen)*
Ōban
Signature: Yoshitoshi
Seal: Taiso
Publisher: Sasaki Toyokichi
Engraver: Chokuzan

In one Kabuki tale, Minamoto no Yorimitsu (948–1021) was seized by fever and tormented in his delirium with visions of monsters. His four loyal followers gathered by his bedside to keep watch and reassure him, but one by one they began to drowse and fall into slumber. When the last of the four had fallen asleep, the Earth Spider, disguised as a seven-foot-tall priest, appeared and stealthily crept up on Yorimitsu with a rope to bind him. The valiant man sprang up in fright, drew his sword called Hizamaru, and struck at the wicked-looking creature, which then disappeared. The four followers awoke and followed a trail of blood to a great mound in the wilderness behind Kitano, north of Kyoto. They entered the mound and found an enormous spider, four feet high, which they succeeded in capturing alive. For its part in the successful outcome, Yorimitsu's sword was renamed Kumokirimaru, The Spider Cutter.

The drama in Yoshitoshi's print lies in the contest between Yorimitsu and the monster. The spider-priest seems to be casting a mantle of lassitude over the already weakened warrior to prevent him from maintaining enough attention to attack.

Yoshitoshi began his series *One Hundred Aspects of the Moon* in October 1885; the last plate was published in April 1892, two months before the artist's death. The prints were very popular, and editions were often sold out the morning they appeared. The publisher Akiyama Buemon is said to have paid Yoshitoshi ten yen for each design. Because the prints were popular, Akiyama carefully preserved the blocks; when the set was finished, he reprinted subjects that had sold out and offered bound albums with a title page, a preface, a double-page decorative table of contents, a memorial portrait of the artist by his pupil Toshikage, and a complete set of the one hundred prints. Because they were bound, the pictures were well-preserved, and fresh impressions of prints from the series are not uncommon. It is uncommon, however, to find fine, fresh, early impressions, since most of the finest prints were put on sale at the time they were issued and suffered the usual vicissitudes of loose single prints (see cat. nos. 56–67). Some collectors must have bought individual prints at the time with the intention of completing the set, and Akiyama may have set aside a certain number of the first impressions to make particularly fine bound sets when the publication was complete. At any rate, some bound sets, including the example in the Cole collection (cat. nos. 48–55), include early impressions of the greatest delicacy and the highest quality and refinement.

For his historical and military sets Yoshitoshi often chose subjects that were unfamiliar to his audience. Some of the subjects of the *One Hundred Moons* are even more obscure because he allowed his imagination to range over the whole field of Chinese and Japanese literature and history and because he adopted a number of pictorial styles that previously had been reserved for painting.

The range of moods in the prints is quite broad, but there is an underlying quality of detachment, serenity, and silence that pervades the set. During the mid-1880s, Yoshitoshi learned to sing the chanted accompaniments to Noh plays, and many subjects in the *One Hundred Moons* are taken from the Noh repertory. In the Noh drama Yoshitoshi found that each gesture, word, and musical phrase contributed to creating a single mood—a parallel to his own work. With the *One Hundred Moons* he used the full range of color, shading, composition, draftsmanship, and engraving techniques to create a series of intensely felt moods, each different from the other, ranging from the sensual to the heroic, from the whimsical to the profound, from humor to melancholy, from awe to tenderness. The titles on the prints are often obscure or difficult to decipher; Yoshitoshi seems to have felt that the subject was simply his point of departure, and that the mood of each picture would be obvious to each viewer. Only in seeing the whole set can one do justice to the breadth, richness, and intensity of Yoshitoshi's vision, but the following prints will indicate some of the quality and variety of the series.

48. The Fox Cry
(Konkai), January 1886

Series: *One Hundred Aspects of the Moon
(Tsuki hyakushi)*
Ōban
Signature: Yoshitoshi
Seal: Yoshitoshi
Publisher: Akiyama Buemon
Engraver: Horikō Enkatsu

Konkai, meaning the cry of a fox, is the title of a
kyōgen, a comic interlude performed between
Noh plays. In the story, an old fox, tired of
being hunted, disguises himself as an old
priest named Hakuzōsu, known for his fondness for foxes. The fox visits the priest's
nephew, a hunter in the region, and speaks to
him about the virtues of foxes and the punish-
ments that await those who take life. He leaves
satisfied that he has convinced the man. On
the way home he begins to change back into a
fox and thus loses the capacities of foresight
and reason. A baited trap looks suddenly attractive, and he takes the bait and is caught.
Yoshitoshi shows the stooped and elderly
priest walking home by moonlight and beginning to change back into a fox. The printing of
this impression is particularly delicate and fine.

**49. and 62. Hakuga no Sammi by Moonlight
at Suzaku Gate**
(Suzakumon no tsuki hakuga no sammi),
February 1, 1886

Series: *One Hundred Aspects of the Moon
(Tsuki hyakushi)*
Ōban
Signature: Yoshitoshi
Seal: Yoshitoshi no in
Publisher: Akiyama Buemon
Engraver: Yamamoto tō

One of the most solemn and serene early
prints in the *One Hundred Moons* series is this
picture of Minamoto no Hiromasa, also known
as Hakuga no Sammi (the Chinese pronunciation of his name and his court rank). Hiromasa
(913–980) was the grandson of the Emperor
Daigo and an accomplished, devoted musician.
On one occasion robbers broke into his house
and, while he hid beneath the floor boards,
took all his possessions except a *hichiriki,* or
wooden flute. When the thieves had gone, he
came out from his hiding place, found the flute,
and began playing a melody which carried
through the neighboring streets. The thieves
heard the music and were so charmed that they
realized their crime, repented, and returned
Hiromasa's possessions. In Yoshitoshi's print,
Hiromasa, dressed in the long-sleeved robes
and lacquered cap of a courtier, plays his flute
at the Suzaku Gate of the Imperial Palace in
Kyoto. The viewer sees only Hiromasa's back
as he accompanies an unknown master,
probably a foreigner because of his unusual
hat and costume.

Los Angeles only.

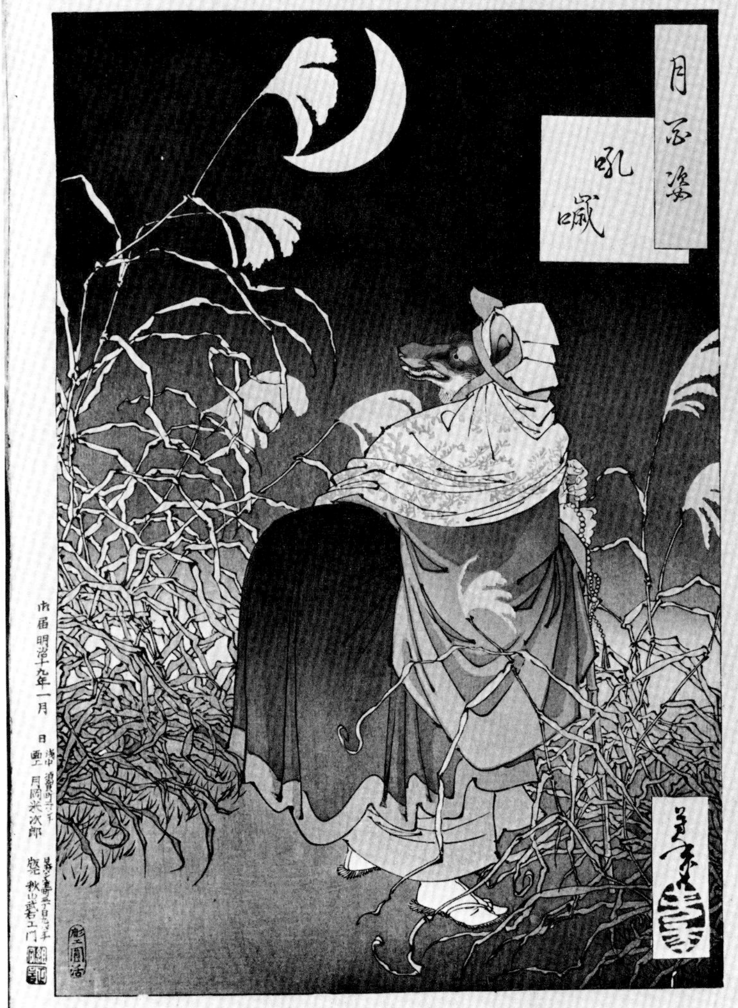
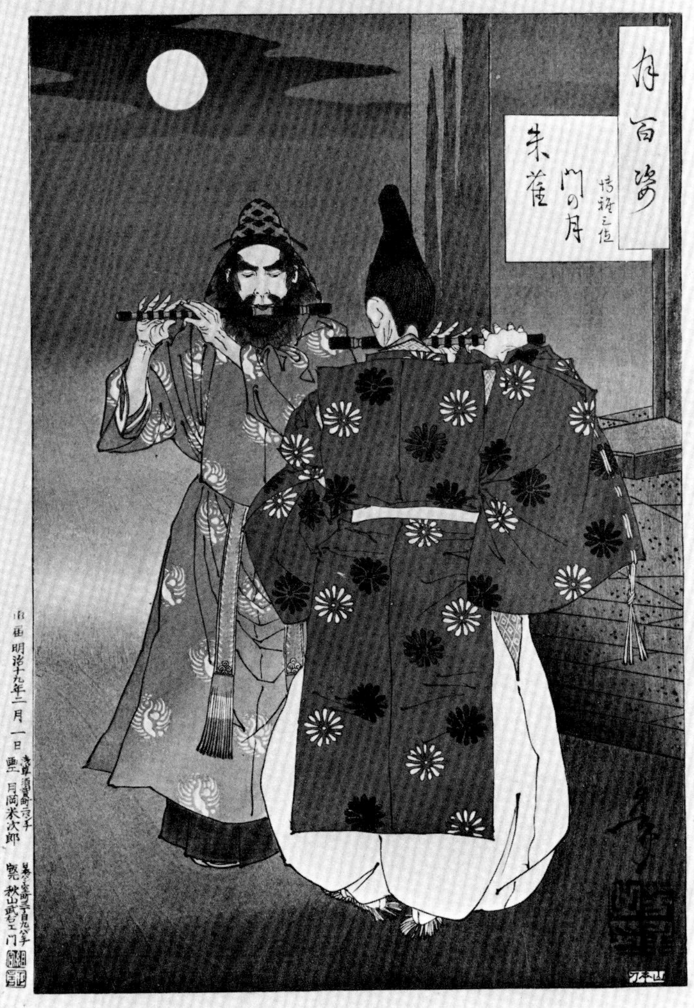

50. Moonlight over Mount Yoshino
(Yoshinoyama no tsuki), January 1886

Series: *One Hundred Aspects of the Moon*
(Tsuki hyakushi)
Signature: Yoshitoshi
Seal: Yoshitoshi no in
Publisher: Akiyama Buemon
Engraver: Enkatsu tō

The ghost of the courtier Sasaki Kiyotaka is the first of several supernatural beings that Yoshitoshi introduced into the *One Hundred Moons* set. Kiyotaka was an adviser to the Emperor Godaigo, whose ambition to restore imperial rule led to the end of the Kamakura shogunate in the fourteenth century. Godaigo was exiled from Kyoto in 1331 but returned in 1333, after his supporters had succeeded in overthrowing the shogunate. In 1336, when Kyoto was in danger of seige from Ashikaga Takauji, Godaigo's leading general, Kusunoki Masashige, advised the emperor to retreat until he had gathered more troops. Kiyotaka and other courtiers with little military experience argued that the emperor should take a stand. In the ensuing battle of Minatogawa the imperial forces were defeated and Kusunoki forced to commit suicide. The emperor retreated to the wilderness of Mount Yoshino and established a second court in opposition to the puppet figure controlled by the new Ashikaga shogun. It is said that Kiyotaka was required to commit suicide to atone for his bad advice, and that his angry spirit haunted the court in Yoshino until it was exorcized by Iga no Tsubone, General Kusunoki's daughter-in-law. Biographical dictionaries, however, say that Kiyotaka, his father, and two brothers died by their own hands in 1333, about the time that the emperor returned from exile, long before the fateful battle.[19]

To the Japanese, ghosts were the spirits of those deceased who were not yet able to find peace of mind. The figure of Kiyotaka is transformed by his violent emotion into a strange, winged creature. Iga no Tsubone, dressed in medieval court dress and hairstyle, stands before him in absolute serenity, and her dignity seems to enrage him even further. The moon here seems to be in eclipse.

51. Hideyoshi by Moonlight at Mount Shizugatake
(Shizugatake no tsuki hideyoshi), October 25, 1888

Series: *One Hundred Aspects of the Moon*
(Tsuki hyakushi)
Ōban
Signature: Yoshitoshi
Seal: Taiso
Publisher: Akiyama Buemon
Engraver: Enkatsu tō

When Oda Nobunaga was assassinated at Honnōji Temple in 1582, disputes immediately arose between his generals, and they took to the field to battle for supremacy. In late April of the following year, Shibata Katsuie brought his forces through the snow to Mount Shizugatake, on the north shore of Lake Biwa near Kyoto, to face Hideyoshi's army. By collusion among his enemies, Hideyoshi himself was drawn away to the castle at Ōgaki when Katsuie mounted his attack, but once the news reached Hideyoshi he immediately returned, covering the fifty miles to Shizugatake in six hours at night. The next morning he pushed Katsuie's troops back. Three days later Hideyoshi took the castle and witnessed his enemy's ritual suicide. This battle was a turning point. Afterward Hideyoshi easily consolidated his rule and unified Japan; peace was kept until his death in 1598.

In Yoshitoshi's print the general has just arrived at Shizugatake in full battle regalia. As the full moon sets just before dawn, he blows his famous war conch to summon his troops for the attack on Katsuie's forces.

Los Angeles only.

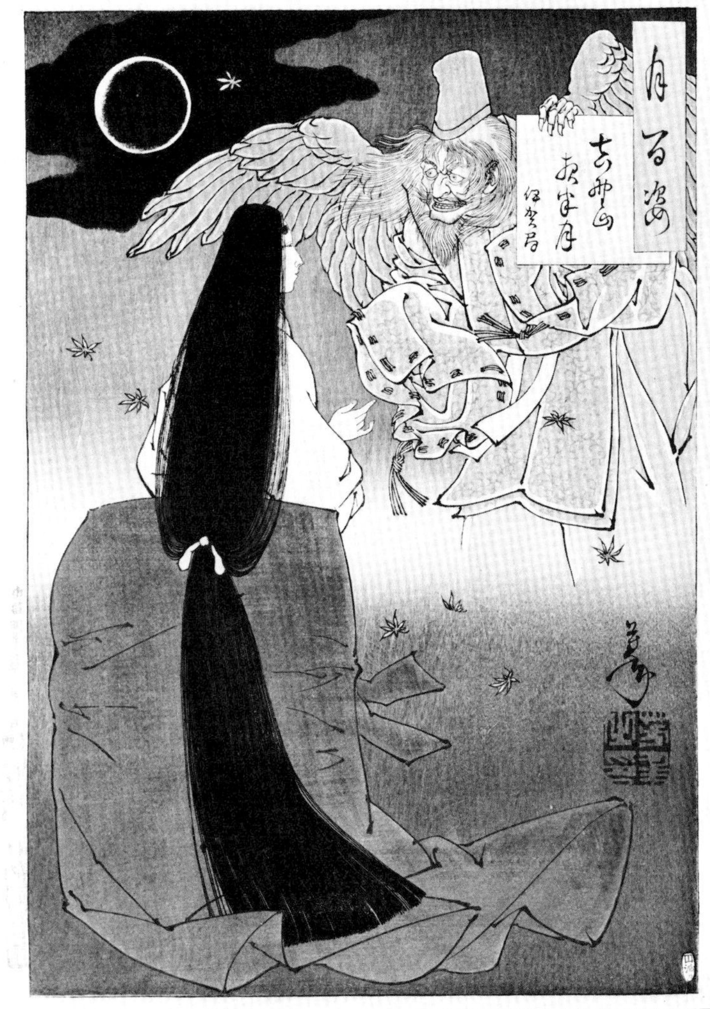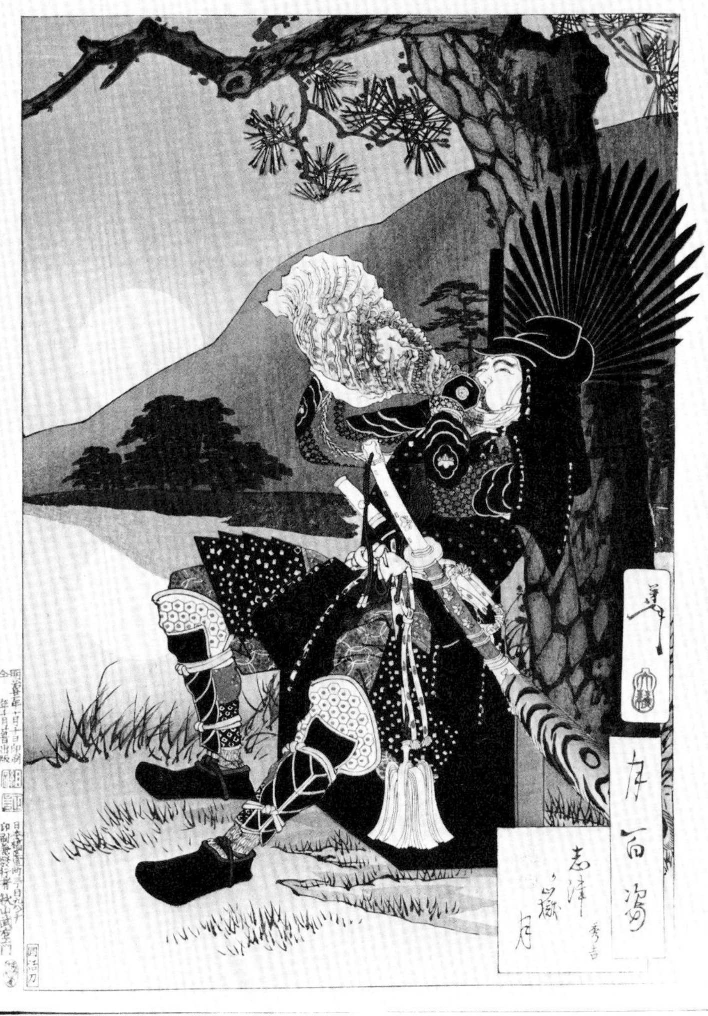

52. The Full Moon! And the Shadow of the Pine Tree on the Floor—Kikaku
(Meigetsu ya tatami no ue ni matsu no kage. Kikaku.), October 1885

Series: *One Hundred Aspects of the Moon*
(Tsuki hyakushi)
Ōban
Signature: Yoshitoshi
Seal: Taiso
Publisher: Akiyama Buemon
Engraver: Horikō Noguchi Enkatsu

The first five pictures in the *One Hundred Aspects of the Moon* series portrayed a variety of scenes: a simple Ukiyo-e portrait of the seventeenth-century courtesan Takao, a picture of the Chinese general Ts'ao Ts'ao, a goddess running through the clouds before a full moon, a quiet picture of the son of the leader of the forty-seven *rōnin* waiting to deliver a message to his father, and this languorous illustration of a haiku by Bashō's favorite pupil, the Edo poet Takarai Kikaku (1661–1707).

53. Benkei Calming the Waves at Daimotsu Bay by Moonlight
(Daimotsu kaijō no tsuki benkei), January 1886

Series: *One Hundred Aspects of the Moon*
(Tsuki hyakushi)
Ōban
Signature: Yoshitoshi
Seal: Taiso
Publisher: Akiyama Buemon
Engraver: Horikō Enkatsu

In the autumn of 1185, Yoshitsune, attacked by his half-brother Minamoto no Yoritomo, was forced to flee to northern Japan by ship (see cat. no. 14). Sailing along the Inland Sea off the coast of Harima province, not far from Kyoto, the ship was struck by a storm which threatened to capsize it at Daimotsu Bay. The storm was said to have been caused by the vengeful ghosts of the Taira warriors Yoshitsune and his men had slain, and many woodblock prints of the scene show the wraiths of the slain threatening the ship. The group was saved by the warrior-priest Musashibō Benkei, who positioned himself in the prow of the ship and pacified the spirits with his prayers. In Yoshitoshi's print the sky has begun to clear but the sea is still high; in the racing clouds and the spray of the waves is a hint of the menace from which Benkei has delivered the ship.

Benkei in the Boat (Funa benkei) is the title of a Noh play, and this was the first of several prints Yoshitoshi did on subjects drawn from the Noh repertory (see cat. nos. 48, 57, 58).

Los Angeles only.

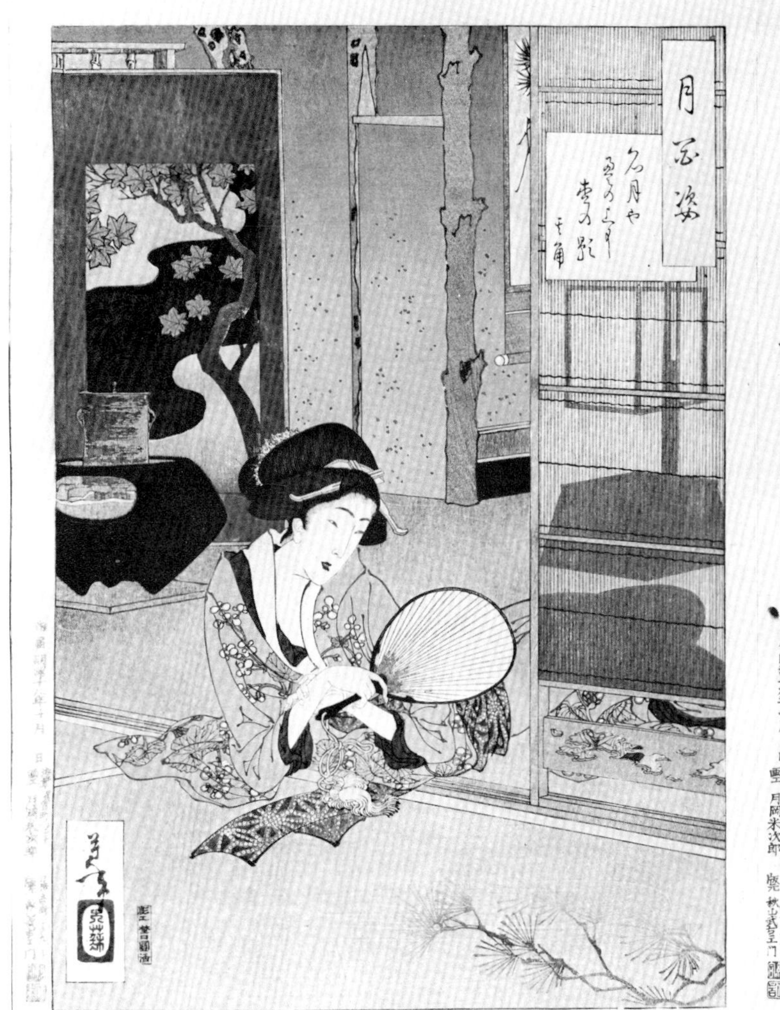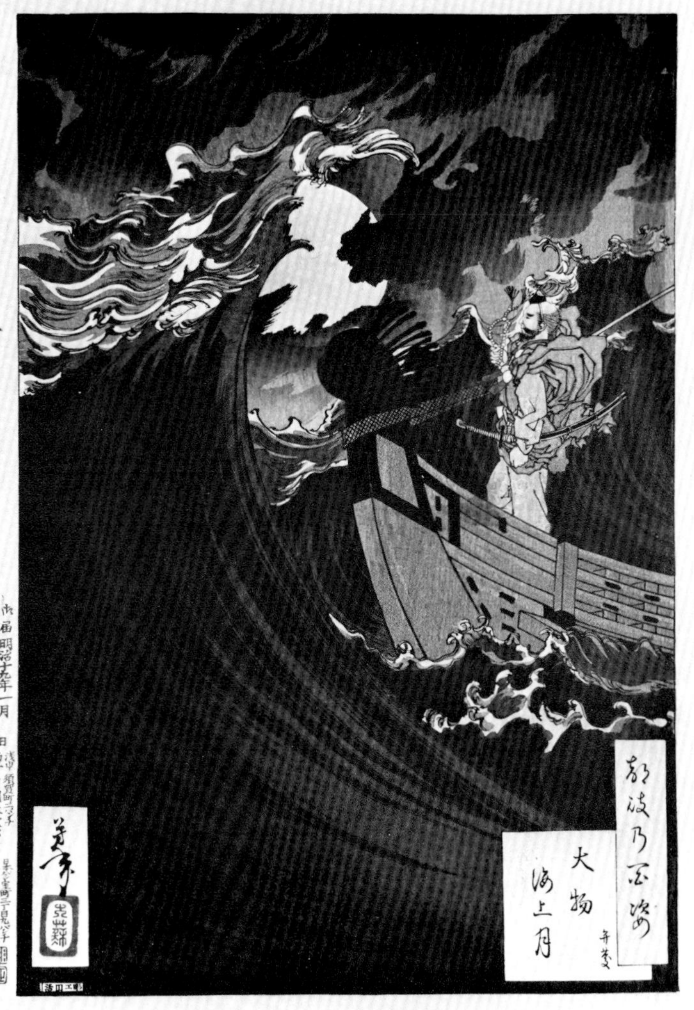

54. The Moon on Musashi Plain
(Mushashino no tsuki), April 1, 1892

Series: *One Hundred Aspects of the Moon*
(Tsuki hyakushi)
Ōban
Signature: Yoshitoshi
Seal: Yoshitoshi
Publisher: Akiyama Buemon
Engraver: Yamamoto tō

The four final prints of the *One Hundred Aspects of the Moon* were published in April 1892, but all of them had been designed and printed earlier. This picture of a vain vixen admiring herself in a pool was printed at the beginning of 1891, more than a year before it was issued. Foxes were thought to take human shapes, and Yoshitoshi had designed an earlier picture in the *Moon* set of a transformed fox returning to his own form (cat. no. 48). The fox's preening gesture in this print still seems quite human. The shadows in the print were hand-painted on the woodblock—as were the clouds in the triptych of Yasumasa playing the flute (cat. no. 24)—and their pattern and intensity varies from impression to impression, like the different inkings of the Whistler etchings from *The Venice Sets*.

55. The Moon over Obasute Mountain
(Obasute no tsuki), December 1891

Series: *One Hundred Aspects of the Moon*
(Tsuki hyakushi)
Ōban
Signature: Yoshitoshi
Seal: Taiso
Publisher: Akiyama Buemon

Long ago a man from Sarashina lived with his wife and an elderly aunt who had raised him. Persuaded by the wife to abandon his aunt, the man carried the old woman to the peak of a nearby mountain one night and left her there. Filled with remorse, he spent a sleepless night and then returned to the mountain to bring his aunt home. The mountain thereafter was called Obasuteyama, the Mountain of the Old Forsaken Woman.

Yoshitoshi designed few landscape prints, and this picture is more a study of a single tree than a landscape. Its composition and brushwork are similar to paintings of the Shijō School from the eighteenth and nineteenth centuries. The Noh play *Obasuteyama* is one of the most mysteriously moving of the repertoire, and it is perhaps the mood of the play that Yoshitoshi has sought to capture in his print.

Los Angeles only.

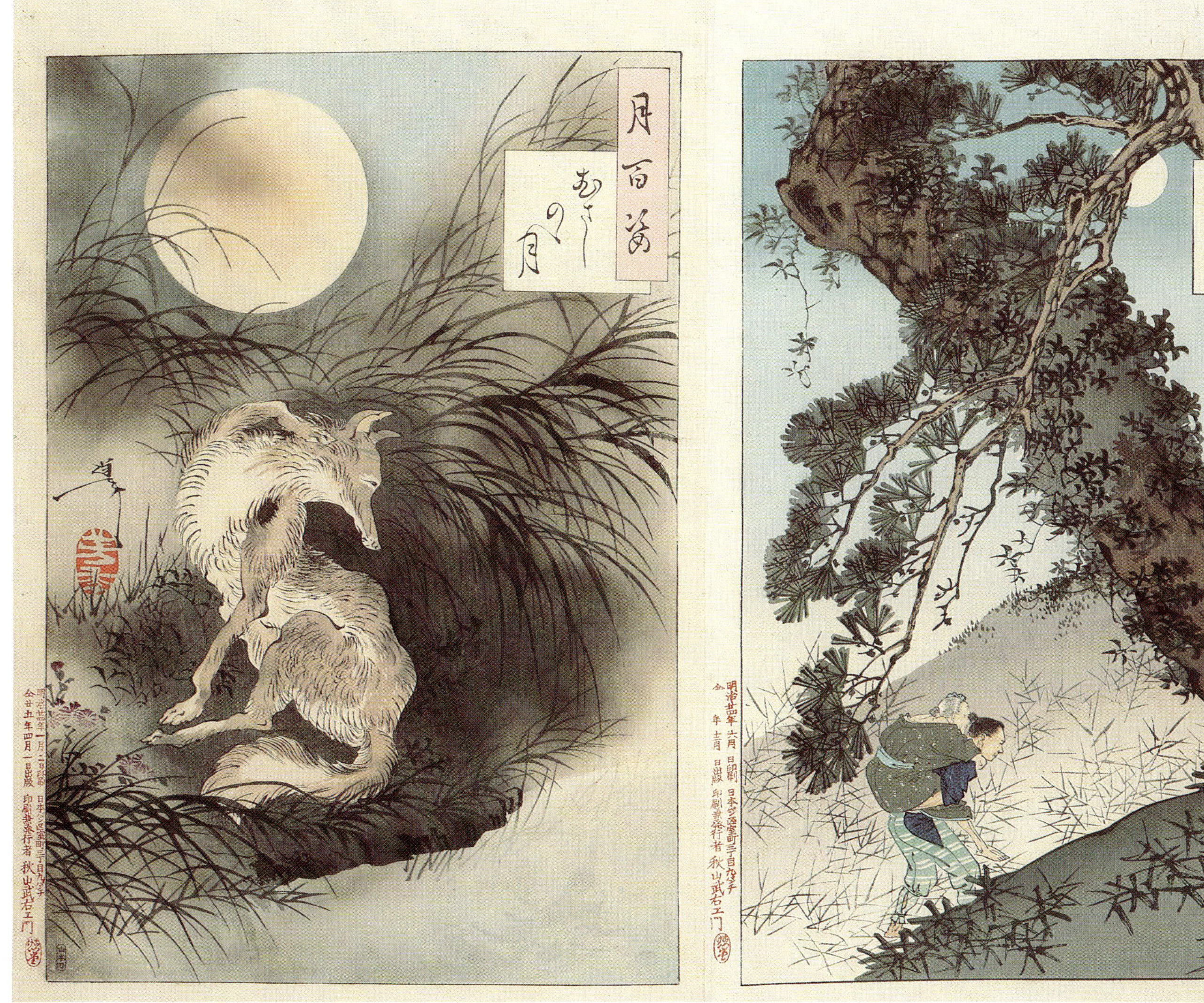
月百姿
むさしのゝ月
月百姿
をぐら月

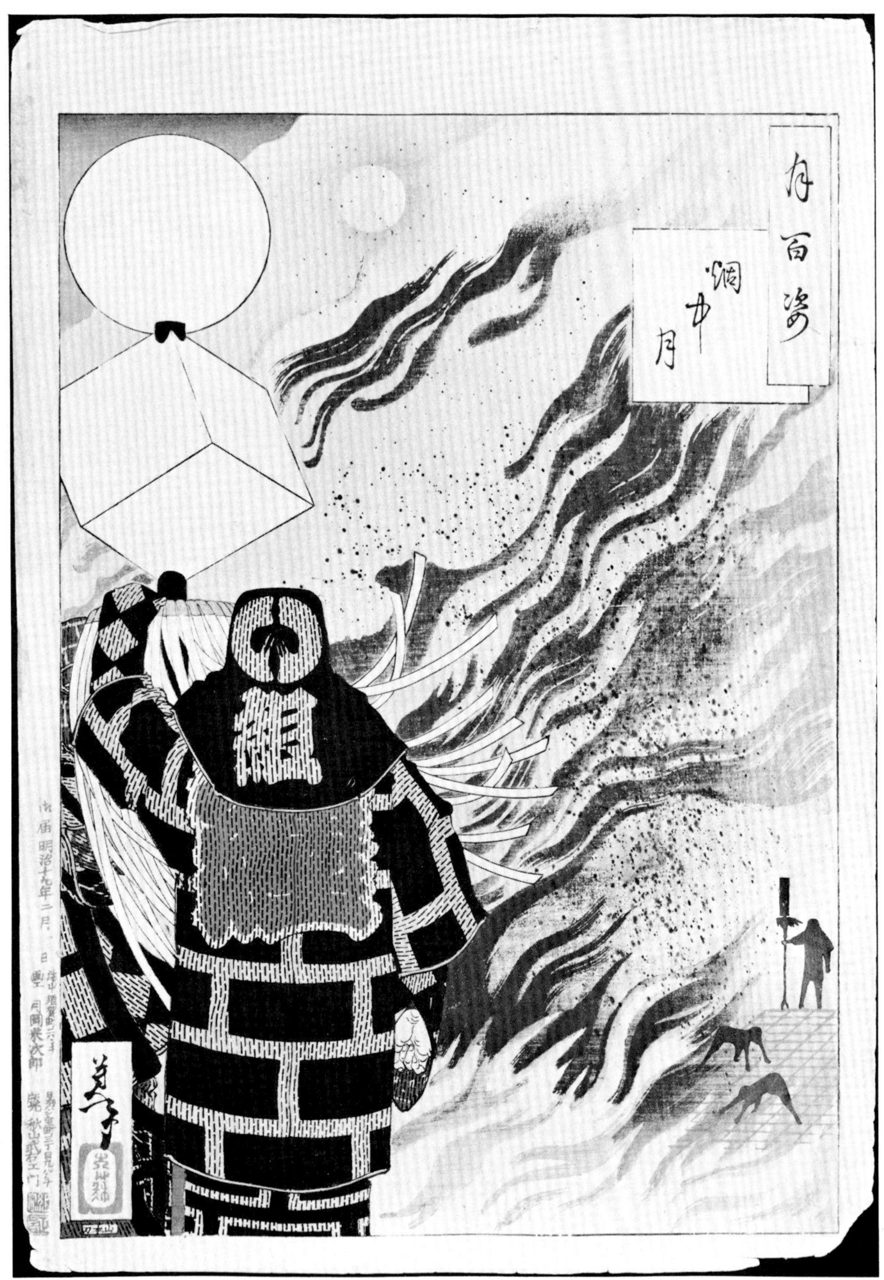

56. The Moon through Smoke
(Enchū no tsuki), February 1886

Series: *One Hundred Aspects of the Moon
(Tsuki hyakushi)*
Ōban
Signature: Yoshitoshi
Seal: Taiso
Publisher: Akiyama Buemon
Engraver: Yamamoto tō

Troops of firemen carried standards, or *matoi,*
by which they could signal to one another in
the noise of a fire and identify themselves
through the flames and smoke. All through his
career Yoshitoshi had designed pictures of
firemen and actors dressed as firemen (see
cat. no. 3). One of his most important prints
was an 1875 triptych of a recent Tokyo fire
whose raging flames are drawn and printed
with the same freedom shown here. The two
firemen on the rooftop at the left of this print
belong to the *I* company, whose circular symbol appears on the cowl protecting the head of
the nearer figure. The character on the back of
his robe reads *matoi,* or standard bearer. The
robe shows the typical *sashiko,* or quilted,
stitching used to make firemen's garments
highly protective and absorbent (water was
cast over the fireman's head when he entered
the burning area). The man in the foreground
has the fingers of his right hand drawn into his
palm for added protection. The keyblock on
this impression is somewhat worn, but it has
shading around the moon and spattered lime,
or *gofun,* which create a texture for the smoke
in the background.

57. The Moon by the Grave Marker
(Sotoba no tsuki), March 1886

Series: *One Hundred Aspects of the Moon
(Tsuki hyakushi)*
Ōban
Signature: Yoshitoshi
Seal: Yoshitoshi
Publisher: Akiyama Buemon
Engraver: Yamamoto tō

Ono no Komachi was a beautiful, intelligent
woman and one of the most accomplished
early court poets. As a young woman she was
pursued by many suitors, most of whom she
heartlessly rejected. In her old age she became destitute and wandered about the out-
skirts of Kyoto reflecting on the world and the
vanity of life. In the Noh play *Komachi and the
Grave Marker (Sotoba komachi),* the aged
poetess sits down on a gravestone to rest. Two
passing priests criticize her disrespect for the
dead, but she refutes their doctrinal argu-
ments. Surprised that this beggarlike woman
should be so intelligent and well read, the
priests inquire her name, but the poetess cannot answer them for shame at her present
state. She falls into a reverie and recalls her
youth when she was being courted by one of
her many suitors; when the memory passes
she becomes calm again. Yoshitoshi's
Komachi is dignified and still intelligent, alert,
and beautiful in her old age. Her robe with its
patches of different rich brocades is like the
costume the protagonist wears in the Noh play.

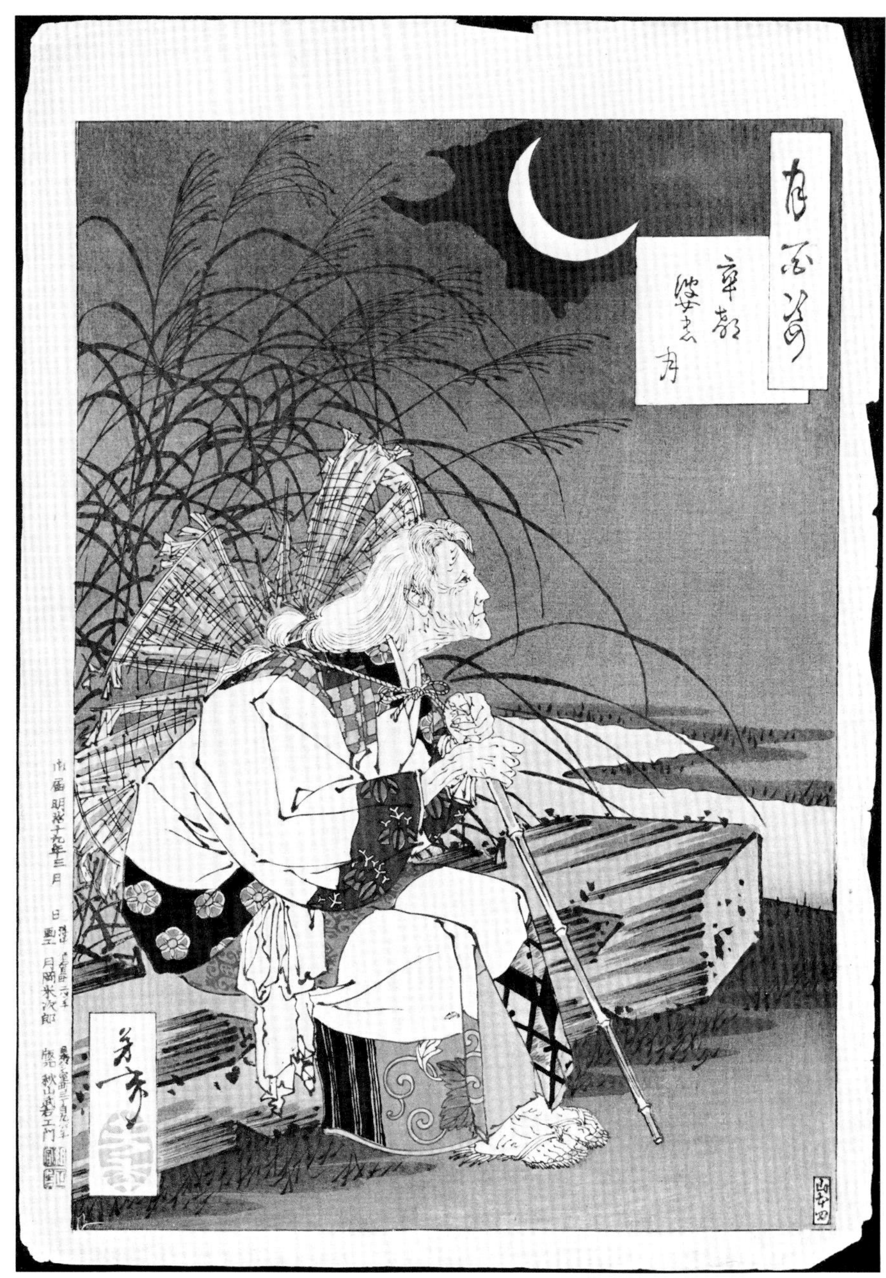

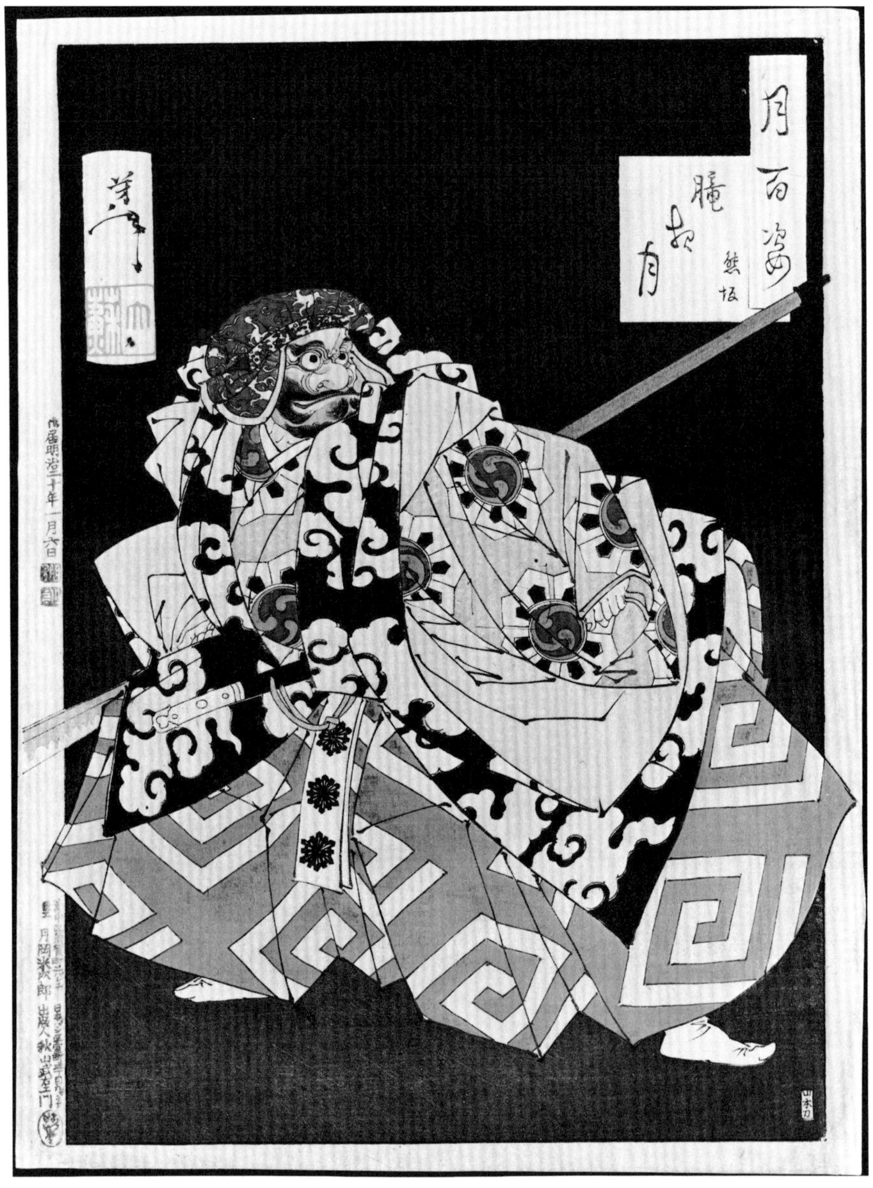

58. Kumasaka in the Misty Moonlight

(Oboroyo no tsuki kumasaka), January 6, 1887

Series: *One Hundred Aspects of the Moon*
(Tsuki hyakushi)
Ōban
Signature: Yoshitoshi
Seal: Taiso
Publisher: Akiyama Buemon
Engraver: Yamamoto tō

As a boy, Minamoto no Yoshitsune was concealed from his enemies in a temple north of Kyoto, but as he approached manhood his guardians decided he would be safer in northern Japan with his uncle Hidehira. In 1174 the youth set out in the armed caravan of a gold and gem merchant. One night at an inn along the way, the group was attacked by an outlaw band led by Kumasaka Chōhan, a lay priest. Young Yoshitsune killed so many of the outlaws that Kumasaka himself attacked the boy and was killed. In the Noh play based on the story, a traveling priest meets another priest who gives him lodging for the night. The traveler falls asleep, and in his dream, his host reveals that he is Kumasaka and describes his own murder. Yoshitoshi portrays a Noh actor in his splendid robes, wearing the mask for the role and holding a long spear. The extraordinary blue of the background is rarely used with this intensity in woodblock prints.

59. The Moon over an Open Moor

(Harano no tsuki), May 20, 1888

Series: *One Hundred Aspects of the Moon
(Tsuki hyakushi)*
Ōban
Signature: Yoshitoshi
Seal: Taiso
Publisher: Akiyama Buemon
Engraver: Horikō Enkatsu

Yoshitoshi's third and last picture of the
brigand Hakamadare Yasusuke creeping up
on the courtier Fujiwara no Yasumasa is drawn,
engraved, and printed in the loose style of
much late nineteenth-century Japanese painting. An earlier version of the subject, one of the
artist's masterpieces, is also included in this
exhibition (cat. no. 24).

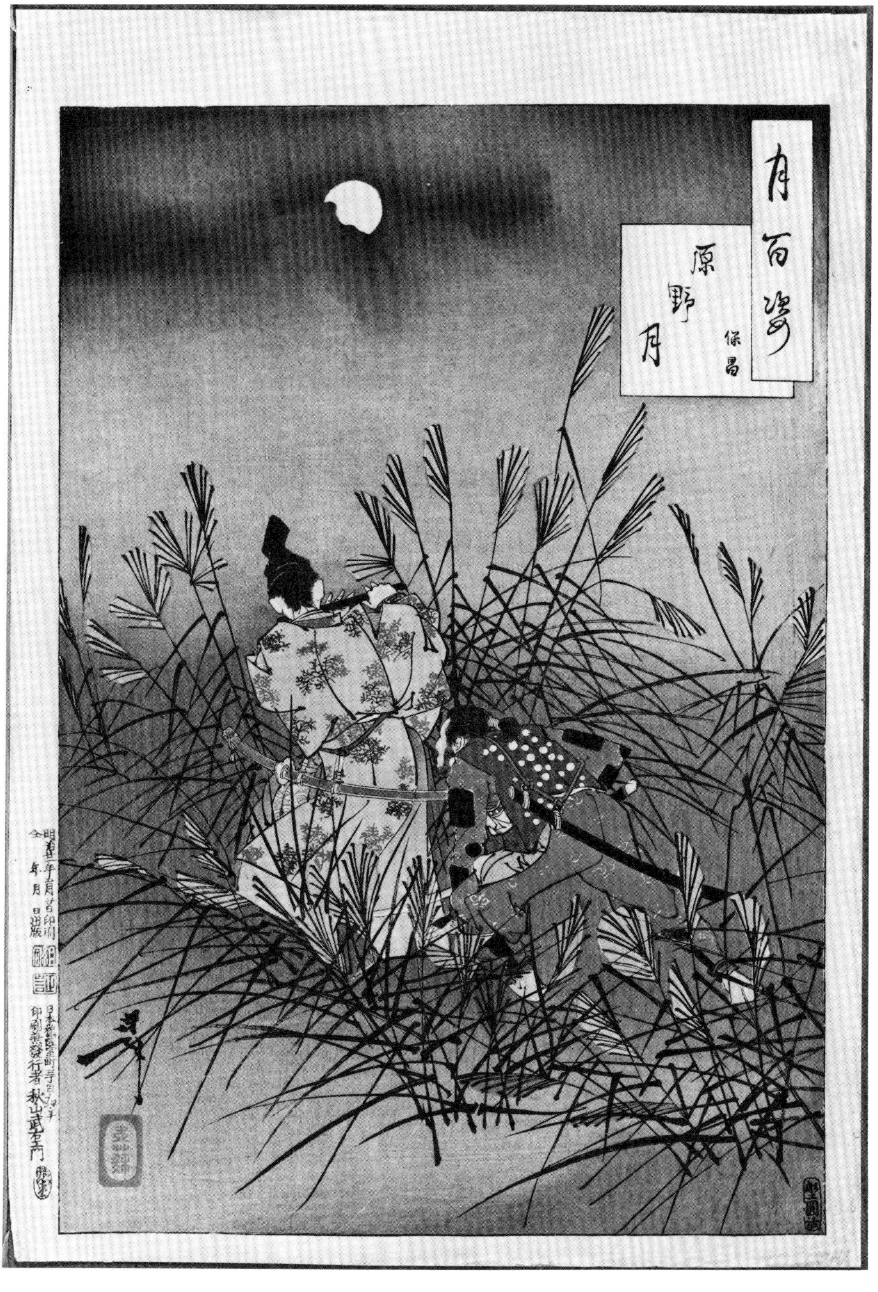

60. Kumonryū on a Moonlit Night in the Shih Clan Village

(Shikason tsukiyo kumonryū), November 1885

Series: *One Hundred Aspects of the Moon
(Tsuki hyakushi)*
Ōban
Signature: Yoshitoshi
Seal: Yoshitoshi
Publisher: Akiyama Buemon
Engraver: Yamamoto

Shih Chin, one of the 108 outlaw-heroes of *Shui hu chuan,* the Chinese novel translated in Japanese as the *Suikoden* (see cat. no. 27), had nine dragons tattooed on his body, and was called The Nine-Dragoned One, or Kumonryū Shishin in Japanese. He was a favorite subject for Kuniyoshi and other artists of his school who invariably showed him locked in fierce combat or performing some prodigious feat of strength.

This was the only print Yoshitoshi designed for the *One Hundred Moons* in November 1885. The first five prints in the set, done in October 1885, had been of subjects unfamiliar to Ukiyo-e. In this print he opened a new range of subject matter: conventional, familiar subjects conceived in an original way.

Not exhibited in Los Angeles.

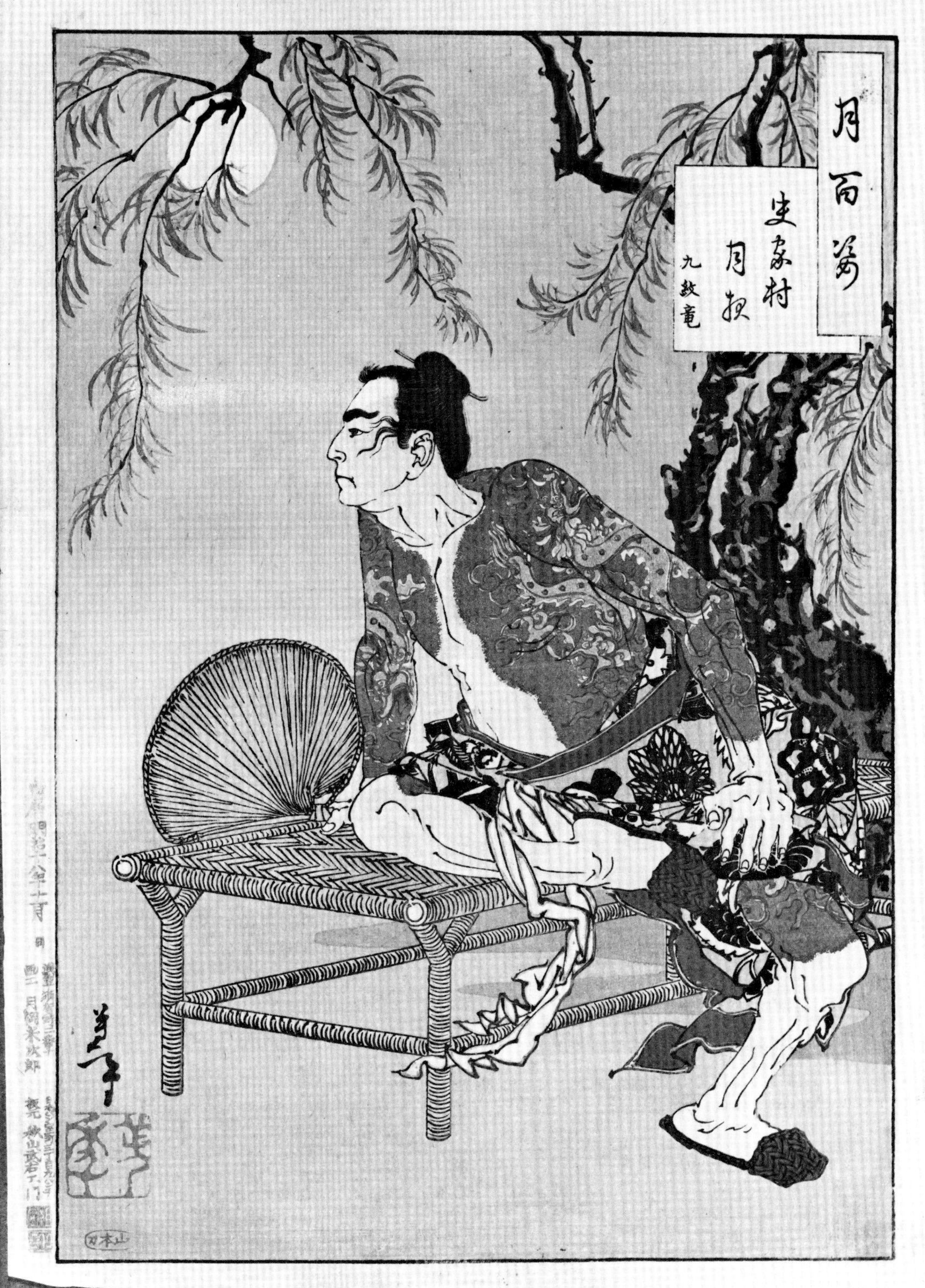

月百姿
生玉村月抜
九紋竜

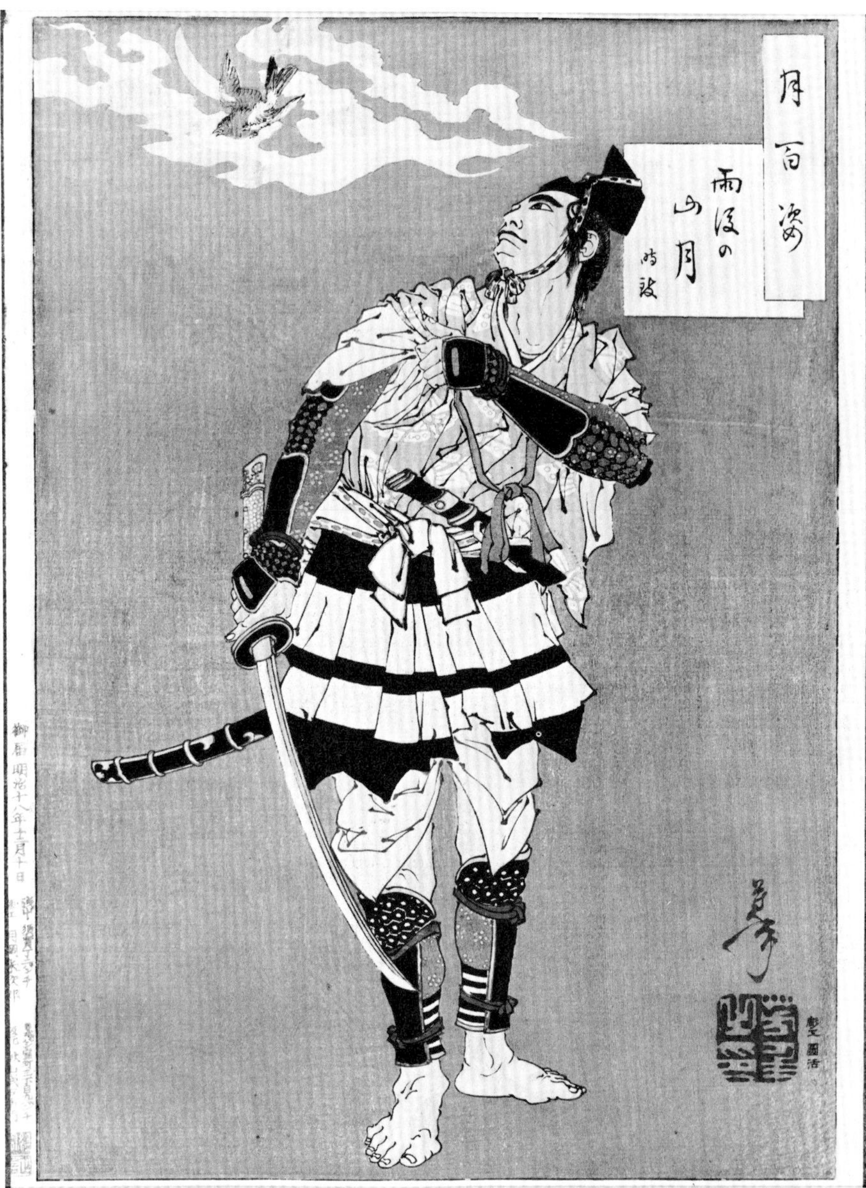

61. Tokimune Viewing the Moon in the Mountains after the Rain

(Ugo no sangetsu tokimune), December 10, 1885

Series: *One Hundred Aspects of the Moon (Tsuki hyakushi)*
Ōban
Signature: Yoshitoshi
Seal: Yoshitoshi no in
Publisher: Akiyama Buemon
Engraver: Horikō Enkatsu

In December 1885, Yoshitoshi continued his exploration of familiar subjects seen in unfamiliar ways (see cat. no. 60). Sogo no Gorō, whose formal name was Tokimune, and his brother Jūrō successfully avenged their father's death in an attack on their enemy's encampment in the mountains of Hakone. The attack took place on a rainy night, and pictures of the attack invariably show the brothers fighting in the rain. Yoshitoshi has chosen instead the peaceful moment after the attack, before Gorō was captured and lost his life. The youth pulls down the sleeve that he had tied back so it would not interfere with his movements during the fight. The clouds part, and he looks up to see a cuckoo flying past the moon in a flight as swift as the remainder of Gorō's own short life. The upper part of his robe is decorated with his personal emblem, the butterfly.

Not exhibited in Los Angeles.

62. Hakuga no Sammi by Moonlight at Suzaku Gate
(Suzakumon no tsuki hakuga no sammi)

See catalog number 49 on page 88.

63. Pleasure is This: A Cool Evening, an Arbor of Yūgao Flowers, a Man in Underwear, a Woman in a Slip
(Tanoshimi wa yūgaodana no yūsuzumi otoko wa tetera me wa futa no shie), September 1886

Series: *One Hundred Aspects of the Moon (Tsuki hyakushi)*
Ōban
Signature: Yoshitoshi
Seal: Yoshitoshi
Publisher: Akiyama Buemon
Engraver: Yamamoto tō

This gentle print of a peasant couple relaxing on a summer evening evokes the mood of the famous painting of a gourd arbor, a Japanese national treasure, by Kusumi Morikage (c. 1620–1690). The unsigned poem must be by Yoshitoshi's friend Keika, who wrote the calligraphic titles and the preface for the set. It is based on another poem by Kinoshita Chōshōshi (c. 1570–1650) which begins, "The feeling of coolness where the gourds break through beneath the eaves" *(Yūgao no sakeru nokiba no shita suzumi)* and ends with a couplet that is nearly identical to Keika's. The picture presents an elegant contrast between the meticulously drawn, painstakingly engraved and printed patterns of the couple's tie-dyed clothes and the soft painterly effects of the gourd vine tendrils and the moonlight.

Not exhibited in Los Angeles.

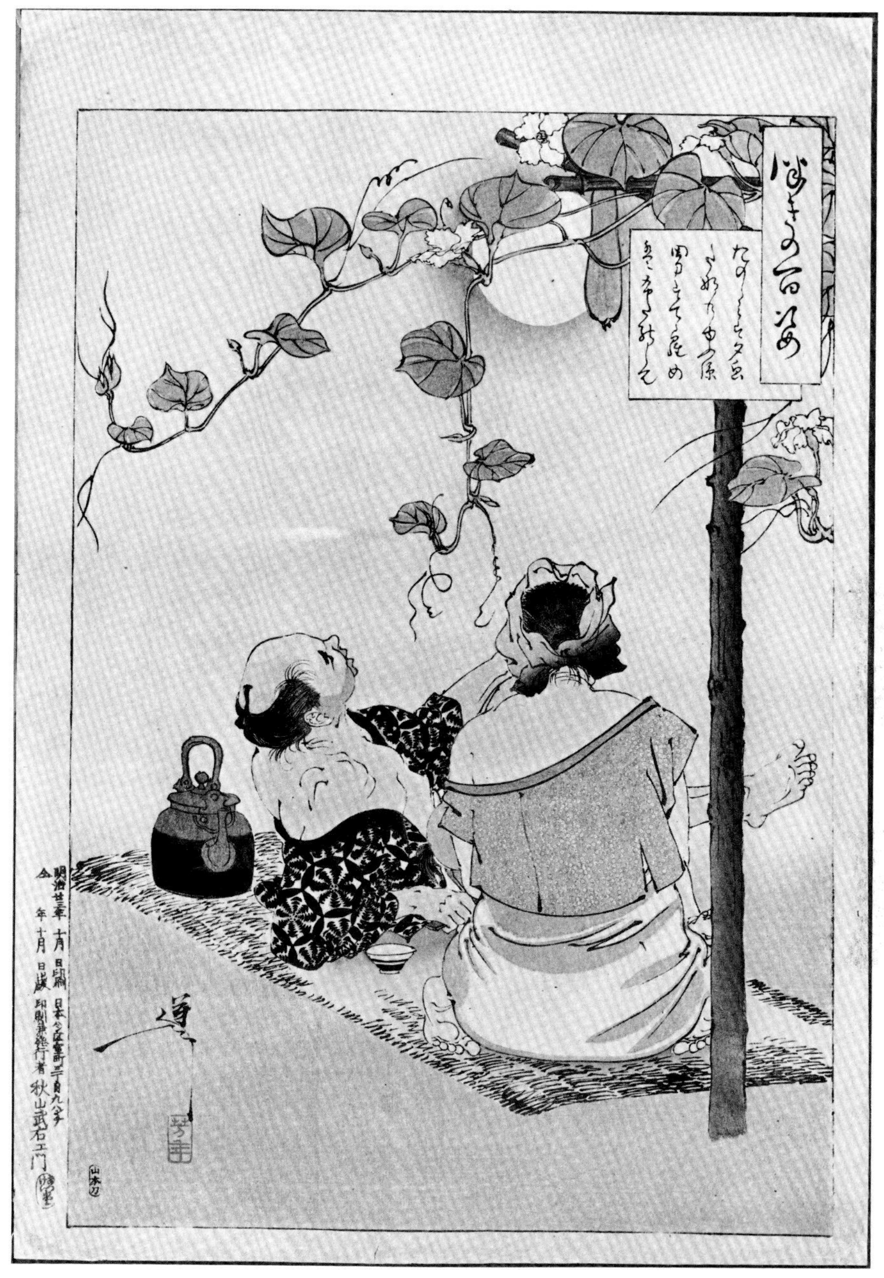

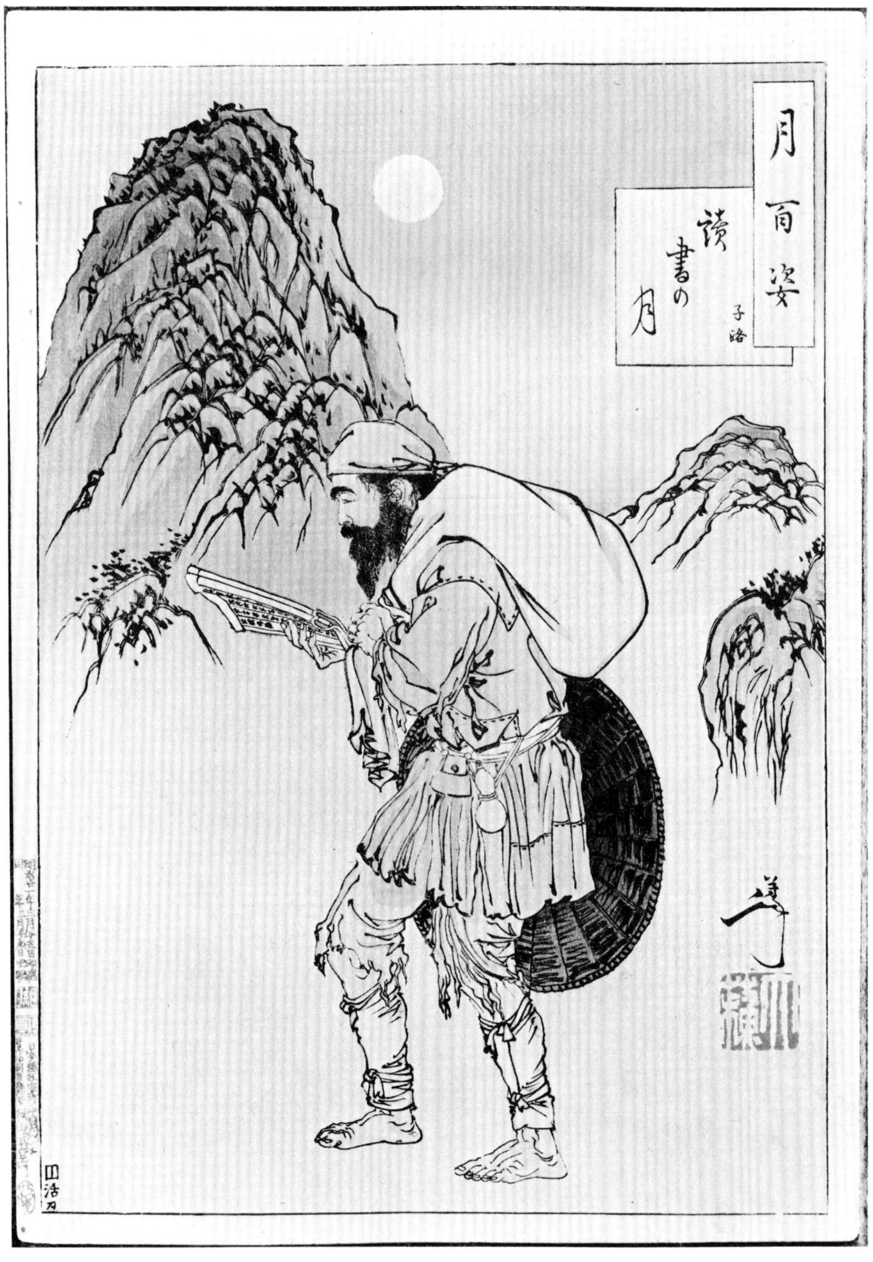

64. Tze Lu Reading by Moonlight

(Dokusho no tsuki shiro), March 15, 1888

Series: *One Hundred Aspects of the Moon*
(Tsuki hyakushi)
Ōban
Signature: Yoshitoshi
Seal: Taiso
Publisher: Akiyama Buemon
Engraver: Enkatsu

Tze Lu (543–480 B.C.), or Chung Yu as he is also known, was one of the Twenty-four Paragons of Filial Devotion and a celebrated pupil of Confucius. He enjoyed a long career as a public official, ending as a magistrate. His family was poor, and as a young man he lived principally on weeds, although he walked long distances to fetch rice for his parents.[20] Despite his poverty he was devoted to learning, and Yoshitoshi shows him here reading by moonlight as he returns to his parents' house with their sack of rice. In contrast to most prints in the *One Hundred Moons* set, the picture of Tze Lu is engraved to imitate the strokes of a dry brush, and the soft colors suggest the effect of a traditional Chinese-style monochrome painting.

Not exhibited in Los Angeles.

65. The Moon at the Lonely House

(Hitotsuya no tsuki), August 1890

Series: *One Hundred Aspects of the Moon
(Tsuki hyakushi)*
Ōban
Signature: Yoshitoshi
Seal: Taiso
Publisher: Akiyama Buemon
Engraver: Yamamoto tō

To anyone unfamiliar with the story of the
Lonely House (see cat. no. 29), the aged figure
with the torch might be puzzling. Is it a woman
or a man? And what does the person look at
so intently behind the screen? A Japanese of
Yoshitoshi's time would immediately recognize
the subject and would be even more affected
by the woman's intensity, knowing that the
wall concealed her knife and that she was
looking down at her victim on the floor asleep.
The broken wall, the pampas grass, the sparse
leaves, the suspended rope, the thatched
room divider, and the dark night are all elements
used by Yoshitoshi in his vertical diptych of the
old woman of Adachi Moor and by Kuniyoshi
in his many earlier prints of the wicked woman
of Asaji Moor.

Not exhibited in Los Angeles.

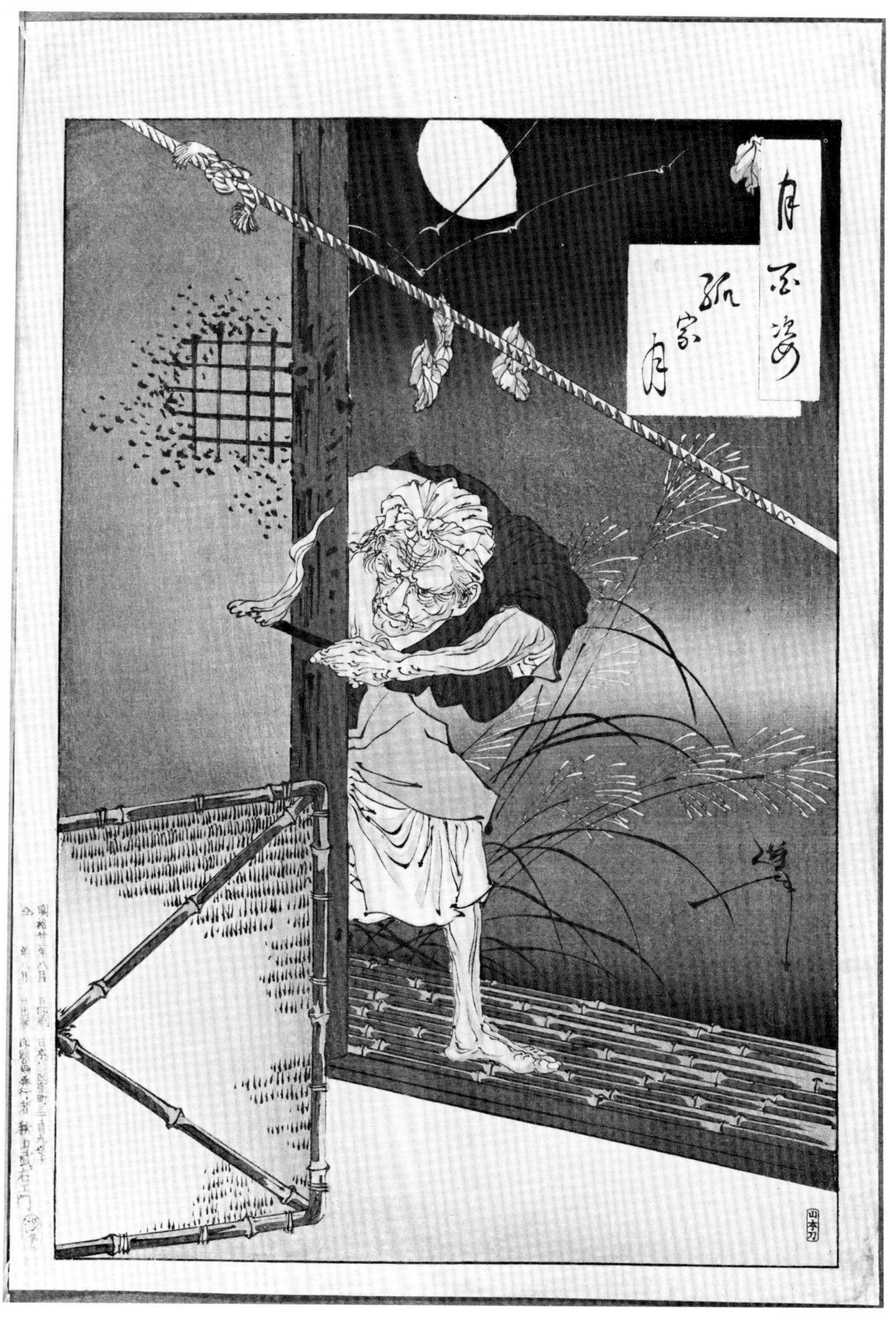

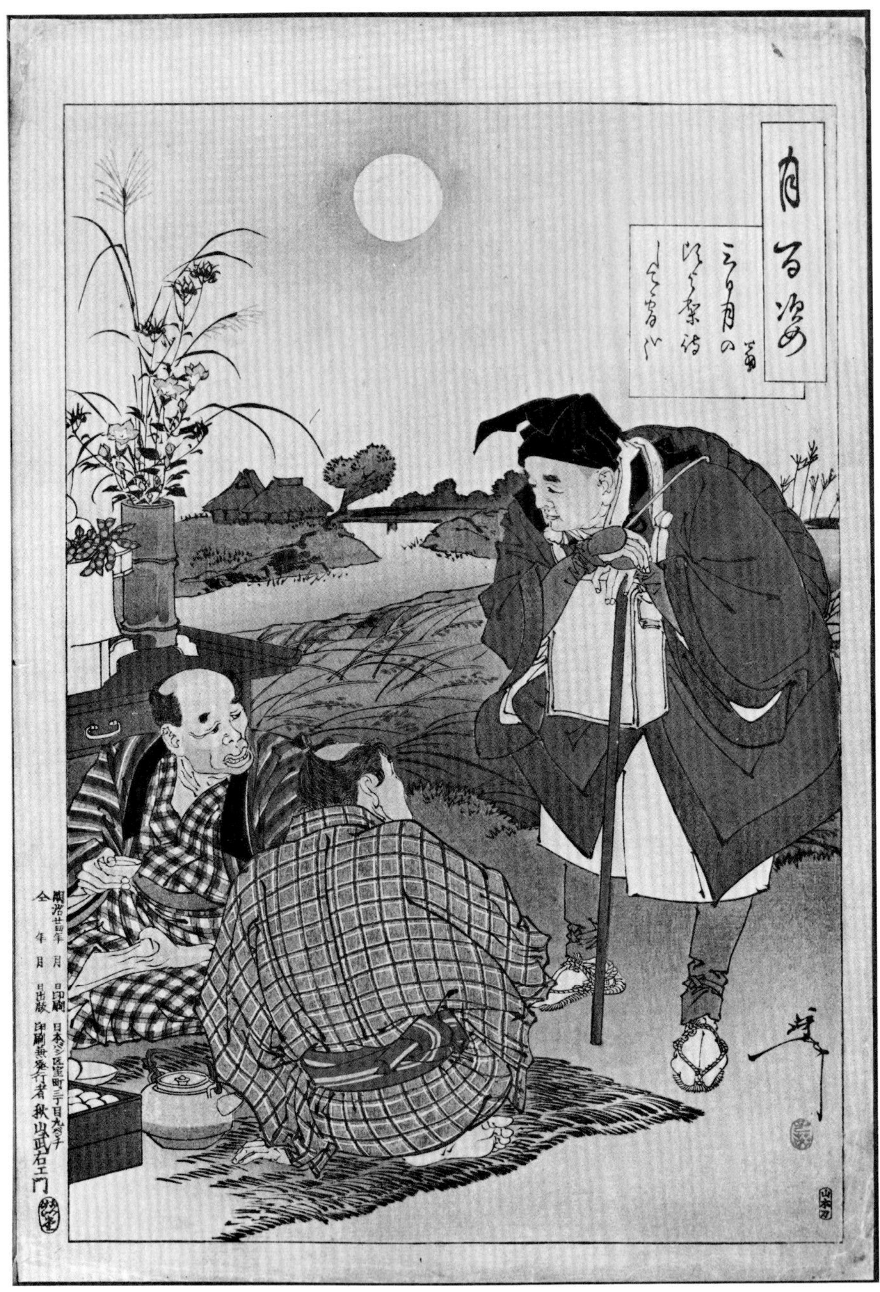

66. I Have Waited for Tonight Ever Since the Crescent Moon—Bashō

(Mikazuki no koro yori machishi koyoi kana ō), 1891

Series: *One Hundred Aspects of the Moon
(Tsuki hyakushi)*
Ōban
Signature: Yoshitoshi
Seal: Taiso
Publisher: Akiyama Buemon
Engraver: Yamamoto tō

Matsuo Bashō (1644–1694), Japan's great haiku poet, traveled throughout the nation, visiting places that had been touched by history and hallowed by visits of earlier poets. As he traveled, the slightest event could become a source of inspiration and the subject of a poem, and he was vividly aware of the contrast between his wise, thoughtful, reflective view of the world and the vision of the common people whom he met on his journeys. In Yoshitoshi's print the Old Man, as Bashō is identified beside his poem, is dressed in the traveling robes of a lay priest. He is talking with two farmers of the countryside who seem oblivious to the flower arrangement beside them and to the moonlight which suffuses the countryside. To Yoshitoshi it was not just the full moon Bashō had waited for, but this convergence of the exquisite and the ordinary, the lofty and the common, the plain and the sublime.

Not exhibited in Los Angeles.

67. Moonlight for a *Sarugaku* Performance

(Sarugaku no tsuki), April 1892

Series: *One Hundred Aspects of the Moon*
(Tsuki hyakushi)
Signature: Yoshitoshi
Seal: Taiso
Publisher: Akiyama Buemon
Engraver: Enkatsu

A samurai of high rank standing in a formal
robe beside a painted screen watches a
crowd of commoners rushing to obtain seats
for an outdoor moonlit performance of
sarugaku, a primitive dance drama which preceded the Noh. Plays were often performed
at the stately residences of feudal lords, and it
is possible that the man in the picture is the
sponsor of the evening's entertainment and is
also on his way to his seat for the performance.
Recent Japanese writers have sensed a feeling of isolation in Yoshitoshi's late work.
Perhaps he expressed his own increasing
separation from the ordinary, everyday world in
the samurai's aloof and dignified detachment.

Not exhibited in Los Angeles.

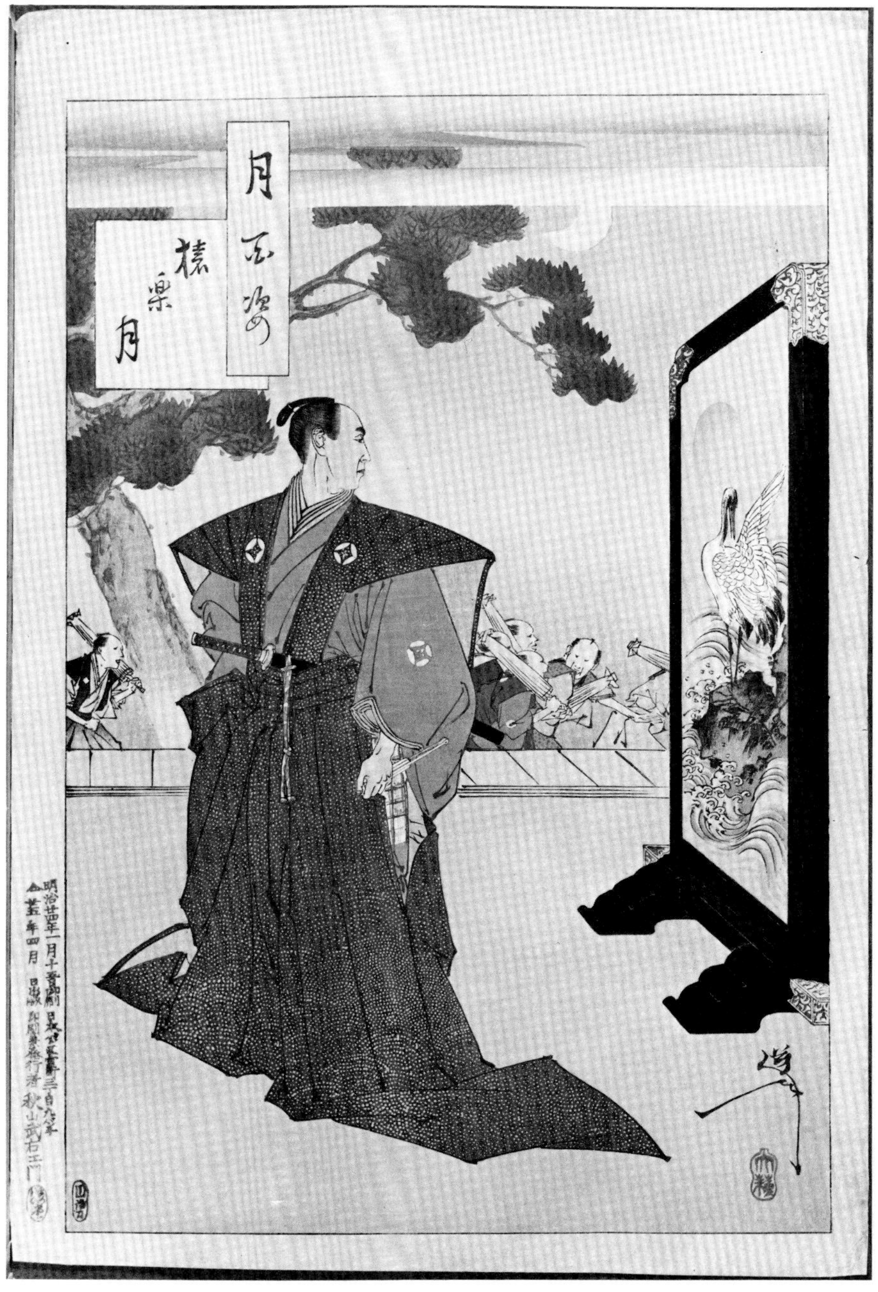

NOTES

Yoshitoshi and His Art

1. Riccar Museum of Art, *Takahashi kore-kushon shinseimen o hiraita meiji ukiyo-eten kiyochika yoshitoshi kunichika* [An exhibition of new developments in woodblock prints of the Meiji period from the Takahashi collection: Kiyochika, Yoshitoshi, Kunichika], exh. cat., Tokyo, 1973.

2. Shinichi Segi, *Tsukioka yoshitoshi gashū* [A collection of pictures by Tsukioka Yoshitoshi], Kōdansha, Tokyo, 1978, p. 116.

3. Seibu Museum of Art, *Saigo no ukiyo-e-shi saisho no gekigaka tsukioka yoshitoshi no zemboten* [A representative exhibition of the works of Tsukioka Yoshitoshi, the last master of ukiyo-e and the first theatrical artist], exh. cat., Tokyo, 1977, unpaginated.

4. Shinichi Segi, "Yoshitoshi no jitsuzo to kyozo" [The truth and misconceptions about Yoshitoshi], *Nippon bijitsu* [Japanese art], no. 8, August 1977, p. 66.

5. Segi, *Yoshitoshi gashū,* pl. 40.

6. Shinichi Segi, "Yoshitoshi no ningen to geijutsu" [Yoshitoshi: the man and his art], Seibu Museum of Art, *Yoshitoshi no zemboten.*

7. Segi, *Yoshitoshi gashū,* pl. 5.

8. Ibid., pl. 11.

9. Shinji Sōya, "Yoshitoshi kenkyu no doko to tenkai" [Current Yoshitoshi studies], *Ukiyo-e,* no, 75, 1978, p. 8. For the *Disasters of War,* see Enrique Lafuente Ferrari, *Goya Gravures et Lithographies,* Arts et Métiers Graphiques, Paris, 1961, pp. 86–168.

10. Toshiko Umezaki, "Yoshitoshi to shibai" [Theatrical themes in Yoshitoshi's work], Seibu Museum of Art, *Yoshitoshi no zemboten.*

11. Kuniyoshi is known to have taught his students to sketch from live animal models. An illustration in *Kyosai gadan* [Illustrated works of Kyosai], vol. 1, 1887, shows apprentices sketching various live creatures, so apparently it was a common practice. Kuniyoshi had amassed a large collection of Dutch graphics with illusionistic illustrations which was accessible to his students. Yoshitoshi frequently used human models: various geisha whom he admired were models for his prints and newspaper illustrations, and several of his students posed for *Oitome saburo no hanashi (The Story of Oitome Saburo).*

12. Seiichiro Takahashi, "Meji hanga to Yoshitoshi" [Yoshitoshi and Meiji prints], Seibu Museum of Art, *Yoshitoshi no zemboten.*

13. A few chūban prints by Hokusai portray violent action.

14. Riccar Museum of Art, *Utagawa kuniyoshi ten* [Pictures by Utagawa Kuniyoshi], exh. cat., Tokyo, 1978, pls. 106, 119.

15. The plays of Tsuruya Nonboku, dominated by the erotic and the grotesque, were very popular then.

16. Unlike other contemporary Ukiyo-e artists, Yoshitoshi did not do landscapes, except for a very few scenic prints. Instead, he displayed his intense interest in realistic renderings in scenes of human drama, showing warriors in battle, legendary heroes, or famous women.

17. Shinichi Segi, "Yoshitoshi ni okeru shakai, rekishi, jinbutsu" [The influence of society, history, and people on Yoshitoshi], Seibu Museum of Art, *Yoshitoshi no zemboten.*

18. Segi, *Yoshitoshi gashū,* pl. 192.

19. The Kanō School was the preeminent school of painting patronized by the shogunate and the court from the fifteenth to the nineteenth century. Yoshitoshi never received any formal training in this style but rather learned it through observation of other artists' work.

20. Segi, *Yoshitoshi gashū,* 1978, p. 134.

21. Ibid., pl. 191.

22. Ibid., pl. 135.

23. Ibid., pl. 197.

24. Shinji Sōya, "Nenpu ni yoru taiso yoshitoshi den" [Yoshitoshi: a chronology of his life and works], *Ukiyo-e,* no. 36, 1969, p. 12.

25. For examples, see *Kohada ohiraji* and *Sarayashiki* from Hokusai's series *Hyaku monogatari (One Hundred Tales),* "Hokusai," *Ukiyo-e taikei* [Complete works of Ukiyo-e], vol. 8, Shueisha, Tokyo, 1974, pls. 49, 50.

26. For examples see Kuniyoshi's *Soma no furudairi* [The old palace of Soma], "Kuniyoshi," *Ukiyo-e taikei,* vol. 10.

27. Segi, *Yoshitoshi gashū,* p. 133.

28. Segi, *"Yoshitoshi ni okeru."*

29. Segi, *Yoshitoshi gashū,* pls. 96–99.

30. Teruji Yoshida, "Yoshitoshi no ketsu no e to bijin-e," [Yoshitoshi's bloody pictures and pictures of women] *Ukiyo-e,* no. 36, 1969, p. 28.

31. Segi, *Yoshitoshi gashū,* pls. 121–23.

32. Ibid., pl. 30.

33. Ibid., pl. 170.

34. Riccar Museum of Art, *Takahashi korekushon,* pl. 155.

35. Ronin Gallery, *One Hundred Views of the Moon by Yoshitoshi Taiso 1839–1892,* exh. cat., New York, 1978.

36. Segi, *Yoshitoshi gashū,* pl. 127; Sōya, "Yoshitoshi kenkyu," pp. 10–11.

The Life of Tsukioka Yoshitoshi, 1839–1892

1. Kodō Yamanaka, "Yoshitoshi nishiki-e nempyō" [A chronology of Yoshitoshi's color woodblock prints], *Ukiyo-e shi* [Ukiyo-e magazine], nos. 11, 12, 1929; "Yoshitoshi den bikō" [Notes on the life of Yoshitoshi], *Ukiyo-e shi* [Ukiyo-e magazine], nos. 15, 17, 18, 20–26, 28–32, 1930–31.

It is difficult to imagine how few contemporary written sources there are for the biography of the most influential and, for much of his later life, the most popular Ukiyo-e artist of the late nineteenth century. Japanese print artists did not keep journals, carry on correspondence, or write memoirs and manifestos like their European contemporaries; nor were there Japanese traditions of commentary or journalistic criticism of popular art. Yoshitoshi's name is mentioned among the pupils of Kuniyoshi on a memorial monument to Kuniyoshi erected in 1873. Yoshitoshi is included in a few printed lists of Ukiyo-e artists published in the 1860s and 1870s. He is mentioned, with modern celebrities in other fields, on the background of a woodblock print designed by Kunichika in the same period. A brief obituary was published in 1892 soon after his death.

But most of what we presume to know about Yoshitoshi's life comes either from the artist's prints themselves or from a lengthy memoir written in 1930 and published in installments in the magazine *Ukiyo-e shi.* It was written by an elderly painter named Yamanaka Kodō, who was born in Tokyo in 1869 and while in his teens apparently studied with Yoshitoshi. After his teacher's death, Kodō studied under a series of more traditional Japanese painters and achieved some recognition after the turn of the century as a painter, newspaper illustrator, and finally as a designer of woodblock prints of female movie stars. Kodō was neither a historian nor a careful writer, and his "biography" is a meandering catch-all of anecdote, reminiscence, and miscellaneous information about Yoshitoshi and any other aspect of the Meiji print world that caught his fancy. Some of his stories about Yoshitoshi are evocative; in others the point seems to be lost in the telling. Indeed, it is difficult to imagine a person temperamentally less suited to writing the life of the artist. Much of Kodō's information sounds plausible, and it is presented in this catalog when it accords with what we know from the well-established sequence of the artist's prints.

After 1930 little new information appeared. The reminiscences of Yoshitoshi's adopted daughter and the embellishments of later writers add little to Kodō's portrait.

2. Yamanaka, "Yoshitoshi den biko," *Ukiyo-e shi,* no. 15, p. 25.

3. Shinichi Segi, biography, entry for 1868, in Seibu Museum of Art, *Saigo no ukiyo-e shi saishō no gekigaka tsukioka yoshitoshi no zemboten* [A representative exhibition of the works of Tsukioka Yoshitoshi, the last master of Ukiyo-e and the first theatrical artist], exh. cat., Tokyo, 1977, unpaginated.

4. Yamanaka, "Yoshitoshi den biko," *Ukiyo-e shi,* no. 25, p. 12.

5. Yamanaka, "Yoshitoshi den biko," *Ukiyo-e shi,* no. 31, p. 12.

6. Yamanaka, "Yoshitoshi den biko," *Ukiyo-e shi,* no. 30, p. 28. *(Yoshitoshi wa bukiyō da ga netsu ga aru. Yoshiiku wa kiyō da ga yoshitoshi no hambun no netsu ga hoshii.)*

7. Yamanaka, "Yoshitoshi den biko," *Ukiyo-e shi,* no. 17, p. 6.

8. Yamanaka, "Yoshitoshi den biko," *Ukiyo-e shi,* no. 18, p. 29.

9. Segi, biographical entry for 1875, in Seibu Museum of Art, *Yoshitoshi no zemboten.*

10. Yamanaka, "Yoshitoshi den biko," *Ukiyo-e shi,* no. 18, p. 29.

11. Segi, biographical entry for 1891, in Seibu Museum of Art, *Yoshitoshi no zemboten.*

12. Segi, biographical entry for 1892, in ibid.

13. Yamanaka, "Yoshitoshi den biko," *Ukiyo-e shi,* no. 18, p. 30.

14. Willibald Netto, "Yoshitoshi und sein Werk," in Museum für Ostasiatische Kunst, *Taiso Yoshitoshi, 1839–1892: Ein Holzschnittmeister an der Schwelle zur Neuzeit,* exh. cat., Cologne, 1971, p. 34.

15. Yamanaka, "Yoshitoshi den biko," *Ukiyo-e shi,* no. 25, p. 13.

16. Yone Nogūchi, "The Last Master of Ukiyoe Art," Transactions of the Japan Society, London, vol. 12, n.d., p. 147. Reprinted in John Murray, *The Spirit of Japanese Art,* London, 1915.

NOTES

Catalog section

1. Will H. Edmunds, *Pointers and Clues to the Subjects of Chinese and Japanese Art,* Sampson Low, Marston and Co., Ltd., London, n.d., pp. 437–38.

2. Kodō Yamanaka, "Yoshitoshi den biko" [Notes on the life of Yoshitoshi], *Ukiyo-e shi* [Ukiyo-e magazine], no. 23, p. 42.

3. Edmunds, *Pointers and Clues,* p. 680.

4. Neither the *Daihyakka jiten* [Great encyclopedia], Heibonsha, Tokyo, 1952, nor the *Nihonshi jiten* [Dictionary of Japanese history], Kodokawa, Tokyo, 1966, mentions the incident.

5. *Heike monogatari* [Tales of the Heike clan], Iwanami Shoten, Tokyo, vol. 1, pp. 408–9. Translated by Atsumi Minami and Roger Keyes.

6. Edmunds, *Pointers and Clues,* p. 608.

7. Seiichi Iwao, ed., *Biographical Dictionary of Japanese History,* trans. Burton Watson, Kodansha International Ltd., Tokyo and New York, 1978, pp. 92, 228. There is some discrepancy over the date of his death; some Japanese encyclopedias say that he died in 1574.

8. E. Papinot, *Historical and Geographical Dictionary of Japan,* Frederick Ungar Publishing Co., New York, 1910, p. 104.

9. Sen'ichi Hisamatsu, *Biographical Dictionary of Japanese Literature,* Kodansha International Ltd., Tokyo and New York, 1976, p. 63.

10. *Kokusho Somokuroku* [Index of national bibliography], Iwanami Shoten, Tokyo, vol. 7, 1970, p. 843.

11. Yamanaka, "Yoshitoshi den biko," *Ukiyo-e shi,* no. 30, p. 25.

12. Yamanaka, "Yoshitoshi den biko," *Ukiyo-e shi,* no. 18, p. 30.

13. Shinichi Segi, *Tsukioka yoshitoshi gashū* [A collection of pictures by Tsukioka Yoshitoshi], Kodansha, Tokyo, 1978, pl. 28.

14. Yamanaka, "Yoshitoshi den biko" *Ukiyo-e shi,* no. 31, p. 10.

15. Yamanaka, "Yoshitoshi den biko," *Ukiyo-e shi,* no. 25, p. 13.

16. R. A. Crighton, *The Floating World,* exh. cat., Victoria and Albert Museum, London, 1973, pl. I–65.

17. Edmunds, *Pointers and Clues,* p. 544.

18. Segi, *Yoshitoshi gashū,* pl. 164.

19. The version of the story in the print is found in Edmunds, *Pointers and Clues,* pp. 443–44. The date of Kiyotaka's death is given as 1333 in Yaichi Haga, *Nihon jimmei jiten* [Dictionary of Japanese biography], Tokyo, 1914, p. 194.

20. Herbert A. Giles, *A Chinese Biographical Dictionary,* [1898]. Reprinted by Literature House Ltd., Taipei, n.d., p. 208.

BIBLIOGRAPHY

Edmunds, Will H., *Pointers and Clues to the Subjects of Chinese and Japanese Art,* Sampson Low, Marston and Co., Ltd., London, n.d.

Hisamatsu, Sen'ichi, *Biographical Dictionary of Japanese Literature,* Kodansha International Ltd., Tokyo and New York, 1976.

Inoue, Kazuo, "Taiso Yoshitoshi," *Zoku ukiyo-e taika shūsei* [Works by masters of Ukiyo-e], part 2, vol. 1, Taihōkaku, Tokyo, 1933.

Iwao, Seiichi, *Biographical Dictionary of Japanese History,* trans. Burton Watson, Kodansha International Ltd., Tokyo and New York, 1978.

Kaasa, Thomas Herbert, "Taiso Yoshitoshi (1839–1892): A Preliminary Study of the Life and Work of a Meiji Ukiyo-e Artist," master's thesis, University of Washington, 1964.

Mitchell, C. H., "Yoshitoshi and Japanese Prints of the Meiji Era," *Ukiyo-e Studies and Pleasures,* Society for Japanese Arts and Crafts, The Hague, 1978, pp. 13–18.

Museum für Ostasiatische Kunst, *Taiso Yoshitoshi, 1839–1892: Ein Holzschnittmeister an der Schwelle zur Neuzeit,* exh. cat., Cologne, 1971.

Nogūchi, Yone, "The Last Master of Ukiyo-e Art, *Transactions of the Japan Society,* London, vol. 12, n.d. Reprinted in John Murray, *The Spirit of Japanese Art,* London, 1915.

Ōmagari, Kuson, "Yoshitoshi to maboroshidayū" [Yoshitoshi and Maboroshidayū], *Ukiyo-e shi* [Ukiyo-e magazine], nos. 14–16, 1930.

Ono, Tadashige, "Yoshitoshi," *Nihon hanga bijutsu zenshu* [The art of Japanese woodblock prints], vol. 7, Kōdansha, Tokyo, 1964.

Riccar Museum of Art, *Takahashi korekushon shinseimen o hiraita meiji ukiyo-eten kiyochika yoshitoshi kunichika* [An exhibition of new developments in woodblock prints of the Meiji period from the Takahashi collection: Kiyochika, Yoshitoshi, Kunichika], exh. cat., Tokyo, 1973.

Ronin Gallery, *One Hundred Views of the Moon by Yoshitoshi Taiso 1839–1892,* exh. cat., New York, 1978.

Segi, Shinichi, *Tsukioka yoshitoshi gashū* [A collection of pictures by Tsukioka Yoshitoshi], Kōdansha, Tokyo, 1978.

Segi, Shinichi, "Yoshitoshi no jitsuzo to kyozo" [The truth and misconceptions about Yoshitoshi], *Nippon bijutsu* [Japanese art], no. 8, 1977.

Seibu Museum of Art, *Saigo no ukiyo-e shi saishō no gekigaka tsukioka yoshitoshi no zemboten* [A representative exhibition of the works of Tsukioka Yoshitoshi, the last master of Ukiyo-e and the first theatrical artist], exh. cat., Tokyo, 1977.

Sōya, Shinji, "Nenpu ni yoru taiso yoshitoshi den" [Yoshitoshi: a chronology of his life and works], *Ukiyo-e,* no. 36, 1969, pp. 10–14.

Sōya, Shinji, "Yoshitoshi kenkyu no doki to tenkai" [Current Yoshitoshi studies], *Ukiyo-e,* no. 75, 1978, pp. 8–29.

Sōya, Shinji, et al., *Chi no bansan yoshitoshi no geijutsu* [The art of Yoshitoshi: A repast of blood], Banshō Shobō, Tokyo, 1971.

Stevenson, John, "Yoshitoshi: Ukiyo-e's Last Star," *Arts of Asia,* vol. 9, no. 4, 1979, pp. 88–96.

Takahashi, Seiichirō, "Jisei no henka o hyōshi suru meiji hanga" [Changes of the time revealed in Meiji woodblock prints], *Ukiyo-e nihyaku-gojunen* [250 years of Ukiyo-e], Chūokōronsha, Tokyo, 1961.

Ukiyo-e Galerie Herbert Egenolf, *Tsukioka Yoshitoshi, 1839–1892,* exh. cat., Dusseldorf, 1977.

Ukiyo-e taikei [Complete works of Ukiyo-e], 17 vols., Shueisha, Tokyo, 1973–76.

Yamanaka, Kodō, "Yoshitoshi nishiki-e nempyo" [A chronology of Yoshitoshi's color woodblock prints], *Ukiyo-e shi* [Ukiyo-e magazine], nos. 11, 12, 1929.

Yamanaka, Kodō, "Yoshitoshi den biko" [Notes on the life of Yoshitoshi], *Ukiyo-e shi* [Ukiyo-e magazine], nos. 15, 17, 18, 20–26, 28–32, 1930–31.

Yoshida, Teruji, "Yoshitoshi," *Ukiyo-e jiten* [A dictionary of Ukiyo-e], vol. 3, Gabundō, Tokyo, 1971.

Yoshida, Teruji, "Yoshitoshi no ketsu no e to bijin-e" [Yoshitoshi's bloody pictures and pictures of women], *Ukiyo-e,* no. 36, 1969, pp. 26–28.